Multicultural Dialogue

Multicultural Dialogue

Dilemmas, Paradoxes, Conflicts

Randi Gressgård

Berghahn Books
NEW YORK · OXFORD

Published in 2010 by
Berghahn Books

www.berghahnbooks.com

© 2010, 2012 Randi Gressgård
First paperback edition published in 2012

All rights reserved.
Except for the quotation of short passages
for the purposes of criticism and review, no part of this book
may be reproduced in any form or by any means, electronic or
mechanical, including photocopying, recording, or any information
storage and retrieval system now known or to be invented,
without written permission of the publisher.

Library of Congress Cataloging-in-Publication Data

Gressgård, Randi.
 Multicultural dialogue : dilemmas, paradoxes, conflicts / Randi Gressgård. — 1st ed.
   p. cm.
 Includes bibliographical references and index.
 ISBN 978-1-84545-666-5 (hbk.) -- ISBN 978-0-85745-648-9 (pbk.)
  1. Multiculturalism. 2. Cultural pluralism. 3. Cross-cultural orientation.
 4. Emigration and immigration. I. Title.
 HM1271.G735 2010
 305.8001—dc22

2010006649

British Library Cataloguing in Publication Data

A catalogue record for this book is available from
the British Library.

Printed in the United States on acid-free paper

ISBN 978-0-85745-648-9 (paperback)   ISBN 978-0-85745-649-6 (ebook)

Contents

Preface	vii
Introduction	1
Chapter 1 Dual Subjectivity and the Metaphysics of Purity	13
Chapter 2 Non-modern Holism and Modern Totalitarianism	40
Chapter 3 Heterogeneity and the Singular Subject	55
Chapter 4 Consequences of Heterogeneity	74
Chapter 5 Conditions for Dialogue	106
Notes	138
References	153
Index	162

Preface

The multicultural dilemma

The overall aim of this book is to scrutinise the underlying cultural and theoretical assumptions from which multicultural dialogue arises, and to establish a theoretical 'ground' for dialogue in the intersection between political theory and a philosophy of difference. The point of departure is the debate on multiculturalism that has been going on for years across academic and political environments in Europe and North America. As I see it, the debate on multiculturalism is structured by certain ideas and values that constitute a particular referential or discursive framework within which particular concepts acquire their meaning. It is my contention that this discursive framework of multiculturalism is made up of a set of component concepts pertaining to modern political ideology, the pivotal element being the tension between equal dignity/equality and cultural distinctiveness/difference. Although these ideas are constituted in opposition to one another, both are considered to be covetable values within this setting. Individuals are considered to be equal, protected by individual rights, while at the same time being culturally distinct by virtue of belonging to particular ethnic or religious communities or groups. Hence, the question arises as to how equal dignity/equality and cultural distinctiveness/difference can be reconciled. How can one call for the recognition of both individual equality and cultural distinctiveness without putting these ideas in conflict or without resolving the one into the other? As this question suggests, the debate on multiculturalism appertains to what might be called a politics of recognition.

The politics of recognition is not, however, a practical-political implementation of resolutions made by democratically elected decision-makers. Multiculturalist politics, no doubt, has a bearing on decision-making processes, yet the politics of recognition is mainly discussed within the fields of philosophy and political theory. Some would say that the debate on multiculturalism invokes the distinction between the abstract philosophical notion of the political (*le politique*) and the more conventional definition of politics as a concrete political event (*la politique*). For instance, when theorists position themselves and propose different, and often contesting, 'solutions' to the dilemma between recognition of equal dignity/equality and distinctiveness/difference, they normally operate on a theoretical level, more or less abstracted from actual material politics. However, the attempt to reach a political-philosophical 'solution' to the dilemmatic relationship between equality and distinctiveness is almost always done with a view to practical politics. For that reason, it is sometimes hard to discern between theoretical, ethical and political discussions within this field.

Politicians, state officials and researchers regularly meet at national and international conventions, and they are, of course, mutually influenced by one another. For instance, policy documents on ethnic minority issues tend to be heavily influenced by the academic discourses on multiculturalism, and, conversely, research expertise is often involved in political processes, not to mention that practical-political problem-solving is a major source of new theoretical problems. Although never complete, my examination of the debate on multiculturalism will exhibit this mutual relationship between political theory and practice. I will draw attention to the conceptions and dynamics constitutive of both the theoretical and the practical field so as to pinpoint a set of common uncontested and uncontestable ideas and values. As part of my critical theoretical analysis, I will endeavour to show how questions about the conditions of possibility for truth, being and knowing are linked with ethical and political questions of justice, hospitality and solidarity.

However, it is not my intention to respond directly to the questions that are being raised in the debate on multiculturalism. Rather, by calling into question the framework within which such questions are made intelligible, my principal concern is with the conditions for multicultural dialogue. A particularly salient aspect of this discussion pertains to the relationship between identity and difference. After a critical investigation of the perceived logic of identity, indicative of Western nation states and at the root of their pluralistic intentions, I take issue with universalist notions of equality, on the one hand, and with cultural relativist notions of distinctiveness, as well as postmodern anything-goes-anti-foundationalism, on the other. I suggest instead a post-foundational stance, with an emphasis on the contingency of foundations. I thereby acknowledge the need for foundations as a basis of dialogue and community, while at the same time I pinpoint the contradiction between accounting for difference beyond identity and nurturing dialogue and community.

The examination of the framework of multiculturalism to which I contribute could perhaps be seen as a critical theoretical intervention. But is it also a political intervention? That depends, of course, on how one conceives of politics and the relationship between theory and practice. As I see it, theoretical reflection does not underlie political action as its neutral ground but is instead a political practice in terms of being an action. So rather than speaking of thought and action, I conceive of thought *as* action. In this respect, my main objective is certainly not conventional political problem-solving and planning, predicated upon a model of thought, but scrutiny of the premises upon which political problems are defined and handled.

Being strongly committed to equal rights and equality, and given the social democratic tradition on which their national policies are based, Scandinavian nation states are particularly interesting with regard to the topic in discussion. In the Introduction, my point of departure is the Norwegian integration policy, which will serve as a stepping stone for the purpose of illustration, before proceeding to the theoretical and philosophical discussions in the subsequent chapters. The empirical examples are drawn from policy documents on integration and cultural diversity. In addition, I borrow some examples from research reports and the media.

As Adrian Favell (2001) demonstrates, there are a variety of facts and elements that must be taken into consideration when discussing integration policies. However, within my analytical framework, it is not feasible to reveal any underlying public theories, or to show how ideas and political argument can work as institutional structures that shape the interaction of interest-driven political actors in the policy process (see ibid.: 19). Such a study would require empirical comparison between different countries in order not to delimit its results and conclusions to one particular context. My identification of a policy framework, related to what Favell reads as 'path dependency',[1] is somewhat different. The aim is not to identify contemporary political forces that serve to reproduce the dominant policy framework, even if this could be relevant to my analysis. By focusing on a more abstract, conceptual level of analysis, my discussion is, by design, principally theoretical, encompassing both symbolic and institutional structures that an empirical analysis alone is unable to capture. These structures are less dependent on social context, even if the discursive framework of multiculturalism is in no way universal or abstracted from practical-political constraints. The analysis takes as its starting point the 'actually existing' patterns in polity processes and the empirical conditions for multicultural dialogue, but it is mainly concerned with the conditions of possibility for such patterns, notably the uncritical preconditions for integration politics and recognition of cultural difference.

A pertinent fact is that so-called egalitarian nation states have been preoccupied with cultural difference and social inequality from the very beginning. Suffice it to say that there has never been an absolute correspondence between formal egalitarianism and substantial equality among groups within this framework, and, as my discussion suggests, nor can there ever be. Political management of differences is a hallmark of Western liberal democracy. As such, difference is at the heart of Western democracies. Intersections of historically, socially and culturally constituted categories, such as race, class, gender, sexuality and age/generation, have formed the basis for social inequality and cultural plurality throughout the modern period. Given the increased immigration and the dynamics of globalisation over the past decades, the social divisions and cultural plurality have become ever more striking and, according to some, more challenging with respect to social justice, public consent and democratic legitimacy. Partly due to this, in the name of public interest, the immigration policies within Europe are generally restrictive. Norway, like several other European countries, has practised an 'immigration stop' since the mid-1970s, and the political decision to restrict immigration radically, supported by most political parties, has made a great impact, not only on the extent of immigration, but above all on its character. As a result of the so-called immigration stop, residence permits are not given to people from countries outside of the European Economic Area unless they have status as refugees, are subject to political persecution, have compelling humanitarian reasons or are qualified for reunion with their families. In any event, strict criteria are observed, in accordance with the Schengen Agreement.

The fact that European immigration policy is restrictive signals that immigrants are considered to pose a threat to the national communities, that is, to what is assumed to be the cultural, religious, ethnic, racial, economic and political unity of the respective countries. In line with the general scepticism towards international and transnational economic and political bodies, often framed as a conflict between the 'people' and the 'elite', the hostility towards immigrants in Europe is often depicted by minority researchers as a reaction to the perceived threat of a lost national community and identity. The reaction is sometimes articulated in terms of nostalgia for lost origins. In most cases, national romantic longings for lost origins, as a response to multicultural diversity and policy, reflect the asymmetry between the so-called ordinary people and the educated elite when it comes to validation of cultural difference.

As Roger Hewitt's (2005) study of 'white backlash' in the UK and the US has demonstrated, white working class people tend to experience the politics of multiculturalism as unreasonable. State support and measures of affirmative action aimed at compensating for former discrimination and institutionalised racism are felt to be 'objectionable for "all reasonable people"' (ibid.: 102). Even equality claims made on purely liberal grounds, such as civil rights demands, are sometimes regarded as unacceptable. In granting black people an equal status, the authorities are taken to be indifferent to the national identities and the special needs of the white working class people. The obverse side of the 'white backlash', also identified by Hewitt, is to deploy the most respectable of liberal claims to overlay hostility and racism. For instance, as several scholars have pointed out, the liberal concept of freedom could easily be used as an instrument of bigotry and coercion vis-à-vis 'others' (see e.g. Butler 2009: 104–105; cf. Brown 2006; Puar 2007). Perhaps the increased tendency across all social classes to conceive of ethnic minorities, Muslims in particular, as a threat signals a more general 'white backlash' in the Western countries.

An eloquent example is the popular vote in Switzerland in 2009 concerning minarets. Fifty-seven per cent of the Swiss voters (and a majority of the units of the federal state) supported the promoters of a change in the Federal Constitution that bans the construction of new minarets on mosques. Due to the Swiss system of semi-direct democracy, the promoters of a ban, provided that they manage to gather at least 100,000 signatures of citizens within 18 months, can force the government to send the initiative to a national vote (irrespective of its support in the Federal Parliament). According to both national and international commentators, the result of the national vote represented an act of mass defiance of the national establishment, which opposed the ban. Right-wing leaders in several European countries depicted the result as a triumph for the people against the elite. Representatives of the National Front party in France proclaimed that the 'elites should stop denying the aspirations and fears of the European people who, without opposing religious freedom, reject ostentatious signs that political-religious Muslim groups want to impose' (*Times Online*, 30 November 2009). This political rhetoric, which seems to be widespread, clearly illustrates a 'white backlash' pertaining to the opposition between the 'people' and the 'elite' in Europe today.

Ethnic minorities are not perceived solely as a threat, however. Positive responses are not hard to find, and most political parties and governments are careful about underscoring the positive effects of immigration, as well as the negative. For instance, in one of its reports to Parliament on integration and cultural diversity, White Paper No. 49 (2003–2004), the Norwegian government describes the present-day ethnic and cultural diversity, emphasising its influence on contemporary society, and makes a normative statement about its positive impact. That being said, cultural diversity is seen as a positive factor only to the extent that it promotes the prevailing values and does not challenge the established institutions and the shared values embodied in those institutions.[2] This is a 'soft' version of multiculturalism, aimed at including immigrants into the common public culture. In the above-mentioned policy document, a tension is outlined between diversity in terms of individualisation and differentiation of values and ways of life, on the one hand, and commonly held goals, shared values and loyalties, on the other (ibid.: 33).

The degree to which immigrants are positively valued is indeed conditioned by the general climate of political debate, which in turn varies on the basis of an entire range of factors, such as the need for labour and the media's focus on negative cases involving ethnic minorities. When I started doing research within this field, prior to the Norwegian municipal elections in 1999, the Conservative Party in Oslo was clearly enthusiastic about immigrants. A few years later, after September 11 in 2001, the policy climate had changed dramatically in a negative direction, as it did in most Western countries – perhaps even more so after the worldwide Muslim reaction to the Danish Muhammed caricatures in 2006, a situation that is enjoying something of a revival in 2010. We have no doubt witnessed an increased hostility to immigrants on a political level, which is reflected in stricter immigration laws and a stronger will to control and regulate the minority population.

This might indicate that the empirical conditions for dialogue between the majority and the minority populations are not constant, and that it is difficult to draw firm conclusions about the validity of premises for discussion beyond the point in time at which research is recorded. However, as I mentioned above, since it is my intent to scrutinise the conceptual underpinnings of the debate on multiculturalism, and thus investigate the debate itself, I have adopted an approach that frees the analysis from the constraints of what empirical analysis by itself is able to reveal. Focusing on the underlying structures and the dynamics behind the multiculturalist discursive framework – its conditions of possibility – enables me to illuminate and discuss otherwise unchallenged assumptions that are constitutive of multiculturalism and multicultural dialogue. A salient inquiry probes into the consequences that the discursive framework has with regard to the relationship between 'us' and the 'others'. How is this relationship constituted and reproduced? What kind of dialogue does it allow? Given that the policy of multiculturalism, at least its 'strong' version, has been under severe attack since 2001, perhaps the most important question is the following: do we still need a concept of cultural difference?

Throughout the book, I relate in both an analytical and explorative manner to a topic area that requires discussion of some founding principles in the political field and in the academic debates within the humanities and the social sciences. In this regard, my approach opens up a broad range of theoretical terms and ways of reasoning, the preliminary questions leading to a successive series of new and often more detailed questions for discussion, and so on. The angle of approach is indeed critical, since my focus on the debate on immigration and integration (i.e. on multiculturalism) calls into question its very conceptual basis. Most readers would probably characterise this attempt to lay bare basic structures as 'deconstruction'. I will not object to such an assignment, but as I have indicated above, my analysis also endeavours to establish viable alternative ways of perceiving the relationship between 'us' and the 'others'. That is why I choose to employ the label 'critical intervention'.

Characteristically, the book plots out a line of argument from chapter to chapter. Based on the acknowledgement that every text is a product of its interplay with other texts, each chapter relies upon sources relevant to the discussion. This is not to say, however, that I lay out my argument by mainly opposing and dissociating myself from other contributions to the analytical fields in which I operate. This strategy of academic writing often involves disparagement and undermining of those texts to which one relates, coupled with a corresponding elevation of the central thinking 'I'. Opposed to such a style, I acknowledge the sources from which I draw my arguments, and I try to let the others speak in my text. This is a methodological strategy that is compatible with my theoretical argument on dialogue. It is not a matter of adoption but adaptation, or, more accurately, a strategy of displacement, in accordance with another point that I put forward. To the extent that I make do with things that were meant perhaps for other ends, I come close to the *bricoleur*, advocated by, among others, Lévi-Strauss (1966; cf. Spivak 1997: xix). However, this is a precarious endeavour, as it is hard to do justice to different texts without reducing them to components of my own line of argument – to instances of the Same. I risk turning against my own argument and analytical aspirations to the extent that I conjoin different perspectives without at the same time being aware of underlying conceptual differences. On the other hand, conceptual displacement is unavoidable, as each repetition inevitably marks a difference.

Line of argument

In what follows, I will give a brief introduction to some of the texts that are particularly central to my approach. These include Scott Lash's *Another Modernity: A Different Rationality* (1999), Jean-Francois Lyotard's *The Differend* (1988) and Hans Herbert Kögler's *The Power of Dialogue* (1999).

Based on *Critique of Judgment*, Kant's ([1790] 1987) Third Critique on aesthetical judgement, Lash argues in favour of a community based on difference ('communities-in-difference'). In the chapter entitled 'Reflexive Judgement and Aesthetic Subjectivity', he draws attention to the subject's singularity and the object's finitude, each characterised by its non-determined, finite qualities. According to Lash, the subject becomes singular in its relation to the finite object. In its singular form, the subject is characterised by a lack of universality, and it is this lack of universal identity that allows the subject to form community. In Lash's view, community demands self-difference, as opposed to self-identity and totality.

Subsequently, I employ Lyotard's philosophy to develop the contention that community based on difference is predicated upon self-difference in terms of a lack of universality. I argue that ignoring this lack, while accepting identity and totality, not only defies the possibility of a difference-based community, but also sacrifices the possibility of dialogue. In line with a philosophy of difference, I contend that the logic of identity obstructs difference/heterogeneity by reducing differences to polar oppositions within one and the same social order. The 'others' are constituted as reverse mirror images of 'us', with the result that their otherness is inevitably silenced.

Kögler's concept of dialogue corresponds, at least partly, to this philosophy of difference. In his view, dialogue implies openness towards the 'others' in such a manner that the 'others' are not depicted as negations of 'our' identity. Rather, dialogue presupposes a critical stance to our own evaluative standards. Accordingly, Kögler's concept of dialogue defies the conflation of understanding and judgement. That is to say, understanding one another's meaning does not presuppose a common evaluative standard. Necessary conceptual bridgeheads do not guarantee a symbolic unity of meaning, Kögler argues, but allow irreconcilable differences in world view to appear. Significantly, his concept of dialogue allows for incommensurability with respect to evaluative standards, which entails a critical reflection upon our own 'truths'.

As this outline suggests, my line of argument implies a profound scrutiny, from different angles, of the underlying assumptions that constitute modern ideologies and truths. As such, the interrogation is, to the extent that it also concerns my own situatedness within the cultural order that is being analysed, a profound self-interrogation. It is a reflexive questioning of prevailing categories and founding discourses of the majority society. However, no matter how self-reflexive one manages to be, the legacy of Enlightenment reasoning seems indispensable. Self-reflexion is indeed a part of this modern legacy. Perhaps Audre Lorde's (1983) often-quoted statement, 'The master's tools will never dismantle the master's house', is pertinent in this context. No doubt I risk falling prey to the structures I aim to criticise, but I affirm this risk – I affirm the complicity of theory with its objects of critique (Spivak 1987: 201). As Jacques Derrida (1997: 24) puts it, the movements of deconstruction do not destroy structures from the outside; the enterprise of deconstruction always in a certain way falls prey to its own work. It is against this background that the following outline of the book should be read.

The Introduction presents the discursive framework that structures the debate on multiculturalism. It deals with the dilemma between equal dignity granted to individuals and cultural distinctiveness pertaining to communities or groups. It is this dilemma, I argue, that sets the premises for what is debated and questioned, and, as such, has an impact on the perceptions and delineations of 'us' and the 'others'. The Introduction includes empirical illustrative examples from the Norwegian debate on integration and cultural diversity. The empirical part of the Introduction is mainly based on an analysis of two policy documents, White Paper No. 17 (1996–1997), *On Immigration and the Multicultural Norway*, and White Paper No. 49 (2003–2004), *Diversity through Inclusion and Participation: Responsibility and Freedom*. Through a critical investigation of these documents, I illustrate how the tension between equality and difference manifests itself in the field of politics. I then elucidate the multicultural paradox that arises from a liberal-democratic 'planned pluralism' in which dialogue is reduced to a means to an end. The analysis raises the question of what happens when the 'others' are assimilated but, at the same time, are depicted as culturally distinct and hierarchically subordinated to 'us'.

Chapters 1 and 2 draw attention to the cultural dynamics that constitute the dilemma between equality and distinctiveness. One question that is being pursued is whether it is possible to understand the 'others' and to recognise them as both equal and different on their own terms. Or does recognition always render the 'others' opposite and subordinate to 'us'? The overall question is whether the multicultural dilemma implies an oppositional logic whereby the 'others' are constituted in negation to 'our' identity by way of culturalisation. If so, are we faced with a modern form of totalitarianism?

Chapters 3 and 4 enquire into this issue of totalitarianism. The modern logic of opposition and totalitarianism is questioned from the point of view of a philosophy of difference, wherein difference or heterogeneity is considered to be prior to identity. This includes a scrutiny of the implications of totalitarianism with respect to conceptualisations of otherness. The argument suggests that totalitarianism implies reductionism by way of ignoring the otherness of the 'others'. A central problem for discussion, which is related to the conditions for dialogue, is whether a community presupposes identity. If not, what does a community based on difference mean with regard to the relationship between 'us' and the 'others'?

The final chapter further develops this line of argument, eventually tying up the loose ends. On the basis of the preceding chapters, the condition of possibility for an open and critical dialogue is discussed in terms of resistance against structures of domination that proceed from and result in a firm cultural identity. However, without identity, is it possible to participate in dialogue? Is there a potential way out of this impasse?

Acknowledgements

An earlier version of this volume was published in 2005 by Spartacus/Scandinavian Academic Press, Oslo, under the title *Fra identitet til forskjell* (From Identity to Difference). The original translation, funded by the Norwegian Research Council, was done in collaboration with Tim Challman. Since then, the book has been rewritten and reworked. This English edition is published with support from the University of Bergen.

My first and largest expression of gratitude for having contributed to the completion of this book goes to Ann Nilsen at the Department of Sociology,

University of Bergen (UiB). Secondly, I want to thank the researchers at IMER/UiB, headed by Yngve Lithman. I am especially indebted to Christine M. Jacobsen for an infinite number of academic and social discussions. I would also like to thank my colleagues and network at the Centre for Women's and Gender Research (SKOK), headed by Ellen Mortensen, and Cathrine Egeland at the Work Research Institute in Oslo for many long and thoughtful discussions. As for the English edition, I owe thanks to the two anonymous reviewers for their valuable comments and to the copy editor from Berghahn Books, Shawn Kendrick, for her careful work on the manuscript. In addition, I would like to thank my parents and grandparents. And last but not least, I want to address a word of thanks to my partner, Sissel Lilletvedt, for being immensely supportive and patient.

Introduction

Individual equality and cultural distinctiveness

Charles Taylor (1994), who is one of the most influential partakers in the debate on multiculturalism, approaches the multicultural dilemma as a tension between equal dignity and distinctiveness. On the one hand, he argues, we find a claim to a democratic form of equality, which presupposes that all humans are of equal value. This means that everyone is entitled to the same rights, and there is an ethical demand that all citizens in a democratic society treat one another as equals. The recognition of equal dignity is, in Taylor's view, granted to individuals. On the other hand, we find a claim to distinctiveness in terms of recognition of individuals as holders of particular cultural identities. When distinctiveness is concerned, Taylor does not distinguish between groups and individuals. He argues that identities originate from different cultural groups in such a manner that both groups and individuals are expected to recognise one another on the basis of their respective cultural distinctiveness.[1] The tension between equality and distinctiveness may therefore be articulated as follows: while the respect for equality points towards a conception of the public arena as a sphere ignorant of differences, cultural distinctiveness points towards a public recognition of cultural identities, with the accompanying claim to differential treatment.

As this brief outline suggests, a pivotal aspect of the tension between equal dignity and distinctiveness is the dynamics between individual and group. The liberal principle of freedom and equality under the law is manifested in individual rights, such as freedom of speech. However, the rights of the individual may undermine the group's distinctive character if, for instance, the group's distinctiveness is based on the premise that women do not have the right of free expression in the public arena. As long as equality is inextricably linked to individual rights and distinctiveness is conceived as a matter of recognition of groups, in some cases manifested in special group rights, then a tension arises between equality and distinctiveness that translates into a tension between respect for individuals and respect for groups.[2] It is mainly the question of recognition of cultural distinctiveness, often articulated as a question of tolerance, that is at issue in the debate on multiculturalism. Where should the majority draw the line in terms of tolerance, provided that cultural practices of ethnic minorities might exist at the expense of the freedom and rights of the individuals? When is it legitimate to criticise cultural practices without being ethnocentric? These questions signify a profound tension in the debate between the positions of ethnocentrism and cultural relativism.

The Norwegian anthropologist Tord Larsen (1979) outlines a tension between cultural relativism and what he calls 'political action'.[3] In some cases, he notes, we invoke a set of governing rules in order to legitimise our moral and political decisions, whereas in other cases we refer to a different set of axioms in order to thwart such decisions (ibid.: 3). In the first case, we act on the supposition that we are all identical as human beings, whereas, in the second case, we act on the basis of being different from one another. Larsen remarks that since there is merit in both positions, they are an incessant source of dilemmas of interaction. If we interfere in other cultural practices, we break with the principle that the moral quality of actions is relative to the culture's own moral norms. If, on the other hand, we refrain from 'getting involved', we deny the possibility of a common communicative and moral universe. Larsen notes that it is only by recognising that all humans are equal, and thereby including everyone in the same moral universe, that we can take a stand against practices such as female circumcision, honour killing and forced marriage, because it is only then that we can morally identify with the victims of (what we might consider to be) inhuman institutions and practices (ibid.: 5). However, as this framework suggests, by interfering in the cultural practices of the 'others', we run the risk of impinging on another cultural and moral universe, disrespecting the group's cultural distinctiveness. Thus, we run the risk of acting ethnocentrically. As long as we stick to an egalitarian framework, such dilemmas of interaction are constant and inescapable. However, in order not to become incapable of acting at all, we might try to distinguish between contexts in which cultural differences are relevant to the interaction between 'us' and the 'others' and contexts in which the interaction is not influenced by cultural differences. Moreover, we might seek to determine which differences are relevant in the different contexts.

Those who oppose a politics of recognition altogether often do so by disavowing the relevance of cultural differences in moral issues. From a liberal point of view, morality is normally conceived of as a matter of right and wrong, pertaining to human dignity and individual rights. Practices such as honour killing, forced marriage and female circumcision are considered to be unacceptable because they violate the rights of the individual. Among the liberal voices is Susan M. Okin (1999), who poses the question of what ought to be done when demands made by minority cultures collide with norms of gender equality (individual rights) that have been embraced, at least nominally, by liberal, democratic states. Her main point is that feminists have been too quick in presuming that both feminism and multiculturalism represent good things and can be easily combined. Okin's objection to the union of feminism and multiculturalism is that they are bound to end up in conflict with each other, because the minority cultures, or ways of life, are inconsistent with liberal feminist ideals about equal status and equal opportunities. She refers to a wide array of practices, not only those mentioned above, but also polygamy and the use of the Muslim veil to illustrate her point (see Gressgård and Jacobsen 2003).

Ethnocentrism and cultural relativism

Okin (1999) is of the opinion that none of the foremost defenders of multiculturalism have actually addressed the disturbing intersections between gender equality (pertaining to equal dignity) and culture (pertaining to distinctiveness). This critique is raised against, among others, Will Kymlicka, who is another influential contributor to the debate on multiculturalism. Kymlicka (1989, 1995) professes the view that cultures are essential for human development. In his view, membership in a rich and secure cultural structure is important both for the development of self-esteem and for providing a context in which people are able to develop the ability to make their own choices on how to live their lives. He asserts that cultural minorities may need special group rights to maintain such a rich and secure cultural structure. However, in order to safeguard the autonomy of individual group members, Kymlicka contends that group rights ought to be limited to groups that are internally liberal. Yet Okin holds that Kymlicka does not go far enough with this demand. When it comes to his insistence on liberal values, on the other hand, Kymlicka seems to be in line with Okin. Notwithstanding his proposal for group rights, a stand that brings up the issue of cultural relativism, he clearly distinguishes between individuals and groups, and, in doing so, demonstrates that group rights are secondary in relation to individual rights. He is of the opinion that cultural distinctiveness is desirable only to the extent that it does not undermine liberal norms and values.

Within the liberal-democratic tradition to which both Okin and Kymlicka belong, freedom of choice is considered to be a basic value. However, by limiting cultural recognition to practices that support liberal norms and values, both Okin and Kymlicka are confronted with a paradox. According to certain critics of liberal ideas, they have to acknowledge that their own rules will not be accepted, because otherwise they break their own rules. For instance, some multiculturalists hold that cultural groups must be recognised and protected even if their cultural practices break with prevailing norms and values. That being said, most cultural relativists confine their relativism to practices that are consistent with existing laws and rights, notably human rights. In this regard, cultural relativists tend to defend individual rights, without calling into question the cultural specificity of concepts such as 'rights' and 'equality'. In most cases, what they target is the employment of *conventional* norms and values, which, in liberal terms, signify cultural particularity as opposed to universality. To the extent that culturally specific conventional norms and values are applied in the evaluation of 'others', it is perceived by cultural relativists – as well as liberals such as Kymlicka and others who subscribe to multiculturalism as a political doctrine – to be an illegitimate interference in others' cultures. With their critical stance towards ethnocentrism, cultural relativists hold that cultures are unique and autonomous. Conventional Western norms and moral standards are hence not considered to be legitimate when it comes to measuring the practices of 'others' (see e.g. Gray 1995; Walzer 1983). In the cultural relativists' point of view, criticising other cultures from a set of Western-liberal values and norms is to assert that Western societies are better than other societies. In opposition to such an ethnocentric assertion, they aim to safeguard cultural distinctiveness by offering minority groups collective protection.

Against this backdrop, it seems evident that we cannot alleviate the tension between ethnocentrism and cultural relativism by simply allowing one consideration to override the other. The tension constitutes a dilemma, inasmuch as any one 'solution' reaffirms – and thereby reproduces – the tension. This does not mean, however, that the different 'choices' do not have different implications for the involved parties. Any potential 'solution' might have a dissimilar effect upon both the individuals and the groups. Thus, most multiculturalists aim for a sound balance between respect for individuals and respect for cultural groups. Unlike Okin, they do not dismiss cultural differences as morally irrelevant by conflating conventional norms and human rights.

From a liberal point of view, Brian Barry (2001) is bent upon distinguishing between conventional and universal norms. Proceeding from this distinction, he counterposes multiculturalists who assert that a cultural group should be able to coin its own concept of justice (ibid.: 132). As Barry sees it, a liberal is someone who holds that there are certain rights against oppression and injury to which every single human being is entitled to lay claim. He argues that any form of cultural relativism existing at the expense of these individual rights runs counter to the liberal position. Like Kymlicka, Barry considers cultural diversity to be acceptable only to the degree that each of the diverse groups functions in a way that is well adapted to advance the welfare and secure the rights of its members (ibid.: 134). However, unlike Kymlicka, Barry concludes that recognition of cultural diversity and granting of group rights is redundant. In his view, the only ways of life that need to appeal to the value of cultural diversity are those that involve unjust inequalities or that require powers of indoctrination and control that are incompatible with liberalism in order to maintain themselves (ibid.: 135).

Once again we see that cultural relativism, which pertains to the recognition of cultural distinctiveness, is challenged from the point of view of liberal equality. The right to interfere in cultural practices that are perceived to be illiberal (even if not illegal) is regarded as legitimate. Barry (2001) maintains that a liberal is a liberal, not a chameleon (ibid.: 137), and that compromise over liberal principles is not, and cannot be, a liberal value (ibid.: 283). Like Okin, he takes a critical stance in relation to Kymlicka, whom, he states, cannot be a liberal as long as he wants to grant special rights to minority groups: 'A theory that has the implication that nationalities (whether they control a state or a sub-state polity) have a fundamental right to violate liberal principles is not a liberal theory of group rights. It is an illiberal theory with a bit of liberal hand-writing thrown in as an optional extra' (ibid.: 140).

In many respects, Barry's and Okin's arguments approach the Norwegian integration policy, as well as other state policies that are based on a universalist justification of intervention. The majority culture's moral judgements assume a common communicative platform and overarching moral standards, relegating cultural differences to the private sphere. In the following, based on an analysis of the aforementioned policy documents, I shall look more closely at the Norwegian policy of integration in order to illustrate the recurrent tension between ethnocentrism and cultural relativism.

Ethnocentric categorisations

I shall point to a simple and yet significant paradox arising from the fact that the cultural norms of the majority set a limit to cultural diversity. In the following, I will treat this paradox as an aspect of 'planned pluralism'. We shall see that the problem is compounded by the fact that national norms may contradict international human rights. For instance, we may ask how Islamic calls to prayer can be regulated by public health legislation, without taking into account religious freedom. In order to pursue this question, which is illustrative of a widespread policy within contemporary Europe, we shall look more closely at the Norwegian integration policy.

Like other Western European countries, Norway is a culturally diverse nation state with a growing number of immigrants from different parts of the world. The increasing cultural diversity is a much-debated issue, in terms of both immigration and integration. As has been outlined above, the debate on integration tends to be structured by the question of tolerance, as expressed in two reports to the Parliament on the integration of immigrants: White Paper No. 17 (1996-1997), *On Immigration and Multicultural Norway*, and White Paper No. 49 (2003-2004), *Diversity through Inclusion and Participation: Responsibility and Freedom*. According to these documents, the government wants to set measures to tolerance so as to promote individual autonomy and freedom. The issues addressed by the policy documents are the extent to which the state should tolerate cultural diversity and the kind of cultural diversity that should be tolerated. This in turn is related to the question as to when respect for the cultural distinctiveness of immigrants impinges upon the individual rights of the citizens.

It is worth mentioning that neither of the policy documents contains arguments for the recognition of cultural distinctiveness (see Gressgård 2005; Gressgård and Jacobsen 2003). This is probably due to the fact that neither Norwegian legislation nor international conventions obligate Norway to take minority cultures into consideration. To the extent that the integration policy promotes cultural diversity, it proceeds from the assumption that respect for the cultural distinctiveness of the 'others' might facilitate the integration process. Respect for cultural distinctiveness is a matter of 'problem-solving' – a matter of managing differences that might pose a threat to the prevailing normative standards. As Wendy Brown (2006) makes clear, liberal-democratic tolerance is a tool for managing – that is, a mode of incorporating and regulating – the presence of the threatening 'other' within. The limit of tolerance is determined by the extent to which this impurity can be accommodated without dissolving the prevailing order (ibid.: 27). Hence, one is tolerant not by law, but in addition to the law (ibid.: 12).

Within a liberal-democratic framework, culture is normally viewed as an obstacle that one needs to be aware of and approach in a constructive manner while working to find feasible political solutions to the problem of difference. For instance, White Paper No. 49 (2003-2004) emphasises consumer rectification of public services and specially designed schemes that cater for various needs (see ibid.: 48, 115ff.). The document underscores that more detailed knowledge about the culture and group is necessary for service providers who largely deal with set target groups (ibid.: 118). Throughout the entire document, emphasis is put on the participation and responsibility of immigrants and their descendants in the process of integration. The immigrants are to be engaged in dialogue in so far as their power of influence may strengthen the legitimacy and effectiveness of the policy (see ibid.: 48, 81, 90, 98, 112, 119). The policy documents employ a multicultural rhetoric that encourages state officials, social workers and others to take into account the immigrants' special needs and diversity and the need for dialogue, and yet it is stated that this should be done only with a view to enhance immigrants' cooperativeness. Respect for cultural distinctiveness is restricted to practices that reaffirm prevailing norms and values, grounded in the ideal of equality. In this respect, the recognition of cultural distinctiveness is subsumed under the ideal of equality, and the ideal of equality is equated with the liberation of individuals from cultural constraints (cf. Brown 2006). From a cultural relativist point of view, this is an ethnocentric stance, since it entails assimilation to the prevailing cultural order.

As indicated above, however, the problem of ethnocentrism does not pertain principally to the legislated limitations, at least not the constitutional laws and articles of the penal code on which the minority and the majority tend to be in agreement. Rather, the problem of ethnocentrism is most often addressed in response to conventional norms and values, some of which are included in the civil statutes. For instance, based on conventional norms and values, citing civil statutes that include these, members of the Norwegian Parliament debated in 1999 whether or not calls to prayer from a mosque in Oslo should be permitted. Similarly, they have, on several occasions, debated whether or not the circumcision of boys should be prohibited. Since these cases involve practices that concern the freedom of religion, and since the freedom of religion is not only a human right but also a right granted by the Norwegian constitution, one may wonder why these questions were raised in the first place. It appears to be the case that neither of the debated issues was processed in accordance with the constitutional rights concerning freedom of religion. Instead, they were discussed as health matters by reference to the public health legislation, which indicates that these issues are not so much legal matters as matters of tolerance (with tolerance understood as a supplement to the law). When the case concerning calls to prayer came up in the community council, it was presented as a noise nuisance complaint, based on normative expectations concerning public conduct. The council was to consider whether or not calls to prayer qualify as a public disturbance that should be sanctioned by the public health regulations. Likewise, it was with a view to health concerns that two Members of Parliament from the right-wing Progressive Party proposed in 1998 a parliamentary bill that would prohibit the circumcision of boys. The representatives of the Progressive Party maintained that the surgical procedure was indefensible on the grounds of health. The same health argument was posed in 2007 by other politicians.

A related case, one that the Norwegian anthropologist Tordis Borchgrevink (2002) analyses, is the ritualistic killing of animals for meat. The politicians are, of course, aware of the fact that Jews and Muslims need to have access to ritually prepared foods in order to practise their faiths. However, the public administration has not taken into account this aspect of their respective religions. Health and security regulations, administered partly by the food control authorities, have taken precedence over religious freedom. That is to say, individual rights, such as freedom of religion, have not been defined as applicable with regard to health and food control regulations. Religious practices have all along been treated as culturally specific traits of groups, and, as stated above, cultural distinctiveness is normally not granted recognition by the state.

In a similar manner, Barry (2001) discusses whether or not male Sikhs in the UK should be allowed to carry the special type of knife that their religion prescribes that they should carry. He notes that prohibiting the carrying of the knife in public is an abridgement of religious freedom. On the other hand, granting permission would constitute a breach of the public order proscribing the bearing of weapons, a breach of general security regulations (ibid.: 152). By the same token, the wearing of the Sikh headgear might be prohibited by reference to health and security, for example, with regard to the regulation requiring motorcycle helmets. In Norway, the concern for health and security always takes precedence over religion in cases that involve religious headgear (SMED 2001). It should perhaps also be mentioned that the regulations are often vaguely defined, so that they can easily be used to impose sanctions against the wearing of such headgear even in situations where it is unlikely to pose a risk. In Western countries, particularly after 2001, security precautions are frequently used to prevent Muslim women from wearing religious clothing, such as the *niqab* and *burka*, that covers the entire body, including the face. Muslim women are also sometimes prevented, allegedly for security reasons, from wearing headscarves, often referred to as *hijab*, that cover their hair and neck. And the security concerns – the issues of public safety – arise not only at airports but also at workplaces, educational institutions, government organisations and public transport systems. As Homi Bhabha (2004) notes in his paper 'Writing, Rights, and Responsibility', security has become a cultural lens through which we view difference.

Cases such as these illustrate not only how health and security issues take precedence over religious concerns, but more generally how para-juridical measures of precaution supplement the law. In line with Brown (2006), we could argue that the production and regulation of subjects take place through a formally non-legal mode of power in both state and non-state institutions and discourses. However, these cases also illustrate how judgements that pertain to conventional norms and values tend to be converted into legal concerns when cultural and religious differences are considered to pose a threat to national identity. Whereas Brown's analyses of tolerance as a regulating practice vis-à-vis 'threatening' differences elucidate how moral-political regulations function as supplements to discourses of legal rights and equality, these examples illuminate how moral-political issues – pertaining to conventional norms and values – are given a legal status and thereby treated as if they were universally valid. With respect to the latter, we may speak of ethnocentric categorisations.

Disintegration of spheres via maintenance of spheres

If we are to pursue the problem of categorisation, we should take a closer look at the political strategies that are being employed when approaching the 'others'. According to Larsen (1979), there are two opposite strategies that emerge as different options. Either one chooses the strategy 'maintenance of spheres', or one chooses the strategy 'disintegration of spheres' (ibid.: 10). The first strategy could be conceived as an expression of cultural relativism, whereas the latter could be seen as indicative of ethnocentrism. As the above discussion has suggested, cultural relativism is characterised by the strategy of maintaining separate spheres by way of upholding cultural borders and boundaries. Culture is taken to mean a group or a community of people who share a set of evaluative moral and legal values. Different cultures are thus depicted as different moral spheres with their own autonomy, and their members are expected to follow the prevailing cultural standards more or less naturally. In so far as people are considered to be cultural products, no distinction is made between individual autonomy and culture.

According to the policy documents White Paper No. 17 (1996–1997) and White Paper No. 49 (2003–2004), cultural relativism – associated with the strategy 'maintenance of spheres' – is not acknowledged in the Norwegian documents. The government's wish to stay clear of cultural relativism is expressed in the way that the document deals with forced marriages, female circumcision and polygamy. Such practices are repeatedly described as illegal, but what interests us in this context is that they are taken to be the potential outcomes of a cultural relativist policy. So, rather than embracing cultural autonomy, immigrant cultural traditions should, according to the documents, be regulated and possibly terminated. Culture tends to be depicted as a potential threat to individual autonomy and liberty, especially to female members of minority communities. Undesirable practices are made into objects of a determined practical and political strategy whose goal is the dissolution of separate cultural spheres. Separate cultural spheres signal disintegration and must therefore be eliminated for the sake of integration. However, the anti-relativist strategy is based on the assumption that cultures are in fact self-contained and closed moral universes. The political defiance of cultural relativism is, as such, predicated upon the cultural relativist assumptions that it opposes. In this respect, cultural relativism and ethnocentrism are mutually constitutive, adhering to the logic of opposition in the relationship between 'us' and the 'others'.

In accordance with this logic of opposition, 'we' are depicted as modern and liberated, in contrast to the traditional 'others', who are taken to be governed by their cultural traditions. In Norway, cultural distinctiveness tends to be reserved for the 'others', and women are notably considered to be subjugated by authoritative traditional leaders. Not only are immigrants defined by cultural attributes and relegated to local moral universes; it is *ipso facto* a self-definition by which 'we' identify with human dignity and universal rights.[4] Such a de-culturalisation of 'us' by means of culturalisation of the 'others' paradoxically excludes the minorities from the dominant moral universe into which integration policy is attempting to enlist them in the first place. This is probably why the state is constantly bent upon integrating the 'others'; the threatening cultural difference is recurrent and has to be managed accordingly.

As mentioned above, the 'others' – immigrant women in particular – are relentlessly depicted in the policy documents as products of their traditional cultural practices, as if those practices were the very core characteristics – the essence – of the immigrant population. This is also true of the national media, in which non-Western immigrants are likely to be portrayed as anonymous members of a group, whereas Western immigrants, alongside of the majority population, are treated as individuals (Lindstad and Fjeldstad 1999). The message seems to be that immigrants belong to closed cultural and moral spheres, and that the supreme authority resides in those who administer culture. For instance, in the wake of the death of the Swedish Kurd Fadime Shindal, killed by her father in January 2002, a number of politicians from various political parties were interviewed by the national media. Their unequivocal message was that imams who practise their profession within the country should take responsibility by publicly condemning cruelty to women and should dissociate themselves from the institutions of forced marriage and honour killing. The Prime Minister at that time, the Christian-Democrat Kjell Magne Bondevik, expressed on camera during the evening news program (*Dagsrevyen*) that the power of the imams is strong, so what they say is important. He encouraged Muslim communities to help prevent prejudice from harming the integration of immigrants, and he emphasised that a positive integration presupposes that the religious leaders have learned and support the values that form the basis of the prevailing society (*Dagbladet/NTB*, 7 February 2002).[5] This type of message indicates that the Prime Minister aims to break down the putative separated spheres and enlist immigrants in the majority moral community. In accordance with the discussion above, we may designate this strategy as a 'disintegration of spheres via maintenance of spheres'. The media debate clearly reveals that the culturalisation of immigrants, by way of maintaining separate spheres, is part and parcel of the national integration policy. Religious leaders, who perhaps otherwise would be less influential, are then granted authority, which risks counter-productively exacerbating the problem at hand.

Planned pluralism

The strategy of 'disintegrating spheres via maintenance of spheres' seems to involve a planned pluralism with respect to the managing of cultural difference.

In her essay 'Immigrant Culture as an Obstacle to "Partnership"',[6] Aleksandra Ålund (1991) defines planned pluralism as a technocratic, effective, rational and scientifically controlled form of integration of immigrants. The plurality is culturalised into a multiplicity of cultural distinctions, while at the same time being ethnocentrically linked to the prevailing standards of normality. In Ålund's view, this amounts to a paradox – a multicultural paradox.

In the Norwegian context, the most significant sign of planned pluralism is the fact that integration is pre-defined. In a report on social integration in Norway, May Thorseth (1995) is critical of a strategy that presumes given standards for successful social integration and communication. Her analysis emphasises that measures for integration are often based on the implicit assumption that the norms and values of the majority are universal. The fact that the majority standards form the basis of a planned co-existence of different cultures, similar to the planned pluralism that Ålund identifies in the Swedish context, suggests that integration takes the form of a unilateral process of assimilation on the part of the immigrants. This indicates that multicultural dialogue is in fact a monologue, and it suggests that cultural renewing forces are ignored in favour of consolidating forces. We may infer from this, in accordance with Ålund (1991: 73), that a planned pluralism entails a standardisation of the 'others', conjoined with a hierarchical dividing line between 'us' and the 'others'.

Ålund argues that the culturalisation of the 'others' constitutes a dual problem. It conceals tensions in the social construction of ethnicity, on the one hand, while consolidating a hierarchical status system, on the other. As mentioned above, within the parameters of the liberal-democratic nation state, social differences are depicted primarily as cultural deviations. Ålund (1991) also points out that proposed solutions to social problems are typically reduced to individual, personal matters, rather than being dealt with as broad socio-political problems of inequality (ibid.: 84–85).[7] In its extreme form, she argues, cultural pluralism is an ideological framework of reference that conceals actual processes of exclusion based on a dominant form of cultural absolutism (ibid.: 84). In line with this argument, we may conceive of the ostensible acceptance – the pseudo-recognition – of cultural distinctiveness in public policy as a normalising measure in a nation-building project. At any rate, the political strategy is that of planned pluralism, whereby the 'others' constitute a cultural difference that must be managed in order to be tolerable (cf. Brown 2006).

In concluding this Introduction, I want to emphasise that planned pluralism seems to promote neither equality nor distinctiveness. Cases that concern equality of a socio-political nature are overshadowed by the focus on cultural distinctiveness, in so far as cultural distinctiveness is equated with deviation and hierarchical subordination. At the same time, recognition of cultural distinctiveness evaporates due to the emphasis on equality, in so far as equality is equated with normalisation and assimilation. This multicultural paradox demonstrates most clearly that the integration policy serves to reiterate and reify the asymmetrical structure between the majority and the minority population – an asymmetry that runs counter to the purported equality among citizens.[8]

Against this backdrop, I shall, throughout the rest of the book, concentrate on the dilemmas, paradoxes and conflicts that adhere to multiculturalism as a political doctrine. Moving from the particularity of Scandinavian integration policy to a more abstract level of discussion, I endeavour to interrogate the conditions of possibility for multicultural dialogue. However, as the following discussion suggests, I do not intend to develop a new model for dialogue, nor is it my goal to improve existing theoretical or ethical formulas for multicultural encounters. As mentioned in the preface, my scrutiny is not aimed at problem-solving at any level; rather, I intend to scrutinise the cultural and philosophical underpinnings of the dilemma between equal dignity and cultural distinctiveness by way of critical intervention. I will proceed by posing the question of whether integration of the 'others', within the parameters of egalitarianism, necessarily entails assimilation and subordination, or whether it is possible to recognise the 'others' on their own terms. In this regard, recognition involves the right and opportunity to speak for oneself and to be entitled to discuss the very terms of recognition (see e.g. Madood 2007). In order to approach this issue, I shall look more closely at the discursive framework that structures the debate on multiculturalism.

Chapter 1

Dual Subjectivity and the Metaphysics of Purity

Is it possible to describe the 'others' and recognise them as equal and distinct on their own terms? Or does recognition render the 'others' opposite and subordinate to 'us'? In what follows, I will pursue these questions by scrutinising the way in which recognition of equal dignity, on the one hand, and recognition of cultural distinctiveness, on the other, converge in a single process of assimilation and culturalisation/subordination. Assimilation denotes a process of conceptual incorporation by way of subsuming the 'others' under the prevailing conceptual framework. To the extent that the 'others' are portrayed as culturally distinct, in opposition to 'us', they tend to be concurrently culturalised and subordinated, whereas 'we' are rendered neutral and superior. Following Tord Larsen (1999), my point of departure will be a quotation from Shakespeare's *The Tempest* (Act I, Scene 2) in which the author permits Prospero to chide Caliban:

> I pitied thee,
> Took pains to make thee speak, taught thee each hour
> One thing or other: when thou didst not, savage,
> Know thine own meaning, but wouldst gabble like
> A thing most brutish, I endow'd thy purposes
> With words that made them known …

Naturally, Shakespeare was not concerned with questions of integration, let alone multiculturalism. Nevertheless, his work seems to prefigure a pivotal dilemma in the modern philosophy of the subject, owing to the fact that

Caliban is unable to articulate his own 'meaning' until Prospero has given him a language by which to express himself. Through the prism of modern constructionism, it could be argued that Caliban's acquisition of subjectivity – his viable subject position – did not exist before his Duke had given him the gift of speech. We may therefore assert that Prospero is Caliban's creator. Prior to this act of creation, which is at the same time an act of incorporation, Caliban is identifiable neither to himself nor to others. Prospero is able to understand Caliban only by assimilating his otherness, which is to say that he must recreate Caliban in his own image in order to recognise him. The Prospero-ised Caliban is thus an effect of recognition by assimilation (Spivak 1988, 1999).

Given this constitutive interaction, two possible strategies emerge. Either one constructs the 'others' as a version of oneself, whereby the 'others' are eradicated through assimilation, or the 'others' are portrayed as an alterity, with the aim of reaffirming the value of one's own dialectical antithesis (Larsen 1999: 91). The latter technique Hayden White (1972: 5) designates as 'ostensive self-definition by negation'. According to White, this seems to be a particularly useful approach for groups whose dissatisfaction is easier to recognise than their programmes are to justify (ibid.). To the extent that the strategy of assimilation entails total effacement of the distinctiveness of the 'others' by way of complete assimilation, either voluntarily or by force, recognition is rendered impossible. My focus of attention will therefore be on the other strategy – that which involves assimilation conjoined with an accentuation of cultural distinctiveness.

In the Introduction, we saw that the recognition of cultural distinctiveness is treated by some as a means to an end. For instance, in the Norwegian integration policy, recognition is encouraged with a view to obtaining the immigrants' cooperation and amenability. This often seems to be the case when integration aims at promoting individual freedom and equality. As it developed, however, we saw that the desire to recognise both equality and distinctiveness is likely to result in neither equality nor distinctiveness. The reason for this, I argued, is that an egalitarian policy, based on individual freedom and equality, entails assimilation, whereas an emphasis on distinctiveness results in culturalisation and subordination. In the conclusion to the Introduction, I pointed out that assimilation conjoined with culturalisation tends to imply a culturalisation of inequality. In this chapter, I attempt to develop this argument.

However, I shall leave the political field for a moment, directing my attention to the cultural logic that underpins the dilemma between equality and distinctiveness. My line of argument is based on a theoretical postulate that recognition of both equality and distinctiveness presupposes a specific standard – or a particular cultural order – that sets the premises for recognition. For this reason, recognition implies assimilation of the 'others' into a specific cultural and symbolic order. And to the extent that the politics of recognition hinges upon a universalised standard for judgement, one may find that multicultural politics of recognition nourishes ethnocentrism.

As suggested in the Introduction, ethnocentrism is characterised in a Western context by a belief in the universal validity of liberal-democratic evaluative standards (cf. Barry 2001), or at least by an assertion that such standards are universally valid by virtue of being better than all other sets of values (cf. Okin 1999). In the latter case, the cultural distinctiveness of the liberal-democratic order is acknowledged, but since the liberal tradition is considered to be more developed, more enlightened, more civilised, and so forth, liberal values are magnified to a universal ideal. In both cases, the 'others' are assimilated in terms of being judged in accordance with norms and values of which they do not necessarily approve, and they end up being judged as inferior.

Inclusive humanity

A crucial question in the debate on multiculturalism is whether the 'others' can be modernised while ensuring their cultural autonomy. Is it possible for them to attain 'the best of both worlds', as it were, and gain recognition as being both equal *and* distinctive? It is this question – whether it is possible to attain both – that makes the issue dilemmatic. By the same token, it is the desire for both equality and distinctiveness that gives rise to the discussion on ethnocentrism. It is not until one attempts to both modernise and ensure the cultural autonomy of the 'others' that the question of ethnocentric imposition is addressed. The pressing question with respect to ethnocentrism is whether the 'others' can be modernised without their cultural distinctiveness being harmed. Another salient question is why the 'others' should be modernised in the first place.

The problem of ethnocentrism has been the object of many discussions in Western political philosophy, and it has led to a number of attempted solutions that have taken various forms and directions. However, there appears to be a common denominator in all of these attempts: all the proposed 'solutions' seem to dismiss the idea of modernisation in terms of civilisation. When associated with civilisation, modernisation is considered to be an illegitimate form of interaction between 'us' and the 'others'. As a consequence of this break with the ethnocentric civilising project of the West, alternative terms and ideas about the 'others' have come to the fore during the last decades. Larsen (1999) groups these new terms and ideas into four categories. The first he refers to as inclusive humanity, which is a replacement for the dichotomy between one party that is not fully developed and another that is completely developed. The second category is that of universal human rights, which holds that all human beings have certain individual rights by virtue of being human. The third concerns the ideal of a dialogue between equal parties, as opposed to a civilising monologue. And the fourth pertains to respect for cultural autonomy, which entails that your world view is as valid as mine, and if we are to speak of development, it should be on one's own terms (ibid.: 95).

All of the attempts at making amends for the legacy of colonial civilisatory enterprises involve a substitution of assimilation and civilising modernisation with ideals of equality and respect, be it between autonomous and unique individuals, or autonomous and unique cultures/groups. All of these efforts seem to involve some sort of idea of an inclusive humanity, which demands equality and respect between individuals. At the same time, the idea of an inclusive humanity presupposes distinct parties, and the distinctions are assumed to be cultural – that is to say, culturally distinct parties ideally constitute a relationship of equality and mutual respect. In this regard, we are left with the desire for recognition of both individual equality and cultural distinctiveness. If we take a closer look at this relationship between equal dignity and cultural distinctiveness, we notice that there is an intrinsic symbolic duality in the human subject, and it is this duality that seems to constitute the dilemma between equality and distinctiveness. Whereas the claim to recognition of equality is laid by reference to humans in an abstract sense – that is, abstract subjects without any particular characteristics or identities – recognition of distinctiveness is based on the idea that all humans, with their particular characteristics and identities, are different and unique.[1]

As the above discussion suggests, equality depends on the notion of an ahistorical, abstract human being, devoid of particular qualities or identities. According to this conception, all humans are equal with regard to dignity. The notion of the abstract human subject can be traced back to the emergence of an individual inner essence as the source for all values and meanings, which presupposes a vital distinction between the inner and the outer world. Alluding to Nietzsche, Foucault, Dumont and others who have scrutinised the historical processes of interiorisation or internalisation, Larsen (1999) paints with broad strokes: 'What occurs on an inner arena (in the form of intention) acquires increased significance in ethics, in pace with a religious inner essence (the Reformation), an aesthetic ideal saying that the work of art is the artist's expression of himself (Romanticism), a psychology of inner emotions as impetuses, reference to inner impulses as legitimate grounds for action ("I had to leave him, because love was dead") and a moral quest that strives for authentic life. Overall: the relocalisation of the sacred from a place out there to a place in here' (ibid.: 97; my translation).

According to Louis Dumont (1986: 37), the Stoics and others acknowledged human equality, anchored in the human mind, but the Christian notion of equality is perhaps even more deeply founded, since it is embedded in the heart of the individual. What characterises Christianity in its Protestant form is that all attempts at perfection are turned inwards in a process of interiorisation. Dumont remarks that this is readily seen, for instance, in Origen's 'tropological' level of exegesis, where all biblical events are interpreted as happening in the inner life of the Christian. Saint Augustine introduces the ideal of equality among humans, Dumont notes, and the idea of the inner life of the individual and of equality among humans becomes further strengthened by Calvinism and the Reformation. Since it is through the soul that the human being relates to God, there exists a chain of subordination from God to the soul and from the soul to the body (ibid.). What is of interest to my argument is the assertion that interiorisation entails a separation between the human being and its social surroundings. This distinction between the inner and the outer life gives rise to the modern notion of human universality alongside differentiation. Another way of putting this would be that the process of interiorisation prefigures a notion of human beings as unique (we are all different) and, at the same time, as comparable to all others (we are all identical).

To a certain extent, this is in line with Charles Taylor's (1989) argument in his book *Sources of the Self*, in which he scrutinises the idea of an inner space to which every individual has privileged access. We think of our thoughts, ideas and feelings as being 'within' us (ibid.: 111). In Taylor's view, this 'inwardness' is the point of origin for the stream of modern thought – the origin of the modern idea of personal autonomy indicative of the Age of Enlightenment (ibid.: 364). Another cultural source of the modern subject is the late-eighteenth-century idea of personal uniqueness, based on the premise that each individual is different and original, and that this originality determines how the individual ought to live (ibid.: 375). The distinction Taylor draws between personal autonomy (Enlightenment) and uniqueness (Romanticism) is indeed pertinent. However, as my discussion will reveal, there are reasons to consider autonomy and uniqueness as two aspects of a more comprehensive category of autonomy. As I see it, to draw a sharp distinction between autonomy and uniqueness is not always illuminating when modern subjectivity is concerned. In Larsen's delineation of the process of interiorisation, the focal point is not the distinction between Enlightenment and Romanticism, but rather the relocalisation of the universal dimension from an outer to an inner world. This delineation, in which human autonomy and uniqueness are grouped together, seems more relevant to my argument about multiculturalism than Taylor's emphasis on the duality of personal autonomy and uniqueness.[2]

With this in mind, I will move on to suggest that the politics of recognition presupposes a universalisation of the configuration of the Western subject, that is, the duality of the modern subject. On the one hand, recognition of equal dignity presupposes universalisation of the notion of an abstract human subject, which unwittingly serves to assimilate the 'others' into the prevailing cultural order. On the other hand, recognition of cultural distinctiveness presupposes a universalisation of the notion of an autonomous or unique subject, for it is only on the basis of the conception that all humans are different that the 'others' can be recognised as culturally distinctive. Alluding to Shakespeare, Larsen (1999: 96) asserts that in order for me to be able to respect your integrity and autonomy, I must create the very integrity and autonomy that I have vowed not to offend. In order to be recognised as both equal/identical and distinctive/different, the 'others' must be made, in principle, identical with 'us'. In this sense, recognition is premised on the incorporation of the 'others' in the dual construction of the human subject. It is on the basis of this rationale that we can understand Larsen's (ibid: 101) assertion that the export of the Western subject configuration could be regarded as the consummation of the idea of an inclusive humanity (cf. Butler 2004a, 2004b).

The problem of opposition

In what follows I will elaborate further on the asymmetrical dynamics between 'us and the 'others'. In line with post-colonial theory, my point of departure is the interaction between the party who speaks first, and who thus lays the premises for comparability, and the party who responds – and possibly articulates opposition – in the medium established by the counterpart (see Spivak 1988, 1999). The asymmetry between 'us' and the 'others' is expressed in a number of doctrines, such as the modern vocabulary of rights concerning the preservation of culture, which purports to protect cultural distinctiveness and the possible granting of specific group rights. This is, according to Larsen (1999: 104), a highly legitimate and morally viable project – and yet the language spoken is that of Prospero.

The relationship between 'us' and the 'others' has been duly discussed and criticised during the past decades, not only within post-colonial studies, but also within various fields of feminism, queer theory, and post-structuralism, notably by scholars who are preoccupied with deconstruction.[3] However, as the preceding discussion on multiculturalism has revealed, the consolidating mechanism seems conspicuously tenacious. Larsen (1999: 105) holds that minority groups are faced with two possibilities: either they end up in a self-effacing homogeneity with the other party, or they retreat to solipsistic uniqueness. In the process of wavering between them, Larsen argues, the 'others' experience a cultural self-objectification due to a unifying eye that comes from the outside. One version of the unifying eye is that of the colonist who objectifies for the purpose of dominating. Another version is that of the anthropologist who objectifies for the sake of knowledge production. Once again, Larsen's elaboration evokes the figures of Shakespeare, stressing that the savage did not exist before the discipline of anthropology was established. The so-called primitive came into being through 'our' discourses, and the 'others' responded from the position that colonialism and anthropology conferred on them, that is, through self-objectification (ibid.).

The assertion that the 'primitive' subject is constituted within a dynamic of objectification and subjugation alludes to Foucault's (1979) depiction of the subject-constitutive dynamics between objectification and subjectification (*asujettement*). The dynamics entrenches the simultaneous assimilation and culturalisation/subordination of the 'others', whereby the 'others' are faced with a dilemma. They can objectify cultural distinctiveness, and thereby become parasites vis-à-vis the group with which they compare their distinctiveness, or they can refrain from objectifying distinctiveness, and thereby find it virtually impossible to articulate difference. This dilemma, which can also be designated as a problem of opposition, suggests that a request for recognition of cultural distinctiveness presupposes a self-culturalisation based on the premises of the majority. One could, of course, try to resist being portrayed as distinct, but that would probably lead to a self-effacing sameness with the majority by way of complete assimilation.

The problem of opposition is akin to the question posed above, namely, how the 'others' can be recognised as culturally distinct without being constrained by the language of the dominant party. This in turn resembles the post-colonial problem elucidated by, among others, Homi Bhabha (1994) and Gayatri Spivak (1985, 1988). Both point to the fact that the formerly colonised must deal with the colonial powers' constructions (stereotypes) of them in their new identities. The post-colonised 'others' appear to have no other choice than to think within the structures that they reject.[4] In Spivak's (1985: 253) view, 'No perspective *critical* of imperialism can turn the Other into a self, because the project of imperialism has always already historically refracted what might have been the absolutely Other into a domesticated Other that consolidates the imperialist self.'

Even though the formerly colonised are in a different situation than disenfranchised groups in the so-called First World, the 'others' risk being perpetually imprisoned in the duality of assimilation and culturalisation/subordination. The process of recognition is likely to entrench discursively what Brown calls 'injury-identity' pertaining to 'wounded attachments' (1995: 7, 21). Recognition involves identity formation whereby some people are depicted as 'others' in need of protection within the very structure that oppresses them. As already mentioned, the consolidation of injury-identities risks reinscribing the structures of domination that they aim to transform, and the injured subjects are likely to be further regulated by those structures. Larsen (1999: 105) is of the opinion that unless we reject the idea of cultural autonomy altogether, the problem of opposition will be perpetually reproduced.

The duality of the subject

In what follows I attempt to show that the antagonistic relationship between 'us' and the 'others' is endemic for a modern metaphysics of purity that gives rise to a disparity between the abstract and the unique human being. It is this disparity or gap, I argue, that energises the logic of opposition constitutive of 'us' and the 'others'. In taking this stance, I move into a theoretical sphere in which the conceptual repertoire is not drawn from the political-philosophical literature that informs the debate on multiculturalism. However, despite this theoretical detour, or perhaps because of it, I am able to delineate a more comprehensive framework within which I question some of the basic assumptions and structural mechanisms that have brought about the dilemma between equality and distinctiveness. On the basis of the duality of the subject – or, more specifically, the intermediating gap between the abstract/universal and the autonomous/ unique subject – I will, in the subsequent sections on modern political ideology, return to the field of political philosophy and the politics of recognition.

Metaphysical purity refers to that which is absolutely whole and devoid of differentiation, that which is indissoluble, that which can be neither depicted nor recounted, that which does not change over time (Eliassen 2002: 22–23). In a certain sense, metaphysical purity is tantamount to undifferentiated chaos. The order of society and nature is, in contrast, a differentiated and impure cosmos. Once the human being has eaten from the Tree of Knowledge, the Fall of Man is an irrevocable fact, and humans are subsequently prone to lapse into sin. The secular world of distinctions and conventions has become humanity's destiny from that very moment: purity has evaporated, and secular impurity is all that there is left. As long as Christianity's founding myth of Genesis is at the heart of Western tradition, metaphysical notions of purity are pivotal elements in modern reasoning.

It is my contention that there is a dynamic relationship between metaphysical purity and impurity in modern configurations of thought. For instance, as will be demonstrated below, the envisioning of a timeless space in terms of a utopian totality is invoked by the certitude of an impure empirical world. Metaphysical purity gives rise to the orderly processes of the secular world of distinctions. Or, put differently, the impurity of the cosmos is the catalyst for the emergence of totalising, regulating ideas of metaphysical purity, such as the Hegelian and Marxist ahistorical epistemologies of the truth and moral theories. The mythical conceit of the Fall of Man seems to be a vital part of all modern grand narratives. Arguably, the 'grand' in grand narratives points to an ahistorical, universal element of metaphysical purity. It is my contention that the teleological view of history that comes to the fore in Enlightenment thinking testifies to the fact that a unifying, mythical structure is (indirectly) operative in modern configurations. I will return to this conflation of nonmodern and modern configurations of thought in Chapter 2.

As for now, we may ask how secular modern reasoning is mythical. Michael Polanyi (1958) identifies a number of features common to magical belief systems and modern secular scientific discourses, arguing that all systems of knowledge rest on basic premises that are sustained by virtue of the actors' commitment to them as true. Likewise, from a slightly different perspective, Adorno and Horkheimer ([1944] 1997) suggest that modern reasoning is imbued with mythical discourse. In their book *Dialectic of Enlightenment*, they point out a continuum between mythical and scientific discourse, via metaphysical discourse. In their view, scientific discourse, in its rationalist and empiricist versions, is unifying and circular in character, because the process is always decided from the start (ibid.: 24). The ideal of Enlightenment is, as they see it, the system from which all and everything follows. Enlightenment makes the dissimilar comparable by reducing it to abstract quantities: that which does not reduce to numbers, and ultimately to the one, becomes illusion (ibid.: 6, 7). Thought becomes mere tautology, they argue, for in its figures, mythology has the essence of the status quo, which means that the new appear as the predetermined (ibid.: 27). Enlightenment is the philosophy that equates the truth with scientific systematisation, and the constitutive principle of science is self-preservation (ibid.: 85ff.). In their view, mythology is inseparable from the profane (ibid.: 28).

Regardless of the particular manifestations of magic, mythical or religious belief systems, secular scientific discourse tends to be contingent upon the knowledge systems that it opposes. As Adorno and Horkheimer (1997: 89) make clear, the principle by which reason is set against all that is unreasonable is the basis of the true antithesis of enlightenment and mythology. This is a commonplace understanding, but it seems nevertheless important to emphasise the oppositional logic pertaining to this Great Divide between the rational and the non-rational that is characteristic of Enlightening thought, as it also directs our attention to the way in which modern secular ideas and subject formations are magnified in a manner akin – although not identical – to religious divinity. We shall return to this topic below, in the section on utopian ideals, before proceeding to the next chapter, in which we will take a closer look at the hierarchical structure that seems to be implied by secular ideologies.

If we keep to the constitutive opposition between metaphysical purity and impurity in modern reasoning, it becomes clear that purity can be experienced only negatively and indirectly – that is, through the impure. Whereas the metaphysically pure is beyond comprehension, the impure world (of differentiations or categorisations) enables us to endow things and human beings with attributes/identities and meaning. For instance, as Foucault (e.g. 1979) and others have demonstrated, it is our categorisations that render subjectivity possible. Above we have seen that the modern subject is marked by a split between a universal and an autonomous element. This split is, as I see it, homologous to the gap between the undifferentiated pure and the differentiated impure within the modern metaphysics of purity. The autonomous element of the subject translates into metaphysical impurity on the grounds that it breaks with the purity of the undifferentiated, universal whole. Conversely, the abstract, universal subject corresponds to metaphysical purity by virtue of being identical to itself and to all others; it comprises an undifferentiated unity.

The universal subject exists, of course, only on a conceptual level, as an abstract individual, whereas the autonomous subject exists in an empirical world as an embodied individual with distinctive qualities and characteristics. In an empirical world, individuals are necessarily differentiated. This constitutes the defining paradox of modern individuality-based ideology. As Joan W. Scott (1996: 5ff.) notes, on the one hand, the individual is the abstract prototype of the human, while on the other, the concrete individual is a distinct person, different from all others of its species. Whereas the former evokes a notion of fundamental human sameness – a set of universal traits – the latter raises the issue of difference. In that sense, individuality requires the very difference that the idea of the prototypical human individual was meant to deny.

The paradoxical relationship between notions of human equality and notions of human distinctiveness also gives rise to the multicultural dilemma between equal dignity and cultural distinctiveness. As the above discussion has indicated, however, this paradoxical relationship needs to be examined more closely with respect to the modern dynamics of purity and impurity. I have suggested that the paradoxical duality of the modern subject – the subject's internal division – is a manifestation of a peculiar modern metaphysics of purity. Significantly, modern individuals are divided by virtue of being self-conscious. As Lars-Henrik Schmidt and Jens Erik Kristensen (1986: 21) put it: "'I am me' is the substitute identity of the humans and not of God: "I am the one I am". Purity, on the other hand, as an absolute quality, does not tolerate the 'I' (Eliassen 2002: 21). The claim 'I am pure' implies that I am self-conscious and autonomous, and hence impure.[5]

Order and disorder

Contrary to metaphysical purity, which is inexpressible because it is devoid of differences, impurity denotes differentiation. In her book *Purity and Danger*, Mary Douglas (1984) remarks that culture is synonymous with impurity because culture entails differentiation from the original chaos (purity). That being said, in a cultural-cosmological context, the impure is normally considered to be pure. This sounds like yet another paradox, but in this case the paradox is principally on a conceptual level and calls merely for conceptual clarification. Given the argument above, it is evident that cultural differentiations – humanly created categories, classifications and distinctions – are necessary in order to make meaning, constitute subjectivity, form cultural identity, and so on. Culture is, as such, predicated on the reproduction of categorical distinctions in a process by which undifferentiated chaos is excluded. Undifferentiated chaos – metaphysical purity – signifies the heterogeneity that must be excluded for the sake of cultural reproduction. In a peculiar way, however, the original metaphysical purity translates into impurity in a cultural-cosmological sense. We produce culturally pure categories by reducing metaphysical purity (undifferentiated chaos) to cultural differentiations. Cultural purity, then, becomes tantamount to metaphysical impurity, and vice versa. According to Douglas (ibid.), cultural systems of order are more or less stable symbolic classification systems. Purity is defined as that which corresponds with the system, while impurity is defined as that which is 'out of place' in relation to the system of order. Order produces disorder through its distinctions, through its exclusion of that which is out of place.

It is worth noting in this context that there are two types of cultural disorder at play in the process of ordering. First, there is the kind of disorder that clearly breaks with the cultural system of order. In this regard, order and disorder are constitutive opposites, in accordance with the logic of opposition. The outcome is a more or less clearly defined order in terms of an identity or a 'we', as opposed to a corresponding 'other' (as in an ostensive self-definition by negation). On this level of negation, the negative is a partial process inasmuch as the 'other' is a clearly defined opposition to 'us'. The 'other' signifies a heterogeneity or difference that can be managed – a controllable and controlled disorder that serves to define and reaffirm 'our' identity.

On another level of negation, the 'pathology' signifies a pure negation that cannot be identified through the cultural system of classifications. This pure negation denotes a second type of cultural disorder that cannot be managed within the system of classifications by virtue of being an undifferentiated, timeless chaos (see Deleuze [1967] 1991: 26f.). Thus, the pathological disorder qua metaphysical purity threatens to radically disintegrate the order of things: it is an uncontrollable and uncontrolled irregularity; it has no form or shape; it is an unidentifiable heterogeneity that simply cannot be identified and managed. Contrary to the partial negation, the pathology qua pure negation refuses incorporation or assimilation.[6] I shall return to this unidentifiable and uncontrollable heterogeneity in later chapters. First, however, I will elaborate on the cultural logics pertaining to partial negation.

Communitas and liminality

The dynamics between cultural order and disorder is sometimes depicted as a relationship between 'liminality' and 'communitas'. The concept of liminality was introduced by Arnold van Gennep ([1909] 1960) in his book *Rites of Passage* and has since been used in a number of anthropological studies of rites.

Liminal situations, phases, stages and spaces signify something that is situated 'betwixt and between' two orders, like a transitional entity. Such transitional entities may include birth, puberty, marriage, sacred rooms, and so on, separate from normal life. In this respect, liminality often denotes something sacred, ritually perilous, vulnerable, impure or exposed to pollution. Liminality is accorded a status as an external determinant of the symbolic order – its more or less clearly defined alterity. The symbolic order, on the other hand, is often depicted as a normative 'communitas', denoting a symbolically distinct cultural community. As such, liminality and communitas are inextricable. The two terms mutually constitute one another by way of opposition, which suggests a symbolic assimilation like the one I have described above. And as long as liminality is depicted as the negation of the normative communitas, it also signifies a concurrent subordination.[7]

Liminality is normally conceived as a space marked by difference. However, it does not always translate into marginality, at least not when marginality is associated with insignificance as opposed to centrality. Liminality tends to refer to a position 'outside' of the community, and yet it is located in the midst of it. In that sense, the liminal space is not marginal but central. However, seen from a different point of view, the liminal space is indeed a marginal space, associated with exclusion. And here emerges a paradox: the centre is an exclusion. Liminality signifies the excluded outside of a normative communitas, which is at the same time its midst. It denotes the disorder on which order is predicated by way of exclusion. According to Victor Turner (1969: 176), liminal places exist as a means for renewal of the society in a process of integration.

If we view liminality in light of the above-mentioned dynamics between metaphysical purity and impurity, the liminal is not pathological but designates instead a reproductive partial negation. The impure possesses an intermediary existence. It constitutes a state associated with liminal phases or thresholds between two stages in which the conditions are highly uncertain, such as birth, puberty, menstruation, marriage, illness, death, and so on (see Hetherington 1998: 111). Eliassen (2000: 21) notes that the social prohibitions that characterise these transitional phases turn them into states of exception. (As we shall see in Chapter 4, however, this does not correspond to Giorgio Agamben's (1998, 2005) concept of 'the state of exception', which signifies radical difference.) According to Eliassen (2000), liminality denotes a 'time outside of time', which is crucial to the symbolic order. Its centrality is mainly due not to its integrating function in a ritual process but, above all, to its constitutive role as an excluded outside.

Liminality tends to be associated with nature, which is seen as the chaos against which modern humans contrast themselves. By the same token, nature signifies those aspects of human life that are not corrupted by modern civilisation: the raw, the wild, the authentic, and so on. However different they might be, the grand narratives of modernity seem to share the objective of mastering nature (cf. Adorno and Horkheimer 1997). But as I mentioned in the previous section, the modern subjects' freedom from external forces is characteristically accompanied by a simultaneous yearning for the (lost) whole from which they have departed. Modern subjects are, according to this approach, prone to strive for infinity. They tend to yearn for the externality that has been abandoned or lost in the secularisation process, and this human proclivity has taken several forms. A common feature is the attempt to reach the whole by transgressing the classifications and boundaries that encompass our secular lives. This pertains not only to institutionalised practices and rituals concerning life and death that are associated with nature. It includes all kinds of practices, arrangements and institutions that aim to transcend the immanent aspects of human life, including the secular will to reach omniscience.

The notion of a metaphysical whole is of vital importance to modern cultural arrangements, including the modern quest for transcendence. When, for instance, 'we' endeavour to transcend the immanent world by means of negative definition of the 'others', the metaphysics of purity seems to be invoked. When 'we' define ourselves as modern in contrast to so-called traditional people, be it in a positive or negative manner, the classifications tend to be prompted by notions of purity. As for critical self-definition by negation, the categorisation of the 'others' is based on nostalgia for an original state of nature. The 'others' are associated with the uncorrupted authenticity that modernity has brought to an end, which means that the 'others' are seen as ambassadors for the vitality that 'our' civilisation lacks. Among other things, the 'others' might be praised for promoting family values and for taking care of the elderly and sick amongst them. In general, they might be acknowledged for being oriented towards areas of life that 'we' (moderns) have dismissed, but allegedly should value to a greater extent. The point is that whether the 'others' are depicted in positive or negative terms, it is 'our' cultural order that forms the evaluative basis. And as I have suggested above, the 'others' are characteristically defined as dual. On the one hand, their shortcomings are accentuated in comparison to modern, enlightened human beings; on the other hand, their dignified, authentic qualities, which the modern humans lack, are underlined.

This duality is prevalent not only in popular speech; it is also prevalent in academic discourses on indigenous people and ethnic minorities. For instance, in Europe there is widespread talk about 'second-generation immigrants',[8] who are believed to be 'split between two worlds'. This characterisation is, of course, a reflection of assumptions in the mind of the beholder – and it is sometimes appropriated by the minorities themselves. Clearly, this conceptualisation invokes a metaphysics of purity, in which the so-called second-generation immigrants are granted an out-of-place status. Attention is directed towards qualities and practices that are considered to be out of place in relation to both the majority culture and their own ethnic and cultural environments. Their cultural distinctiveness is emphasised when at school or in other public arenas, while their Western characteristics are emphasised when at home or elsewhere within the private sphere (see e.g. Jacobsen 2010). Notwithstanding their impure status, however, ethnic minorities certainly do not constitute a pathological impurity. As mentioned above, a pathological impurity would threaten to dissolve the very cultural order, due to its uncontrollable or unmanageable nature. But even though undifferentiated chaos poses a threat to the cultural order, it is nevertheless essential to it. In the next section I endeavour to show how metaphysical ideas constitute utopian ideals within modern systems of order. To the extent that the undifferentiated whole poses a threat to the cultural order, it is, I argue, because the ideals of purity are inherently self-destructive.

Foundational grounds and utopian ideals

Whereas non-modern systems of order are generally based on mythical or religious ideas of origin, such as God and the sacred, modern conceptions of purity are more likely to be secular. However, this does not mean that modern thought is devoid of mythical conceptions. On the contrary, secular ideas tend to hinge upon notions of metaphysical purity akin to religious ideas of divinity. Modern metaphysical concepts normally function as regulating ideals, constituting secular standards of judgement. But unlike religious or mythical ideas of origin, these modern ultimate foundations are only indirectly operative. They are foundational grounds upon which social classifications are based, and, as such, they are not articulated. Examples of secular ultimate foundations are non-articulated ideas of history, nation, race, health, hygiene, the natural, the body, and so on. These regulating ideas are characteristically concealed in what purports to be merely practical regulations.[9] For instance, within the parameters of modern metaphysics, the 'others' might be depicted as more or less natural, more or less healthy, more or less clean, and so forth (see Eliassen 2002: 18f.).

Because modern foundational grounds are regulating elements in narratives, they characteristically take the shape of end-goals, forming the basis for grand narratives (Lyotard 1992a: 61).[10] Modern grand narratives are universal and totalising structures that purport to encompass and reveal the true significance of all other narratives – of first-order narratives. As opposed to non-modern myths, grand narratives do not seek legitimacy in an original event or 'founding' act. Rather, they seek legitimacy in a future to be brought about – an idea to be realised. The idea, be it of freedom, enlightenment, socialism or general prosperity, has legitimising value because it is perceived as universal. According to Lyotard, it is the (regulating) ideas that give modernity its characteristic mode: the project – the will that targets a goal (ibid.).

If we link this end-goal orientation to the term 'utopia', we may – in line with Thomas More's description of utopia in the sixteenth century – speak of a conceptual relationship between 'eutopia' and 'outopia'. 'Eutopia' refers to the concept of a good place, whereas 'outopia' refers to a non-place. The chasm between the good and the non-place is designated by More ([1516] 2003) as 'the neutral', which refers to an area of difference. The neutral is an impossible space, and the insoluble tension that lies within eu/outopia gives rise to an endless deferment of meaning. In Bruno Latour's (1988) terms, the neutral denotes, rather than a place, an obligatory point of passage, a stage through which things pass, a gap that has no ontological basis. In many respects, the neutral is akin to the concept of liminality. However, the term 'liminality' is usually deployed in relation to the concept of communitas, denoting a cultural community that belongs to the empirical world of experience. The point of passage, on the other hand, transgresses our cultural classifications and is perhaps thus more akin to Foucault's (2000) concept of 'heterotopia'. According to Foucault, heterotopia designates the gap between the conception of the good and the non-place. Order is never achieved but rather becomes a series of endless new forms of ordering. Heterotopia signifies a spatial room in which difference and ambivalence are encountered and ordered. The orderly process is based on utopian ideas through which the radical unknown is transformed into something known. Heterotopia is a place of changing order, propelled by a desire to transform a non-place into a good place – a desire to bridge the gulf between eutopia and outopia. Places that, from the end of the seventeenth century onwards, comprise the spatialisation of utopian ideals are many: gardens, scientific laboratories, urban spaces, factories, museums, and so on. In these arrangements a 'not-yet' is tentatively transformed into a 'there', which of course can never (literally) take place. The hope for a better life will ultimately end in disappointment, although the disappointment will form the basis for new hope.

The social imaginaries of the utopian end-goal denote an absolute purity that is beyond the empirical world of experience. We may therefore wonder what would happen if the utopian ideal was to be accomplished or realised. An evident answer is that the end-goal would dissolve or self-destruct. As has been pointed out, the utopian ideals involve a withdrawal from (this) life; so, if the end-goal was to be reached, it would entail a 'utopia of death'. A 'utopia of death' denotes a quest for identical pure being, which is at the same time a striving for nothingness (Schmidt and Kristensen 1986: 20). The fact that metaphysical purity is tantamount to death is of course a paradox, one that is fundamental and pertains to any utopian narrative.[11] As noted above, utopias cannot exist without impurity in a metaphysical sense, for the very idea of purity presupposes a world of differentiations. As long as impurity signifies the dynamic character of metaphysical purity, the impure cannot be estranged from the ultimate, timeless chaos. That is why the intention to expel the impure is likely to assume the character, not of a mundane destructive instinct, but of an ultimate Death Instinct (see Deleuze [1967] 1991: 30).

If we transfer this cultural dynamics to the duality of the subject, a substantial resemblance emerges. We recall from the above discussion that the gap between the pure and the impure corresponds to the gap between the universal and the autonomous subject. The autonomy of the subject is an irrevocable fact in the modern world of reasoning, inasmuch as concrete subjects belong to the secular world of distinctions. Furthermore, we recall that it is this destiny that gives rise to the quest for a universal, undifferentiated element, often manifested in ideas of omniscience or man's sovereignty over existence. To Kant ([1781] 1996), utopia signifies genuine universality whereby men organise themselves as universal subjects and overcome the conflict between pure and empirical reason in a conscious solidarity with the whole.[12] Utopian ideals characteristically determine human beings by subordinating them to the universal whole that constitutes the utopian end-goal. And yet, in line with the dynamics between metaphysical purity and impurity, individual distinctness is the very condition for utopian ideas about the undifferentiated whole. Without the impurity of the autonomous subject, utopian ideals would immediately dissolve.

If we take this one step further, we may ask what happens when a cultural order is programmed to eliminate differentiations by assimilating them – that is, when an imagined community purports to constitute an inclusive humanity. As long as the inclusive humanity functions as a utopian ideal, self-destruction seems likely. However, as I will endeavour to show in the next section, a cultural order that claims to encompass all of humanity is not doomed to implode into nothingness. The reason for this, it seems, is that the universal subject is incorporated into the autonomous subject, and not the other way around, as it were. The autonomous subject has been granted a universal dimension without eradicating its autonomy and cultural particularity. The issue concerning modern subjectivity, which has thus far been elucidated in light of the logic of purity/impurity, will by this move return to its starting point: the field of political theory. In the next two sections I will draw attention first to the republican ideology and then to the liberal political ideology, since these modern political configurations are crucial to the social order within which modern subjectivity and the politics of recognition are enfolded.

The subject in republican ideology

The republican and the liberal political ideologies are in different ways aimed at bridging the gulf between the autonomous and the universal subject. Common to both ideologies is the idea of a universal subject, comprising a metaphysical horizon. However, as we shall see, the metaphysical horizon does not eliminate autonomy. On the contrary, as I aim to show, modern ideologies incorporate the universal ideal into the autonomous subject so as to overcome the breach between the autonomous and the universal subject. In the preceding sections, I suggested that the modern subject is a carrier of universal equality.

Through the process of interiorisation or internalisation, I argued, the human being is constituted as both autonomous/unique and identical with all other human beings (universal). By virtue of being autonomous, the modern human being is a self-conscious individual, free from external forces. Accordingly, to act as a person in the modern, autonomous sense entails seeking a private consciousness, rather than donning an identity mask and playing a public role (cf. Foucault 1979; Sennett 1976). In ancient Roman society, by contrast, identity was conferred, and one's rights were based on membership in a family or clan. According to James Donald (1996), being a person in Roman society was not a universal attribute of humanity that belonged to a person per se; rather, it was a status defined by law. Personal status was accorded to some, while excluding others, in a ritual of naming. Slaves, for example, were not considered to be persons, while corporations and religious institutions sometimes were (ibid.: 176–177). Christianity, in conjunction with secular cultural and institutional structures, inaugurated a social change with respect to personhood. Personal status became a universal structure, constitutive of the individual and defined by the relationship between each person and a personal God. As Donald points out, the 'new' person does not exist as a mask (*persona*); it exists as an abstracted position of ethical apperception, which appears to lie behind the mask (ibid.: 177). The (internalised) person came to signify the universal human being.

In so far as modern individuals tend to strive for infinity, they yearn to become whole, complete persons, and this search for completeness emanates from the gap between the autonomous and the universal subject. Autonomous subjectivity is, in other words, a lack that motivates the quest for the original whole. Within republican ideology, the category of subjectivity signals, via its nexus to democratic sovereignty, a symbolic equality of all citizens. This is due to the fact that all citizens are perceived to be the nominal source of the authority of democratic sovereignty, as well as being subject to that authority. Donald (1996: 178) notes that the sovereign equality of democratic authority institutes citizenship as a certain kind of freedom that is anchored not in a relationship to God but in the nature of Man. Clearly, this institution of citizenship touches upon the above-mentioned process of interiorisation or internalisation, whereby equality and freedom are constituted as inherent in human nature. Consequently, denying freedom is not only conceived as unjust, but also considered to be unnatural – an idea that is, above all, promulgated by the works of Jean-Jacques Rousseau.

Against this backdrop, we see that what initially is a rift between two opposing elements – one autonomous and unique, the other universal – is in modern republican ideology transformed into a unity, whereby the autonomous and unique subject is the carrier of the universal element, amounting to personal integrity. However, this does not mean that the autonomous subject is universal at the outset. Rather, it means that the subject can become universal, provided that the gap between the two elements is bridged. One way of elucidating this process of reconciliation between the universal and the autonomous subject is to emphasise the liminal duality indicative of the modern conception of the child.[13] In modern configurations of thought, the child symbolises the natural and the humane, yet also the uncivilised and the non-humane. The duality of the child suggests that we are born humane but are at the same time incomplete, led by nature, not programmed, as it were (see Lyotard 1991: 3). It is the presumed natural humanity of the child and its concurrent innate lack that brings about the quest for the transparent, true human/citizen, which thereby functions as an end-goal in modern reasoning. The objective is to become fully human in terms of being good, civilised citizens.

According to Lyotard (1991), it is the institutions that constitute culture that supplement the native lack in modern societies, notably education. As for the republican ideology, the political, civic culture replaces the native lack in the subject, while at the same time allowing for the Rousseauian dream of a universal civic identity in a transparent, rational and harmonious society.[14] Because things are ideally public and transparent, the republican ideology does not firmly differentiate between private and public spheres. Following Lyotard (1992a), we could view the dream of transparency in light of the tension between the distinctive, on the one hand, and the universality, self-determination and transparency that the future represents, on the other (ibid.: 37). The crux of the matter is the 'overcoming' (*dépassement*) of the particular cultural identity in favour of a universal civic identity (ibid.: 44–45). When seen in light of the whole, the self is surely incomplete, and as long as this abstraction comprises the metaphysical horizon or the ideal, everything particular – any distinctive identity or social characteristic – is considered to be a deficiency in the subject. Among these deficiencies are race, class and gender.[15] With regard to gender, '"[m]asculine" and "feminine" are ... the two modes of the subject's *failure* to achieve the full identity of Man. "Man" and "Woman" together do not form a whole, since *each of them is already in itself a failed whole*' (Salecl in Donald 1996: 186).

In a similar vein, Hannah Arendt (1973) contends that the reason why political communities such as modern nation states so often insist on ethnic homogeneity is that they hope to eliminate natural and always present differences and differentiations. Differences all too clearly indicate those spheres where people cannot act and change at will – the limitations of the human artifice (ibid.: 301). However, as Arendt also points out, a man who is nothing but a man has lost the very qualities that make it possible for other people to treat him as a fellow man (ibid.: 300). We are not born equal; rather, we become equal as members of a group on the strength of our decision to guarantee ourselves mutually equal rights, she explains (ibid.: 301). Those who symbolise the natural and unfree are thus 'civil dead' (cf. Agamben 1998, 2005); they are not fully human. Without a profession, without citizenship, without deeds by which to identify and specify oneself, one loses all significance. Within the parameters of nation states, one does not have any political and legal status without a social identity (Arendt 1973: 302). As such, identity is a precondition for equal rights, a fact that republicanism amply demonstrates – although from a different angle than Arendt's – when ideologically incorporating the universal subject into the civic, autonomous subject. The ideal of the true, equal human being, the inclusive humanity, is intrinsic to the civic cultural order of republicanism.

Thus far we have seen that any distinctive trait of a human being is considered to be a lack by way of marking the gap to the undifferentiated whole. The abyss is to be overcome through an educational process, leading towards a universal human identity – an inclusive humanity. In this respect, the republican ideology targets a utopian ideal that, in principle, does not allow for individual autonomy. However, it is not autonomy per se that must be eliminated in order to reach the end-goal, since the good citizen is indeed an autonomous individual. The discussion suggests that autonomy is both the starting point and the outcome in modern egalitarian ideology. As a starting point, autonomy is inhuman; as an outcome, it is fully human, having incorporated the universal element. In accordance with this cultural logic, it is only the civil subject – the mature citizen (cf. Dean 1999: 134–135, 146) – that can possess the attributes required of the equal human being in a modern world. This means, firstly, that equality cannot be dislodged from the cultural order within which it is constituted. Secondly, it means that a supposed accusation that the civic cultural order does not promote universal equality – that the inclusive humanity is in principle as well as in practice exclusionary – would be in vain. Such an accusation would make no sense within a cultural order that purports to embody humanity.

The subject in liberal ideology

The second political ideology that has defined Western democratic societies, namely, the liberal, is normally seen as the antithesis of the republican ideology. However, despite its foundation in the utilitarian model of John Locke and Thomas Hobbes, with which Rousseau takes issue, there are several similarities between the two ideologies. Notwithstanding that liberals regard the individual as formed prior to its social life, which is surely at odds with the republican ideology, both ideologies proceed from an idea of an original, universal subject. Within the liberal ideology, the original human being is considered to be threatened by the external social environment that Rousseau saw as a precondition for the formation of the true self. Generally speaking, for liberals, the objective is to resist being levelled down and worn out by the outer sociotechnological mechanism that creates a transparent society. It is a matter of preserving one's autonomy and individuality, which gives rise to a high degree of individualism (see Donald 1996: 183). Writes Donald: 'Modern man dedicates his power of invention to hiding his sense of an interior, intimate self from the world' (ibid.; cf. Sennett 1976). Contrary to the Rousseauian ideal of transparency, a mask of anonymity conceals distinctiveness, such as race, class and gender. A common identity is created among fellow citizens, as a result of which one adheres to the public norms of behaviour that constitute modern individuality. These norms are believed to be universal standards of evaluation.

The division between the public and the private spheres lies at the core of liberal political ideology. In Arendt's view, it is especially the human qualities associated with the given – remote from human will or autonomy – that are relegated to the private sphere and obliterated from public, political life. In liberal ideology, the public sphere is based on equality and should ideally represent the general interest of individuals. This is similar to the republican order, which is to ensure the common good for its fellow citizens. Both ideologies assume a universalist civic public that denies or represses differences. Writes Arendt (1973: 301): 'The whole sphere of the merely given, relegated to private life in civilized society, is a permanent threat to the public sphere, because the public sphere is as consistently based on the law of equality as the private sphere is based on … difference and differentiation.' Because the public sphere is based on equality, it does not permit distinctive identities, especially not traits that clearly mark the gap to the universal human being. The public sphere is defined as general, in which all particularities are abandoned, while the private sphere houses the particular – feelings, needs, the body, and so on (see Young 1990: 181).

As my delineation suggests, one striking similarity between the republican and the liberal ideologies pertains to their universalist basis and their will to unity. These aspects are particularly evident in the duality of the subject. In both ideologies the universal, undifferentiated subject is incorporated into the autonomous subject. However, the liberal ideology departs from the republican when it comes to the actual process of humanisation. As opposed to republican ideology, liberal ideology does not require an institutionalised education, inasmuch as a person's individuality is considered to be prior to her or his social life. Practically speaking, however, liberal ideology entails humanisation, since the qualities that correspond to the universal ideal constitute a specific evaluative standard – a norm for the cultivated human being. We may therefore speak of a common civic identity, a civically collective subject, which marks the limits for inclusive humanity and equality.

In this sense, the notion of an inclusive humanity is inextricably intertwined with the notion of Man, predicated upon the duality of the subject, or, to be more precise, predicated upon the gap between the universal and the autonomous subject. When this divide is bridged, the civic subject transcends immanence and becomes universal, and the civic subject may, in a collective sense, claim the status of being a universally inclusive 'we'. Roland Barthes ([1957] 1993: 140) describes this universalisation of particular norms as a normalisation of bourgeois representations. He contends that these 'normalised' forms attract little attention by the very fact of their extension: the further the bourgeois class propagates its representations, the more normalised they become. In a similar manner, although in a different context, Bruce Kapferer (1988: 195) demonstrates how national identity in egalitarian societies becomes integral to one's being, a part of one's very substance or a manifestation of the essence of the individual. He notes that whereas class is merely identity, nation is spirit. By bridging the gap between the particular identity and the abstract human being, the paradox of modern subjectivity is (dis)solved.

However, as the above discussion suggests, the universal status of the modern subject is highly distinctive. If the civic cultural order had *de facto* been universal and inclusive, rather than being a cultural-specific ideal to which certain conditions are attached, the political ideologies would have been superfluous. They would have been eradicated before being established, because the ideal would have been realised prior to the social, empirical world of distinctions. The most significant point is not, however, that a metaphysical ideal is self-destructive by virtue of defying autonomy and individuality, which is to say that the ideology necessarily has to be cultural-specific in order to be maintained. Rather, the point is that an ideal that purports to be universal forecloses all other alternatives (see MacIntyre 1988: 334), making it virtually impossible for 'others' to lay claim to equality on their own terms. What is more, 'others' risk being silenced or stigmatised when complaining about unfair treatment, since the premises for equality are defined by the order against which they protest. Arendt (1973: 302) sees it as follows: 'The danger ... is that they are thrown back, in the midst of civilisation, on their natural giveness, on their mere differentiation.... The danger is that a global, universally interrelated civilisation may produce barbarians from its own midst by forcing millions of people into conditions which, despite all appearances, are the conditions of savages.'

It seems reasonable to infer from this that the 'others' are viewed as barbarians to the extent that they do not submit to the demands made to the autonomous (fellow) citizens in the presumed universal civilisation. The 'others' are treated as uncivilised, non-autonomous, natural (savage) people, determined by their culture, bodies, feelings, gender, sexuality, and so on. In sociological terms, they are considered to lack propriety or respectability, which brings together discourses of hygiene, sexuality and morality (Skeggs 1997: 42; cf.

Linke 1999; Mosse 1985; Skeggs 2004; Young 1990, 1995). A central aspect of this orderly process is the reproduction of 'our' identity, which is supported by a number of polar, hierarchical opposites, such as individual-group, normal-deviant, soul-body, and so on. Iris Young (1990: 99) remarks: 'The first side of the dichotomy is elevated over the second because it designates the unified, the self-identical, whereas the second side lies outside the unified as the chaotic, unformed, transforming, that always threatens to cross the border and break up the unity of the group.'

One could perhaps object that because the modern, egalitarian ideologies have incorporated the idea of an undifferentiated human being, they allow for a critical self-definition via negation more than a positive one.[16] I will not reject such an assertion, but neither do I consider it to be a profound objection to my argument. Both the critical and the positive self-definitions via negation presuppose the logic of opposition pertaining to the modern metaphysics of purity. Like a self-flattering negation, a critical self-definition, which emphasises the uncorrupted character of the 'others', serves to reaffirm dialectically the civic identity. Put differently, both the self-critical and the self-flattering identifications of the 'others' involve projection.

One might also object that the modern grand narratives were abandoned long ago in favour of a plurality of narratives. I will not defy this assertion either. However, to the extent that the multicultural politics of recognition is located within the parameters of the civic, collective subject, recognition implies assimilation in terms of incorporation. In order to be recognised, the 'others' have to be granted a civic status, and they need to be included in the humanity defined by the civic identity. The ideological motivation for integration and recognition seems to be that the 'others' are non-autonomous, that they are in need of the transcendence of immanence. This is most particularly the case in liberal democracies, where transcendence translates into liberation from so-called traditional practices and cultural boundaries.

Ethnocentric fallacy

In the following, I shall draw attention to the mechanisms that constitute a particular cultural self-image as universal and inclusive. Subsequently, in order to illustrate these mechanisms, I will propose some paradigmatic examples from the Norwegian context. These in turn will extend the theoretical argument and point to some central dimensions of the multicultural dilemma that have not yet been scrutinised. My contention is that there are specific norms of universality that the civic order embodies. As such, the civic order is granted a universal status with an exclusive right to define equality. Hence, an ethnocentric fallacy emerges: the ideal of equality is confounded with substantial equality. The fact that the universal subject is incorporated into the autonomous civic subject enables the collective civic subject to emerge as *de facto* equal. The civic cultural order is equated with the ideal in such a way that equality becomes ideal and real at the same time. Due to this conflation, the civic culture acquires a status as universal and all-inclusive.

In order to elucidate the ethnocentric fallacy and its totalitarian implications, I shall draw attention to a study of minority pupils in the Norwegian school system, conducted by Joron Pihl (2001). The focal point of the study is the dynamics of inclusion and exclusion with regard to ethnic relations. One of the main lessons to be taken from this study is that the policy of inclusion serves to exclude the pupils who are to be included (ibid.: 21). The exclusion occurs, first of all, because the pupils that are targeted for inclusion are expelled from ordinary classroom instruction and given special education in separate rooms. Secondly, the evaluative standard for determining whether or not the pupils need special education is grounded in mono-cultural and mono-linguistic norms, which are assumed to be universal. Pihl maintains that the courses of study for pupils with minority backgrounds are developed on behalf of the minorities without their involvement. An ethnic 'minority/incompetent' conceptualisation is developed, and the 'others' are constituted as inferior. In general, Pihl notes, the relationship between 'us' and the 'others' is characterised in public rhetoric by a self-flattering comparison in which the dominant Norwegian ethnic group and culture are elevated (ibid.; cf. Pihl 2005; White 1972). The 'others' are rendered opposite and subordinate to 'us', which is to say that they are being assimilated and culturalised/subordinated.

The school example suggests that the majority culture constitutes a universal, inclusive humanity, in line with the modern, civic ideologies. The 'myth' of Norwegian neutrality is, in other words, perceived as real, and the formal equality before the law is conflated with substantive social equality or social justice. Justice is made into the very constitutive element of Norwegian culture. However, as the school example reveals, the postulation of the majority culture as inherently just makes the state school both ethnocentric and totalitarian. The ethnocentric fallacy enables 'us' to be conceived as an aggregate of equal, autonomous individuals, while the 'others' are conceived as traditional and inferior. 'We' are constituted as universally inclusive, while the 'others' are seen as exclusive. 'We' are in the position to accuse the 'others' of undermining the autonomy and equality of the individual, and their deficiencies, in contrast with 'us', eventually call for integration measures.

The way in which ethnic minorities are depicted in the school system borders on caricature, and yet it is not at all exceptional. For example, in her book *Mot en ny norsk underklasse* (Towards a New Norwegian Underclass), social anthropologist Unni Wikan (1995) asserts that our Western liberal tradition is inclusive, neutral and universal, while the 'others' are reactionary, traditional and collective (ibid.: 88, 91, 183, 190). Wikan establishes a hierarchical opposition between 'us' and the 'others' based on a culturalisation and subordination of those who depart from the majority population. She proposes that inclusion in the majority society implies adaptation to the prevailing standards. Integration is a question of duty, she maintains, whereupon she emphasises the immigrants' duty to live in conformity with Norwegian core values and to acquire knowledge of the Norwegian language (ibid.: 146). She moves on to suggest that integration involves the right to be human beings – the right to be taken seriously as individuals. This in turn is linked with the immigrants' obligation to demonstrate loyalty towards the society in which they are included (ibid.: 191; cf. White Paper No. 49 2003–2004: 33). Immigrants should either live according to 'our' (Norwegian-Western-universal) standards, or go home (Wikan 1995: 91).

Wikan eventually asserts that all reasonable, rational individuals with a free will must choose to adapt to Western values. In this respect, she universalises the standpoint of the privileged, in line with Rousseau's political ideology. In his book *The Social Contract*, Rousseau ([1762] 1989) depicts French civic values as *the* universal values that correspond with the interests of every individual (see e.g. Barthes [1957] 1993). The same seems to hold true of the Norwegian policy documents on integration, in which Norwegian values are equated with universal values.[17] The majority 'we' purports to be all inclusive, but it is *de facto* reserved for the chosen few. Those who do not wish to integrate, or are incapable of doing so, are excluded within the parameters of modern nation-state ideology. Yet even if the 'others' are excluded by virtue of being told to return to their home countries, they are not excluded in a symbolic-structural sense. As the above discussion reveals, one has to be included/assimilated into the civic order or jurisdiction in order to be excluded. In this respect, the 'others' have a symbolically integrating function in relation to the community or communitas from which they depart. As mentioned, the 'others' comprise the negation – negation as a partial process – that serves to create the positive identity of the majority population. At the same time, however, the majority culture must be abstracted from cultural particularity and granted a universal status. In order to do so, Wikan (1995) conceives of the majority population as an aggregate of autonomous individuals. She thereby unwittingly illustrates my point that equality implies incorporation into the order in which equality is an attribute of the individual's autonomy.

Multicultural paradox

The above argument suggests that a cultural order that revolves around the autonomous subject characteristically ascribes equality only to individuals. Recognition of group-based distinctiveness is an opposite value of individual equality. Accordingly, recognition of group-based distinctiveness is associated with conventional norms and values, as opposed to universal norms and values. If distinctiveness is recognised at all, it tends to be of secondary value. As the Norwegian integration policy illustrates, cultural distinctness is recognised to the extent that it promotes individual autonomy and equality. What is also characteristic for a social order that revolves around the autonomous subject is its egalitarian structure. Hierarchical differences are not taken to be 'natural'. That is to say, one's status and position are not considered to be innate, naturally endowed or God-given; rather, they must be rationally justified. Accordingly, any inequality in the treatment of individuals qua individuals requires justification. As Alasdair MacIntyre (1988: 344) makes clear, justice is *prima facie* egalitarian. Within the parameters of modern political ideology, inequality is characteristically justified by defining hierarchical difference as a result of non-natural attributes, such as individual skills and abilities, conditioned by the assumption that all members of a society are equals from the outset (see Young 1990: 200ff.). It is pertinent to ask, therefore, whether the inequality that follows from the recognition of distinctiveness is paradoxically justified by reference to equality. Does the ideal of equality legitimate inequality? To follow up this first question, we may also ask whether non-natural hierarchies are paradoxically justified by reference to human nature. I shall begin the discussion by addressing this second question.

The above analysis has revealed that the ideal of innate equality or equal dignity is conflated with substantive equality for all citizens. Furthermore, we have seen that the ideal of universal equality is constitutive of the modern, civic cultural order. What concerns me here is the fact that non-natural hierarchy tends to be justified by reference to human nature – to the putative natural, universal attributes of the individual. This can be illustrated by the earlier cited examples from the Norwegian school system, in which special education purports to produce social justice and equal opportunities for all. Pihl (2001: 23) notes that a formal inclusive school system meets the demands in higher education and the job market, which require academic qualifications and competency certified by a selective school system. The rationale is that when everyone enjoys equal conditions, the subsequent selections will be socially just. This conception of fair selection seems to arise directly out of the modern idea of an innate equality of the individual, which is taken to be embodied in the cultural order, including the school. It is not that the school system does not manage to establish equal conditions by fully incorporating the pupils into the prevailing order, regardless of their ethnicity, race, class, gender, able-bodiedness and other markers of difference. It is more that the dominant cultural order is taken to be just – and justified – by a universal element. As I see it, the concept of justice that is endorsed by the school authorities is indicative of the metaphysical notion of a natural equality of human beings. The school system is, by reason of this, considered to be just per se. In my view, this is a far more severe problem than, conversely, erroneously inferring from difference/distinctness to injustice. The latter problem has attracted some attention among academics within this field of research (e.g. Morken 1996), but as the above examples suggest, the inference from ideal to real equality is likely to generate more severe problems for those who fall short. One reason for this is that the school system cannot be called into question as long as justice is guaranteed by the system itself. If, for example, parents of pupils who are given special education criticise the school for being discriminatory towards minority pupils, the parents are likely to be accused of being hostile to the majority culture, and therefore to equality per se.

If one is to criticise the school system profoundly, the critique must be grounded on premises other than those from which the system itself emanates. However, in reference to the problem of opposition, that might prove difficult. We may ask whether it is possible to obtain social justice as long as the ideal of equality constitutes a foundational ground, inextricably linked to the national order. A related question is whether a metaphysical ideal of equality inevitably reproduces social inequality. At this juncture, we touch upon the first question that was posed above. Is the inequality that follows from the recognition of cultural distinctiveness justified by the ideal of equality? To approach this issue, I shall once again recapitulate some of the above argument. We have seen that recognition of equality involves incorporating the 'others' into the inclusive humanity by imposing on them the civic (dual) subject form. The duality of the modern subject renders possible the recognition of fellow human beings as both equal and autonomous. Furthermore, the politics of recognition aims at consolidating the fundamental equality of individual human beings by this process of incorporating the 'others' into the inclusive humanity. Incorporation into the putatively inclusive humanity requires, among other things, that specific measures be undertaken, such as special education. The 'others' may require special treatment, given their supposed lack of autonomy and underdeveloped will (cf. Brown 2006: 153). The supposed lack of autonomy and individual will among the minority population is indeed prevalent in the policy documents on integration, in which the recognition of cultural distinctiveness is used as a means to integrate the minority population and provide them with personal autonomy. I have argued that the integration policy seems to originate from the idea that the egalitarian system is the reification of inclusive humanity, whereby ideal equality emerges as real. Hence, assimilation becomes the very condition for equality. And to the extent that cultural distinctiveness is regarded as an impediment to assimilation, culture or ethnicity is depicted as a challenge to the dominant order – a difference or impurity that must be managed – in accordance with the oppositional logic of the multicultural dilemma. Significantly, within the parameter of liberal democracy, subordination is not considered to emanate from biased standards of judgement. Attention is not directed to how the prevailing standard renders the 'others' subordinate to the majority population. Rather, subordination is depicted as an effect of the distinct and exclusive cultural inclinations of the 'others'. To the extent that the 'others' do not perform equally well as the majority, it is seen as a result of their inferiority, that is, their remote cultural traditions. Immigrant culture is, within a liberal-democratic framework, depicted as a collective obstacle to immigrants' personal autonomy and self-development. Equality, on the other hand, is allegedly warranted by the state, in so far as the state institutions provide everyone with the same opportunity to develop the qualities necessary for proper achievement, liberated from patriarchal cultural sediments.

The answer to the first question posed above is thus that the ideal of individual equality does in fact justify inequality. At this point, we also approach – or rather return to – the paradox that was pointed out by way of introduction. It has now become clear that the paradox of (in)equality arises as the boomerang effect of equality unfolds. Adorno ([1951] 2005) aptly asserts that if one wishes to proclaim the equality of all those who bear human features as an ideal, instead of establishing it as a fact, this would be of little help. The abstract utopia would be all too easily reconcilable with the most devious tendencies of society. The idea that all human beings would resemble each other, he moves on to argue, is exactly what suits such tendencies, since it regards factual or imagined differences as marks of shame. This humiliates the 'others' in a benevolent manner by a standard that they cannot attain (ibid.: §66). Against this backdrop, we may conclude that the paradox is not the effect of an empirical divergence between the ideal and the real. Rather, the paradox emerges because the ideal is inherently counter-productive.

Chapter 2

Non-modern Holism and Modern Totalitarianism

※

In Chapter 1, we saw that one characteristic feature of the modern systems of order is that order emanates from an undifferentiated whole, comprising a totalitarian horizon. However, the utopian character of the modern systems of order does not always entail implosion into nothingness. The autonomous subject is not always sacrificed to a higher cause and made into universal substance. On the contrary, the autonomous subject is at the heart of Western egalitarian ideologies. As we saw in the preceding chapter, both the republican and the liberal ideologies nourish individualism, and yet they proceed from a metaphysical notion of the whole. In this chapter, I will enquire into this paradoxical character of the modern configurations in order to elucidate its consequences with respect to the dynamics between 'us' and the 'others'.

Within the modern logic of opposition, difference is the opposite – the negative reflection – of identity. And qua negation, difference acquires a negative value. Difference is inferior by comparison with identity, which in turn acquires a positive value. We could conceive of this process as an 'ideologisation' of the terms 'pure/identity' and 'impure/difference' (see Eliassen 2000). What interests us in this chapter is how this process of ideologisation comes about. How does difference acquire its negative value, or, put differently, how is it that culturalisation of the 'others' coincides with their subordination at one blow, so to speak? I argue that the subordination of 'others' is the effect of a peculiar conflation of modern and non-modern elements, amounting to modern totalitarianism. To be more precise, I endeavour to show that the paradox of (in)equality – the fact that the ideal of equality leads to a subordination of those who are not identified with the whole – issues from a non-modern, hierarchical structure. Modern totalitarianism, I argue, is a transformed non-modern holism. It is noteworthy that the 'non-modern' in this context does not designate a historical epoch – a pre-modern era – but denotes a configuration whose defining feature is holism.

As for the non-modern, holistic element in modern thought, it seems pertinent to proceed from the critique of Enlightenment made by Adorno and Horkheimer ([1944] 1997), which I referred to in the preceding chapter. I accede to their depiction of the mythical, hierarchical structure that is intrinsic to modern systems of knowledge, and I share their view on the reductive effects of such totalitarian knowledge systems with respect to difference. Accordingly, I subscribe to their critique of the implied social holism that executes the particular and separates notions of harmony and fulfilment from their hypostatisation in the religious Beyond, and transfers them as criteria to human aspiration (ibid.: 88). As the following discussion will reveal, however, my line of argument diverges from their theoretical framework in several ways. Suffice it to say, my thesis is not that the unity of the manipulated collective consists in the negation of each individual, or that enlightenment reverts to mythology due to a fear of truth, that is, due to false clarity (see ibid.: xiv, xvi).

Rather than proceeding from the theses of Adorno and Horkheimer, I intend to draw on Louis Dumont's (1986) essay, 'On Value, Modern and Nonmodern'. In my view, this text illuminates quite clearly how holism is a constitutive element of modern egalitarian ideologies.[1] Among other things, Dumont's line of argument brings out the symbolic structures that ideologise impurity by assigning it a negative value. It must be noted, however, that I draw on his argument only to the extent that it serves to develop my own, and I endeavour to rework aspects of his conceptual repertoire to make it fit with my own analytical framework.

Modern and non-modern configurations

Within the modern configuration, the distinction between 'idea' and 'value' is of paramount importance. It is due to this division, Dumont (1986) remarks, that differences are defined in rigid black-and-white categories. By the same token, differences are depicted as consolidating oppositions to privileged identities. As long as differences are defined in accordance with the logic of opposition, the structuring horizon comprises a totality. When the relationship between idea and value is seen as a unity, on the other hand, we are – according to Dumont – dealing with a non-modern holism.[2] As opposed to a totality, characterised by a rigid oppositional logic, holism entails differences that are defined relationally within a hierarchical whole.

My approach to the distinction between holism and totality takes as its starting point the distinction between the two forms of pure-impure configurations that I delineated in Chapter 1. As I see it, the metaphysical dynamic of purity-impurity implies a holistic relationship between the whole and its parts. In a metaphysical sense, purity refers to an undifferentiated whole in terms of an original chaos, whereas the impure denotes its differentiated, autonomous parts. The binary-oppositional logic of purity-impurity, on the other hand, signifies a relationship between pure and impure cultural categories that comprise a cultural system of classifications. Allegedly, within modern cultural orders, the ordering processes take place without any explicit external point of reference. Modern classifications are presumably not grounded in an authority of metaphysical being. That is to say, in a modern system of classifications the whole does not denote an external force, prior to the classifications, but points to a differentiated totality of pure categories, clear distinctions. And yet, as Chapter 1 suggests, the two different pure-impure configurations seem to be intertwined.

By exploring the conflation of modern and non-modern configurations in greater depth, I hope to be able to extend our understanding of multicultural dilemmas and paradoxes a bit further. In Chapter 1, we saw that the two configurations, in principle, run counter to each other. Purity within the former amounts to impurity within the latter, and vice versa. However, as was also made clear, the conception of an undifferentiated chaos is the condition of possibility for modern secular classifications. I argued that the modern system of classifications tends to emanate from metaphysical notions of purity. We also saw that the modern conceptions of undifferentiated purity are manifested in various foundational discourses and unarticulated standards of judgement. The latter take the shape of ultimate foundations that set the standards against which everything else is evaluated. In the following, I intend to demonstrate that these modern conceptions of the whole, which forms the basis of modern grand narratives, are characteristically non-modern. Qua foundational grounds, they are superior and external to the cultural classifications, which in turn are parts of – yet also opposites of – the whole.

The question as to whether it is possible to describe the 'others' on their own terms will now be addressed in Dumont's terminology. Touching on the problem of opposition, Dumont (1986: 247) poses the question of how to build a bridge between our modern ideology, which separates values from ideas/facts, and other ideologies, which embed values in their world view. Is it possible to build a bridge between modern and non-modern configurations of thought without subsuming the one into the other? Or is this task compounded by the fact that modern ideology comprises a concealed holistic element? What seems to be implied by Dumont's question is the assumption that a reconciliation of modern and other ideologies presupposes an overall holistic framework. He seems to presume that multicultural dialogue implies a holistic structure, which forms the basis of the encounter between modern and non-modern ideologies.

I do not adhere to this presupposition, but, in line with Dumont's argument, I do find the modern configuration problematic with respect to the relationship between 'us' and the 'others'. My critical remark will focus on the holistic element that seems to be inherent in modern ideologies, because it is this factor, I contend, that serves to confine dialogue to monologue and render the 'others' opposite and subordinate to 'our' identity.

In his critique of modern ideology, Dumont (1986: 244) remarks that modern society wants to be 'rational'; it wants to break away from nature and set up an autonomous human order. This is an argument most scholars can agree upon. In connection with the liminal duality described in the preceding chapter, it was pointed out that 'nature' is normally considered a generic term for the chaos against which our identities are defined. One separates oneself from the original whole through a process of differentiation or autonomisation. As for autonomisation, Dumont is particularly preoccupied with the modern separation between the true, the good and the beautiful. His main concern is the insurmountable separation between 'is' and 'ought' within modern ideology. Due to this separation, he contends, it is impossible to deduce what ought to be from what is (ibid.: 243): no transition is possible from ideas/facts/knowledge to values.[3] It is well known that the separation of knowledge from value is paradigmatic for modern reasoning and is inextricably linked with people's separation from nature.[4]

The crux of Dumont's (1986: 244) argument is that the separation of people from nature is synonymous with a commanding concern with the individual actor, which in turn has led to the internalisation of morality. As was pointed out in Chapter 1, morality is, in the modern world, localised in the consciousness of the individual. This interiorisation implies a separation of the inner world from the outer world, which is closely related to the liberal distinction between the public sphere and the private sphere, whereby religious matters are defined as private. With regard to the privatisation of religion, Dumont asserts that a physical homogeneous universe has replaced a non-modern holistic universe. He notes that the dimension of value is relegated to human understanding, feelings and will – that is, to the individual. Furthermore, whereas the individual parts are atomised, he argues, it is evident that the whole, in a modern world, cannot be understood as a hierarchical whole (holism).[5] On the contrary, the modern configuration is 'flat': 'Rather than relating the level under consideration ... to the upper level ..., we restrict our attention to one level at a time.... [I]n modern ideology, the previous hierarchical universe has fanned out into a collection of flat views of this kind' (ibid.: 249). That is to say, we cannot distinguish between various levels of values, nor can we establish a ranking of first-, second- or third-order values.[6] Dumont goes on to suggest that 'where non-moderns distinguish levels within a global view, the moderns know only of substituting one special plane of consideration for another, and find on all planes the same form of near disjunction, contradiction, etc.' (ibid.: 239). He opposes this modern autonomisation by maintaining that facts and values cannot be separated from the whole to which they belong. Significantly, values do not concern the more suitable or desirable. Strictly speaking, the whole is not preferable to its parts, but is simply superior to them (ibid.: 249). The value of something is dependent on a hierarchy of levels of experience in which that entity is situated. This is, Dumont notes, perhaps the main perception that the moderns unconsciously miss, ignore or suppress (ibid.: 250).

The unity of value and idea

In a footnote, Dumont (1986: 250n) poses the following questions: 'Is it possible that what is true of particular entities or wholes is true also of the great Whole, the universe or whole of wholes? Is it possible that the Whole in its turn needs a superior entity from which to derive its own value? That it can be self-integrative only by its subordination to something beyond itself?' Of interest to our study is the fact that, in this passage, Dumont seems to allude to a metaphysical conception of purity when speaking of the Whole. In order to examine his concept of hierarchy and holism more closely, we have to take into consideration his delineation of the holistic entity of idea-values or value-ideas.[7]

To begin with, Dumont (1986: 252) emphasises that value-ideas are 'ranked' in a particular fashion. Secondly, he points out that ranking includes 'reversal' as one of its properties. And finally, the configuration is normally 'segmented'. With respect to ranking, Dumont notes that 'high' ideas will both contradict and include 'low' ideas. He refers to this special relationship as an 'encompassment'. That is to say, an idea that grows in importance and status acquires the property of encompassing its contrary (ibid.). For instance, the category 'goods and services' comprises commodities, on the one hand, and something quite different from commodities but assimilated to them – namely, services – on the other. And the one is characteristically ranked beneath the other (ibid.). Another example of encompassment can be found in Dumont's (1970) book *Homo Hierarchicus*, in which he elucidates the relationship between Adam and Eve. God creates Adam first, Dumont notes, the undifferentiated man, the prototype of 'mankind'. Then God somehow extracts from that undifferentiated being a human of different sex – Eve. In this operation, Adam has changed his identity: from being undifferentiated (metaphysically pure), he has become a male (impure) (ibid.: 239–241). In his essay 'A National Variant I', Dumont (1986) explicates: 'Adam – or 'man' in our language – is two things in one: the representative of the species, and the prototype of the male individuals of that species. On one level, man and woman are identical; on a second level, woman is the opposite or contrary of man. These two relations together characterize the hierarchical relation, which cannot be better symbolized than by the material encompassing of the future Eve in the body of the first Adam' (ibid.: 119). Another version of this example was accounted for in the preceding chapter, in connection with the republican-ideological quest for the original whole. What concerns us in this context is that the yearning for a lost whole seems to invoke a hierarchical relationship between the whole and its elements, the elements being parts of the whole. On the one hand, the elements are identical to the whole, while, on the other, they are segregated from, and in opposition to, the whole.

This brings us to the next aspect of the non-modern configuration, namely, reversal. Dumont (1986) illustrates reversal by pointing to the relationship between the priest and the king. In matters of religion, he argues, the priest is superior to the king, but *ipso facto* the priest will obey the king in matters of public order, that is, in subordinate matters. The reversal element is an intrinsic principle, which means that the moment the second function is defined, it entails reversal for the corresponding situations. Due to this bi-dimensionality, it does not suffice to speak of different 'contexts' as distinguished by us. Rather, the situations are foreseen, inscribed or implied in the ideology itself. We must therefore speak of different 'levels' hierarchised together with the corresponding entities (ibid.: 252–253).

The meaning of difference

The third – and, for my purpose, the most important – aspect of value-ideas is that values are segmented in their application. Dumont (1986) exemplifies the contrast between modern and non-modern cultures with respect to the way in which distinctions are organised or configured: 'Impressionistically, on one side [the non-modern] …, distinctions are numerous, fluid, flexible, running independently of each other, overlapping or intersecting; they are also variably stressed according to the situation at hand, now coming to the fore and now receding. On the other side, we [the moderns] think mostly in black and white, extending over a wide range [sic] clear either/or disjunctions and using a small number of rigid, thick boundaries defining solid entities' (ibid.: 253)

Once again, Dumont underscores that modern differences are based on clarity and distinctions rather than interrelationships, and that multifaceted and transparent symbols have become one-dimensional and opaque emblems. In order to amplify the contrast between the modern and non-modern ideologies, he refers to the psychologist Erik H. Erikson. In his discussion of adolescents' identity formation, Erikson contrasts two possible outcomes of this process. These are two forms of entireness, designated as 'wholeness' and 'totality', respectively. Dumont cites from Erikson's (1964) book *Insight and Responsibility*: 'As a Gestalt ... wholeness emphasizes a sound, organic, progressive mutuality between diversified functions and parts within an entirety, the boundaries of which are open and fluent. [Note the plural!] Totality, on the contrary, evokes a Gestalt in which an absolute boundary is emphasized; given a certain arbitrary delineation, nothing that belongs inside must be left outside, and nothing that must be outside can be tolerated inside. A totality is as absolutely inclusive as it is utterly exclusive: whether or not the category-to-be-made absolute is a logical one, or whether the parts really have, so to speak, a yearning for one another' (Erikson in Dumont 1986: 254; Dumont's commentary in brackets). As this cited passage suggests, the totalitarian type of entireness is characterised by a rigid boundary within which one is either included or excluded. The alternative form of entireness is, for its part, characterised by an internal interdependence between separated functions within the whole. As for the latter, Dumont contends that these, non-modern boundaries are open and fluent. The point he makes is that whereas the totalitarian concept of entireness is modern and arbitrary and somewhat mechanical, the other is traditional and structural (ibid.). It is the latter concept of entireness that Dumont designates as holistic.

Against this backdrop, it becomes evident that the difference between modern totalitarian and non-modern holistic understandings of entireness is decisive for the conceptualisation of difference. Dumont (1986: 256) emphasises that the holistic hierarchy entails acknowledging differences while at the same time subordinating them to, and encompassing them in, unity. In order to illuminate the distance to the modern understanding of difference, he refers to the modern American 'colour bar' (without suggesting a homology between this and the holistic hierarchy – as the former is limited to human beings – but rather to underscore the characteristic aspect of the modern way of understanding difference). In the American 'colour bar', he remarks, instead of being divided into a number of estates, conditions or statuses in harmony with a hierarchical universe, all people are equal, but from one discrimination. Dumont notes that it is as if a number of distinctions had coalesced into one absolute, impassable boundary, namely, the binary division of black and white (which is a racist construction in so far as it is constructed to emphasise that distinction).[8] Characteristic is the absence of the shades still found elsewhere or previously (ibid.: 256): that which is not pure white is black. In other words, the modern configuration is constituted by rigidly defined, binary pure-impure categories. As Dumont puts it: 'Clearly we reach here the perfect opposite of segmentation. The contrast is so decisive that one might as well speak of antisegmentation, and the similarity with the other examples adduced tends to show that this form is characteristic of modern ideology' (ibid.).

Significantly, when the categorisation of purity and impurity evolves within the modern logic of opposition, holism is, according to Dumont, transformed into totalitarianism. Within the non-modern holistic framework, on the other hand, the opposition between purity and impurity is the structuring principle that forms a whole series of open and fluent distinctions, which, in turn, form the basis for the hierarchy itself. In his most comprehensive work on hierarchy, *Homo Hierarchicus*, Dumont (1970) analyses the Indian caste system and its dynamics of purity-impurity. The pure and the impure, he contends, are complementary entities that constitute a hierarchical status (a caste system), in which Untouchables' impurity is conceptually linked with the Brahmans' (priests') purity. Dumont goes on to suggest that the two poles, although unequal, are equally necessary (ibid.: 55). And since the holistic pure-impure categorisation is of a more fundamental, permanent nature, the people cannot cleanse themselves of impurity through their own will and actions. Impurity may, in certain cases, be a temporary malady that can be overcome through certain rituals, but above all it is intrinsic to the system. Accordingly, people are classified not on the basis of individual qualities or capacities, but on the basis of sects. Compared with Douglas's (1984) conceptualisation of impurity as disorder, Dumont's delineation of non-modern impurity does not denote something 'out of place'. Rather, impurity – when conceptualised within a holistic-hierarchical system of classifications – is the defining feature of the structural order.

This brings us to another discrepancy between modern totalitarianism and non-modern holism. While a constituting element in totalitarianism is the autonomous and equal individual, this is not the case with regard to holism. In Chapter 1, we saw that when a modern egalitarian society operates in accordance with a hierarchical logic, individuals are subordinated in relation to a privileged identity. Individuals who do not comply with the system are deprived of their autonomy and intrinsic value. Following Dumont (1970), we may add to this argument that totalitarian systems of order come into existence when individualised societies operate hierarchically. The point is not to say, however, as do Adorno and Horkheimer ([1944] 1997: 13), that collectivity and domination constitute a unity, and that individuals are being manipulated, alienated and finally negated by the totalising logic of calculation. The point is more formal or conceptual. Hierarchy, I contend, when operable within the parameters of modern individuality, is able to undermine the intrinsic value of individuals because that value is a constitutive element of modern societies. This is perhaps the most central aspect of totalitarian ideologies, as Hannah Arendt (1973) maintains in her book *The Origins of Totalitarianism*. In totalitarian ideologies, she notes, individuality – indeed, anything that distinguishes one man from another – is characteristically intolerable (ibid.: 457). Personal traits are unacceptable because no ideology that aims at explaining all historical events of the past and at mapping out the course of all events of the future can bear the unpredictability that springs from the fact that humans are creative. Arendt moves on to argue that human creativity can bring forward something so new that nobody ever foresaw it, and that poses a threat to any totalitarian order (ibid.: 458).

To the extent that individuals do *not* lose their autonomy and intrinsic value in relation to the ideological whole, as in republican and liberal ideologies, it is because human autonomy and equality are defined by the ideological whole. However, as noted in Chapter 1, these ideologies subordinate the 'others' by assimilating them into the prevailing order, judging them under the prevalent standards or excluding them completely, which is sometimes articulated as a request that they return 'home'. Regardless of the strategy, the 'others' are excluded in one way or another and are thus deprived of the opportunity to become autonomous and equal. However, those who are excluded completely do not exactly 'lose' their autonomy and equality. Since they are not included in the ideological whole that defines autonomy and equality, they cannot lose their status as autonomous and equal, nor can they be excluded (cf. Agamben 1998, 2005). Rather, they are deprived of the opportunity *to become* autonomous and equal, as the modern subject has not (yet) been established. As for those 'others' who are encompassed/assimilated by the ideological whole in the first place, their autonomy and equality are virtually 'lost' in the process of culturalisation and subordination. They are excluded, albeit not in every sense of the word, since they are symbolically constitutive of the cultural order from which they depart (as demonstrated in the preceding chapter).

Drawing on Dumont, social anthropologist Knut Odner (2000) elucidates this internal exclusionary mechanism in the Norwegian society. His study reveals how minorities who do not share the values of the majority population are excluded (subordinated), due to their deviance from the dominant normative standards. Odner attributes this fact to the holistic structures that are operative within the Norwegian society. He argues that the reprisals that affect those who wish to be recognised as different indicate that people in Norway are thought of not as individuals but as identical parts of society. It is the public interest that is given priority (ibid.: 192). This might indicate that all individuals 'lose' their autonomy (and equality) within this whole. As I see it, however, the loss applies mainly to the 'others', who are conceived as anomalies within the cultural order that defines autonomy (and equality). One is constituted as autonomous and equal only to the extent that one is an identical part of the normative communitas. Autonomy and equality vary according to the degree to which one serves the needs of society. Viewed in this way, Odner's study resonates with my postulation that a hierarchical-holistic structure does not exist at the expense of autonomy and equality as long as they emanate from the whole. The proviso is, of course, that one does not pose a threat to the structuring whole.

Modern paradoxes

In the preceding chapter, I pointed out some dilemmas and paradoxes that pertain to the parameters of multiculturalism and integration policies in modern ideology. In this chapter, I endeavour to show that these paradoxes are related to the operative hierarchical structure within modern, egalitarian configurations of thought. Modern ideology, in its rational-secular arrangement, aims to suppress holism, but the hierarchical structure nevertheless interposes itself through the back door. In what follows, we shall see how the dilemma between equality and distinctiveness encapsulates the paradoxes that arise from this concealed holism.

To develop my argument, I will start with a short summary of Dumont's line of reasoning. As we saw above, Dumont (1986) outlines two alternative configurations: either value attaches to the whole in relation to its parts, with value being prescribed by the very system of representation, or value attaches to the individual, which results in the separation between idea and value. Dumont illustrates the latter, modern configuration by making a reference to Ferdinand Tönnies' distinction between *Naturwille* and *Kürwille*. Freedom of choice – *Kürwille* – is, according to Dumont (ibid.: 261), exercised in a world without wholes or, rather, in a world in which the empirical wholes are deprived of their orientating function or value function. Subsequently, Dumont turns to the complex nexus between humans and nature. He maintains that the relations between humans have to be subordinate for the individual subject to be autonomous and 'equal'. The relationship of humans to nature acquires primacy, but this relation is *sui generis*, he argues, as modern human beings are separated from nature: subject and object are absolutely distinguished (ibid.). *Naturwille* is replaced by *Kürwille*, the latter denoting an independent will, which is to say that the subject has become autonomous.[9] But notwithstanding the absolute distinction between the subject and the object, there is some homology in the way that we regard both sides (ibid.: 262). Like autonomous subjects, modern knowledge is distributed into a number of separate compartments. This entails, among other things, a high degree of division of labour and scientific specialisation. According to Dumont, the modern configuration results from the break-up of the value relation between the elements and the whole (ibid.). As he sees it, the objective world is made up of separate entities or substances in the image of the individual subject (ibid.: 263). Hence, we could speak of autonomous spheres that are homologous to autonomous subjects.

It is the distinction between nature and individual (will) that enables us to distinguish between various spheres, including 'is' and 'ought' in modern ideology and life. Because the modern configuration does not include a world order (value holism), Dumont (1986) argues, it is left to the individual subject to establish a relation between representations and her or his own actions – that is, between 'is' and 'ought'. According to Dumont, this modern world, devoid of value, is a world of objects, of things that we can know exactly, and we can act on this world provided that we abstain from any value imputation. However, a significant paradox emerges: it is a world from which humans have deliberately removed themselves and on which they are able to impose their will (ibid.: 262). In other words, the autonomous subject is constituted in contrast to an objective world, which in turn is reduced to an object of the subject's will, like in the modern utopias. As indicated above, this paradox is sustained by the fact that the notion of an undifferentiated whole – holism – is indirectly operative in egalitarian ideology, whose bedrock is the individual.[10]

Dumont (1986) goes so far as to assert that there is in each concrete society or culture the imprint of this universal, holistic model. He states that the modern configuration is in fact an exceptional variant of the general model (ibid.: 265). So, what, then, are the features of this universal model? A first answer is, according to Dumont, that there are things that equality can and cannot do. He brings up an illustrative example from France that touches upon the debate on multiculturalism.[11] It appertains to recognition of 'difference' – recognition of the 'other' as 'alter'. Dumont contends that in so far as recognition is a matter of enfranchisement in general, such as equal rights and opportunities, as well as equal treatment of women and homosexuals, there is no theoretical problem (ibid.: 266). In such cases, the difference is subordinate, which means that cultural distinctiveness is not recognised. Nevertheless, there is a definite aspect of differentiation at the core of these kinds of egalitarian demands, since it is the distinctive – alter qua alter – that calls for recognition of equality. Dumont's assertion, in line with my argument in the preceding chapter, is that recognition can only be hierarchical, because the act of recognising means placing value on, or integrating into, a whole. In a footnote, Dumont points out that the difference between hierarchy and equality is not at all 'what we are wont to suppose' (ibid.: 266n).[12] If the advocates of difference claim for both equality and recognition (of distinctiveness), he states, they claim the impossible (ibid.: 266).

This is a position that probably strikes a multiculturalist as ethnocentric and perhaps even racist. As Dumont (1986) notes, nothing is more remote from our common sense than Thomas Aquinas's dictum that 'order is seen to consist mainly in inequality (or difference: *disparitate*)' (ibid.: 266). Yet it is only by a perversion or impoverishment of the concept of order that we may believe contrariwise that equality can by itself constitute an order. Dumont specifies: 'To be explicit: *alter* will then be thought of as superior or inferior to Ego, with the important qualification of reversal.... That is to say that, if *alter* was taken as globally inferior, he would turn out as superior on secondary levels of consideration' (ibid.).

This argument is based on the holistic purity-impurity configuration that Dumont (1986) considers to be universal and hence the constituting principle for the hierarchical order (of which reversal is an essential trait). Modern egalitarian society, on the other hand, concludes – from the concept of identity between people on a higher order's (abstract) plane – that all humans are in fact equal. This is, according to Dumont, a fallacy. In Chapter 1, I argued that when an individual-based order operates in accordance with an ideal of equality, it inevitably leads to a subordination of the 'others'. The concept of equality is a legitimising authority for the hierarchical order as long as equality is grounded in Man/Human as an ultimate foundation. I argued that the ideal of equality is defined within a totalitarian horizon, which makes it virtually impossible to bear witness to unjust conditions within an egalitarian system. We may infer from this that the modern, egalitarian order – based on the autonomous subject – keeps the holistic structure adequately at bay. However, the concealed holism is led in through the back door by way of ultimate foundations. As long as the idea of the universal subject – the notion of a common human identity – is operative within the egalitarian order, hierarchy is inevitable. Accordingly, we are left with two alternatives: either we acknowledge the hierarchical structure in terms of a holistic universe, or we defy the hierarchical structure that is operative within the egalitarian order and thereby dismiss altogether the conception of a universal whole/horizon. The latter option requires of us that we ground equality on something other than the idea of an abstract, universal subject (or any other foundational basis).

From Dumont's (1986) point of view, we have no choice, in so far as he conceives of the holistic hierarchy as universal. For him, the solution is to renounce the rigid, 'flat' pure-impure classifications that characterise modern ideology in favour of a hierarchical pure-impure conception within a holistic structure. As indicated above, this solution seems to imply a metaphysical conception of purity. The pressing question, then, is whether or not we are to accept Dumont's assertion that the hierarchical configuration is universal in order to speak of an indirectly operative hierarchy within the modern configuration. A related question is whether a social order is hierarchical per se. In response to the former, I will argue that it is possible to admit Dumont's argument that orders are hierarchically structured without assuming a universal model. My line of argument has suggested that a number of orders can exist without taking on such an overarching hierarchical structure, and I will address this topic in a later chapter. In response to the second question, I will, for the present, look on it as an empirical issue. However, in the following chapter, I will pose the question as to whether a social order can derive from difference rather than identity, a position that allows for community to be based on difference.

Conflation of modern and non-modern configurations

What remains to be summed up in this chapter is how the hierarchical structure impinges upon the dilemma between equality and distinctiveness. In my view, when it operates within a modern, egalitarian order, the hierarchical structure not only is shrouded but also has changed its character. Because the hierarchical structure is prevalent in an ideological order that explicitly disavows hierarchy as an organising principle, differences are understood in accordance with egalitarian principles. As noted in Chapter 1, one does not conceive of social divisions as effects of external forces, such as naturally endowed or God-given human capacities. On the contrary, hierarchical differences are perceived to be legitimate effects of individual (lack of) qualities or competences. According to Dumont (1986), the transformation from a non-modern to a modern frame of reference occurs when the holism is confounded with the egalitarian principles, that is, when non-modern idea-values acquire meaning within the modern political ideologies.

With this in mind, I will return to the distinction between the two forms of purity-impurity configurations that were introduced in Chapter 1. When 'our' identity is imbued with positive value, it is because it is conceived as pure, in opposition to the 'others', who have a negative value by virtue of being impure. This is exactly what happens when the two configurations are conflated. The modern configuration gives rise to binary oppositions imbued with value: everything that is not categorised as pure is concurrently determined as negative in a normative sense. In one stroke, the 'others' are constituted as different and inferior – as negative mirror images of 'our' identity. In this respect, difference and identity are simultaneously descriptive ideas and normative values. The descriptive categories (ideas) are permeated with normative values so that ideas and values merge into a single unit. But unlike the non-modern configuration, in which the dimension of value emerges out of a holistic unity with super- and subordination in relation to the whole, the modern variant of this unity is individualistic. As mentioned earlier, in the modern ideologies values are internalised, and the autonomous subject is at the heart of the egalitarian social order. We could argue, therefore, that both because of and in spite of the concealed presence of the non-modern unity between idea and value, the values are discarded on the basis of the subject's individualistic preferences, determined by what is (un)desirable. Modern ideologies tend to comprise individualistic preferential hierarchies, rather than holistic idea-value hierarchies.

Given that the ranking of values takes place within the modern configuration, the idea-value unity is not simply a tenacious remnant of non-modern times. Firstly, as mentioned above, the term 'non-modern' does not denote a historical epoch or era. Secondly, the unity between idea and value is an integrated (holistic/universal) element of the modern configuration. The normative dimension is indeed based on a non-modern unity of idea and value, but as long as the value is individualised, the configuration is characteristically modern. Within the modern configuration, differences are ordered hierarchically based on what is considered valuable, which enables us to judge the 'others' as second-class citizens and, additionally, exclude them on the basis of being undesirable in 'our' society (cf. Wikan 1995). The wish to exclude 'others' on the basis of their being undesirable would make no sense within a holistic-hierarchical configuration.

It is, in other words, the universal, metaphysical foundations in modern ideology that constitute the idea-values. As we saw in the preceding chapter, in modern ideology, foundational grounds are undifferentiated, universal elements; they are self-evident, superordinate standards against which everything else is evaluated. The fact that non-modern orders exist independently of such legitimising ideas (see Lyotard 1984) suggests that these foundational grounds are perfectly modern, and yet they are non-modern through their composition. And precisely because foundational grounds are non-modern in their composition, they cannot be communicated or articulated. If articulated, the modern configuration risks defeating its own rational, secular character. Any ultimate foundation must appear as self-evident in order to be a catalyst for social dynamics, and it must be constantly reinstated by the social dynamics and the social institutions from which modern nation states arise.

There is, however, a question that persists. How does the intrinsic holism manifest itself in the relationship between 'us' and the 'others'? In Chapter 1, we saw that the liminal duality attributed to the 'others' rests on the notion of non-modern, uncivilised and natural 'barbarians', defined in opposition to 'us' modern, civilised and rational beings. The 'others' are, in a normative sense, people from whom one dissociates oneself, on the one hand, and to whom one aspires, on the other. However, regardless of whether the normative attribute is negative or positive, the other side – in every sense of the word – is in a subordinate position. As I see it, the hierarchical relationship between 'us' and the 'others' is a manifestation of the modern division between idea and value that has been fused with the incomprehensible normative dimension of ideas. However, as long as the modern configuration does not allow the normative dimension of ideas to come to the fore, and as long as foundational grounds continue to operate as self-evident evaluative standards, the unity of ideas and values escapes scrutiny. The prevailing order is left unchallenged, and the normative relationship between 'us' and the 'others' is reinscribed in morally viable attempts at integrating the 'others'.

In taking this stance, I suggest that the paradoxes pertaining to multiculturalism issue from the non-modern element in the modern configuration. It is this non-modern element that – paradoxically – permits 'us' to construct the 'others' as non-modern. The 'others' are depicted as the opposites of 'our' identity, while in fact they are the product of the cultural identity to which they are subordinated. The 'others' are, in other words, rendered opposite and subordinate through the conflation of modern and non-modern conceptions. It follows that the conflation of modern and non-modern elements is also the impetus behind 'the problem of opposition', as described in Chapter 1. There we saw that the problem of opposition brings about the question of how the 'others' can assert their distinctiveness without being confined by the language of their counterparts. How can they refuse incorporation? This question is akin to the one Dumont (1986) takes as his starting point. As noted above, his formulation of this question focuses on how we can build a bridge between our modern ideology, which separates values and 'facts', and other ideologies, which embed values in their world view (ibid.: 247). Given the modern framework within which this question is posed, the possibilities are limited. Cultural differences tend to be consolidating as long as the 'others' are constituted in negation to 'our' identity. The otherness of the 'others' is reduced to a mere function of 'our' identity, and the 'others' are thus deprived of their otherness (e.g. Spivak 1988, 1993, 1999).

Against this backdrop, we may draw the conclusion that totalitarianism will exist as long as the holistic structure continues to be concealed within the egalitarian order. As Dumont (1986) sees it, if we are to avoid totalitarianism, we need to come to terms with holism and acknowledge that holism is prior to egalitarianism. Alternatively, as I have suggested above, we need to rigorously interrogate and eventually relinquish the non-modern element, so as to ground equality in something other than the metaphysical conception of a universal human identity incorporated in the autonomous civic subject. As long as equality is derived from a metaphysical ideal – a foundational ground – the principle of equality will perpetually reproduce and legitimise a subordination of those who are not a worthy part of that order. My argument in favour of an alternative concept of equality is based on the premise that we should conceive of the human lack – the human subjects' non-universal qualities – as something other than a gap between the autonomous and the universal subject. What this alternative understanding of the lack entails, with regard to difference and otherness, will be accounted for in the next chapter.

Chapter 3

Heterogeneity and the Singular Subject

✳

In this chapter I will pursue the question as to whether the construction of the subject and the object needs to accord with Dumont's description of the modern framework. Do we have to conceptualise difference within the logic of opposition if we defy holism? Would it be possible to conceptualise difference as other than the negation of identity? I intend to investigate whether difference can be a source of openness and critical reflection, as opposed to a consolidating counterpart of identity. As indicated above, I do not assume a holistic structure such as the one proposed by Dumont. My point of departure is heterogeneity that does not correspond to a superordinated whole.

In Chapter 2, we saw that the modern autonomous subject inaugurates a differentiation of spheres: nature/science, freedom/morality and art/aesthetics. In this chapter, I will enquire into this heterogeneity of spheres, proceeding from Kant's partition between different human faculties or mental powers (*Kräfte*). Dumont links this division of spheres (and the corresponding faculties) to the modern separation of idea and value, and from this he infers that a holistic way of thinking within the modern configuration leads to totalitarianism. Although my argument concurs with his assertion about an operative holism within the modern configuration, I take issue with his account of modern heterogeneity, which I think is somewhat unbalanced. Contrary to Dumont, I argue that Kant's separation of spheres and faculties prefigures a radical heterogeneity in terms of incommensurability in modern thought. Needless to say, such heterogeneity defies any notions of holism. By calling into question holism, I also call into question the metaphysical regulative ideas, utopias or grand narratives on which modern ideology is based. Anything that presupposes a universal horizon or a totalising identity is repugnant to the kind of heterogeneity that is emphasised in this chapter. I intend instead to enquire into the very lack of a determining, self-identical totality so as to discuss whether this lack enables us to conceptualise an open and non-determinate community, rather than consolidating the logic of opposition pertaining to communitas.

My point of departure is Scott Lash's 'Reflexive Judgement and Aesthetic Subjectivity', in his book *Another Modernity: A Different Rationality* (1999: 197–230). In this text, Lash demonstrates how the modern subject is transformed from being universal to being singular – a transition he finds in Kant's Third Critique, *Critique of Judgment* (*Kritik der Urteilskraft*) ([1790] 1987). Subsequently, Lash elucidates how the singular subject allows for community based on difference, rather than community based on identity. Before examining Lash's interpretation of Kant, however, I shall give a brief account of those aspects of Kant's philosophical framework upon which Lash bases his argument. These aspects concern the context of judgement, notably the heterogeneity of spheres and faculties.

Heterogeneous faculties

In his Third Critique, Kant ([1790] 1987) defines judgement as the ability to think the particular as subsumed under the universal. He distinguishes between two types of judgement. The first one progresses from the universal to the particular, as when we subsume something particular under a rule, principle or law (some universal). Accordingly, Kant calls this judgement 'determinative'. The second type of judgement, which proceeds from the particular to the universal, comes into effect when it encounters something that cannot be subsumed under a principle or a given rule. The inference from the particular to the universal occurs when an event, behaviour or object exceeds the determinate concepts. Judgement must then try to find a universal – to find a rule. Kant names it 'reflective judgement' or 'indeterminate judgement', in so far as it does not determine objects. Against this backdrop, Kant defines determinative and reflective judgement in opposition to one another.

Reflective judgement is the focal point of Kant's Third Critique. In this text he addresses judgements for which the particular is given, so that judgement must try to find a universal, a rule. The Third Critique concerns, more precisely, the conditions for making rational aesthetic judgements, that is, the conditions for aesthetic judgement of taste. Kant finds these conditions between dogmatic objectivism/rationalism and sceptical subjectivism/empiricism (which is termed by Lash the 'critical third way'). The main challenge is to establish the validity of the judgements of taste in this environment between subjectivism and objectivism. Aesthetic judgement is indeed a matter of subjective experience, and yet Kant must demonstrate its universal validity. He has to establish that the judgements cannot be diverted or substantiated in relation to experience. In other words, he must show how 'subjective universal validity' is possible. In his Introduction to the English translation, *Critique of Judgment*, Werner S. Pluhar poses the following question: 'How, if at all, is it possible to judge something in nature (or in art) as beautiful on the basis of something very subjective ... and yet demand for our judgment a universal assent?' (Kant ([1790] 1987: xlvii).[1] According to Kant, the general precondition for the universal validity of a proposition is that it is articulated in 'synthetic a priori judgments' (ibid.: xxxii) – judgements that articulate something necessary about reality without being grounded in experience and thus made trivial.[2]

In addition to judgement (*Urteilskraft*), Kant postulates two basic faculties or powers (*Kräfte*)[3] in the human being that synthesise a priori judgements: understanding (*Verstand*) and reason (*Vernuft*). The faculty of understanding legislates a priori for nature, as an object of sense (Kant ([1790] 1987: IX:195–196), and synthesises cognitive, theoretical judgements (the concepts of understanding, which are logical principles, are called 'categories'). The faculty of reason, for its part, legislates a priori for freedom and for freedom's own causality, and synthesises moral, ethical judgements (the concepts of reason are called 'ideas'). As already mentioned, the third faculty, the power of judgement, synthesises aesthetic judgements of taste. The power to judge with the aid of aesthetical judgements is, in other words, called 'taste', and to Kant this faculty comprises the bridge between the other two.[4] In addition to these powers, there is the imagination (*Einbildungskraft*), which is the power of intuition. This power does not synthesise judgements; instead, it synthesises presentations or representations. Lash (1999: 207) briefly summarises Kant's four faculties/powers as follows: 'If the imagination ... apprehends objects; if the understanding ... subsumes objects; and if reason ... directs subjects; then judgement *searches* for rules.'

I do not intend to discuss Kant's foundation for the validity of judgement in a systematic manner. Rather, I will restrict myself to touching upon those moments – or, more accurately, those portions of Kant's moments and deductions[5] – that are of interest to my study. First of all, I want to emphasise that since each faculty involves an a priori power that produces judgements, so that every capacity has its own rules of synthesis, the faculties are incommensurable. As Kant ([1790] 1987: I:171) notes in the introduction to his Third Critique, philosophy contains principles for the rational cognition of things through concepts, usually divided into theoretical and practical, and these are essentially different. Without being different in kind – as opposed to different in degree – the concepts would not justify a division (since a division presupposes that the principles of the rational cognition pertaining to the different parts of a science are opposed to one another) (ibid.). Kant maintains that the concept of freedom determines nothing with regard to our theoretical cognition of nature, just as the concept of nature determines nothing with regard to the practical laws of freedom. It is not possible to throw a bridge from one domain to the other (ibid.: IX:195–196). This heterogeneity – this difference in kind – is the focal point of both Lash's and my own study. In Kant's Third Critique, heterogeneity is the existential justification of judgement, and it is the very gap between the different spheres that allows judgement to function as a bridge.

Faculties in unison

As opposed to the First and Second Critiques, the Third Critique concerns judging, whereas the others concern only judgements. Judging, according to Lash (1999: 204), is an operation of measuring, estimating, determining and proportioning, which calls for a singular (non-universal), knowing subject. In contrast to the ancient, natural order, the modern order is jurisprudential. It is not God but humankind or reason that determines and judges from its 'critical tribunal' (ibid.). Thus, judgement is to be understood in light of the human autonomy described in the preceding chapters. To the extent that humans are free from external forces, they are impelled to judge.[6]

In his Second Critique, *Critique of Practical Reason* (*Kritik der praktischen Vernunft*) of 1788, Kant focuses attention on human freedom. As he sees it, freedom implies the transcendence of the limits of understanding. Contrary to his First Critique, the *Critique of Pure Reason* (*Kritik der reinen Vernunft*), first published in 1781, in which he addresses the sphere of necessity, his Second Critique draws attention to the sphere of freedom in which reason is not determined but may directly constitute the world. However, as Lash (1999: 205) points out, this act of constitution can be done only under a 'hypothetical' or an 'as-if' mode, due to the fact that the ideas of reason cannot subsume, or be applied to, such world-constituting experience. Lash remarks that reason can subsume under a rule and can recognise whether or not a phenomenon stands under a rule, but reason cannot give itself a rule for subsuming under a rule. 'Thus when subjectivity must take itself and its being as its own creations, the upshot is not ancient order but modern lack. The upshot is what Benjamin called *Lücke*, an unbridgeable gap, between intuition and intellect, and most of all between the intellect's sphere of determination and reason's sphere of freedom' (ibid.: 206).

As the above quotation emphasises, there is an unbridgeable abyss between the different spheres, including the gap between the categories of understanding (necessity/nature) and the ideas of reason (freedom). What is essential in this context is that we – as subjects – are faced with a series of *aporias*. Aporetic conflicts are far more complex than oppositional encounters. Whereas the latter compel us to choose between alternatives, the former constitute an insoluble antinomy, a deadlock, as it were. The concept of *aporia* normally refers to a figure of undecidable ambiguity – an insoluble internal contradiction or a logical disjunction in a text, argument or theory, which is often articulated in terms of lack, confusion or dilemma.[7]

In Kant, the *aporias* ensue from the lack of homogeneity between faculties and the corresponding spheres to which they are applied (nature, freedom/moral law and art). In conjunction with the unbridgeable gap between 'is' and 'ought' – the divide between the necessary (cognitive knowledge, reason, truth) and the free (reason, morality) – the critical philosophy of Kant establishes, in the words of Lash (1999: 206), an 'island of truth' in the 'sea of freedom'. Lash notes that philosophy's critical question 'What can I know?' is situated in the midst of the moral question 'What should I do?' (ibid.). The moral question is uttered in darkness – in the presence of the *noumenon*[8] – in which subjectivity seems to be lost. Lash moves on to suggest that it is in this context, given the limits of cognitive reason and the indeterminacy (freedom) of moral reason, that a few signposts for practice are sought. In the attempt to bridge the gap between understanding and reason, he asserts, the subjectivity that dares to ask 'What can I hope for?' will look for these signposts in aesthetic judgement, which thereby function as a 'light in the tunnel' for subjectivity (ibid.: 206–207). We clearly see that it is modern heterogeneity and the concomitant *aporias* that make up the context for judgement. Kant endeavours to establish aesthetic judgement as a nexus between his first two Critiques – between understanding (nature) and reason (freedom, morality), with the faculty of judgement as the mediating power – in an attempt to bring them into harmony.

Lack of harmony

As the outline above demonstrates, the aesthetic judgement of taste has a mediating function between 'is' and 'ought'. It is in situations where an object cannot be subsumed under a concept, and hence made intelligible, that judgement can bring necessity (as determined and determining) in conjunction with freedom (Lash 1999: 209). According to Kant, the judgement of taste is found in two variants, and only one of them appertains to reconcilement and harmony, namely, the judgement of beauty. In this form, the imagination (the power of intuition) and understanding are brought into harmony, and a feeling of pleasure arises. In the other variant of the judgement of taste – the judgement of the sublime – harmony is broken due to a lack in our cognitive powers. Our concepts fail to grasp the sublime because, according to Kant, the faculty that mediates our relationship to the world, the power of intuition, is overwhelmed and put out of play by the phenomena or objects we encounter. Among the examples that

Kant ([1790] 1987: §28:261) brings forward are overhanging, threatening rocks, thunderclouds piling up in the sky and moving about accompanied by lightning and thunderclaps, volcanoes with all their destructive power, and hurricanes with all the devastation that they leave behind. Because the power of intuition is not capable of synthesising presentations or representations of such phenomena, the sublime is, in principle, not representable. It signifies an abyss that cannot be bridged, and the imagination's confrontation with this gap results in a feeling of discomfort and pain, albeit combined with a sense of pleasure – a negative pleasure (ibid.: §23:245).

Even though the power of intuition is unable to create a representation of the sublime, there is nevertheless a symbolic identification of imagination and reason through its very unpresentability, and this non-identity moves us (we experience the peculiar negative pleasure). In observing nature's omnipotence, we are indeed confronted with our own limitations and inability to make an aesthetic judgement. In our encounters with overwhelming phenomena and objects, however, we come to recognise the infinity in ourselves. According to Kant ([1790] 1987: §27:258), the heterogeneity between the powers of intuition and reason brings forth the feeling that we have a pure and independent reason. And in comparison with this, everything in nature is small (ibid.: §27:260, cf. §28:261). In other words, we become aware of the superiority of our mind over nature, that is, our strength as human beings (which is not nature) in relation to nature. According to Kant, nature is called 'sublime' merely because it elevates (*erhebt*) our imagination, making it exhibit those cases where the mind can come to feel its own sublimity, which lies in its vocation and elevates it even above nature (ibid.: §28:262). Writes Kant: '[Alt]hough the irresistibility of nature's might makes us, considered as natural beings, recognize our physical impotence, it reveals in us at the same time an ability to judge ourselves independent of nature, and reveals in us a superiority over nature that is the basis of a self-preservation quite different in kind from the one that can be assailed and endangered by nature outside us' (ibid.: §28:261).

We may infer that the experience of the sublime, perhaps more than the experience of beauty, makes us aware of our independence from nature. The sublime marks the gap between nature and culture – between nature and human beings – and this gap makes us recognise our autonomy as cultural beings. It seems pertinent to ask, therefore, whether the sublime experience also makes us aware of our inadequacy – the human lack – in relation to the omnipotent or to a metaphysical externality. In my view, we should hold open the possibility that this might be the case, since the sublime marks the limitations of our mental powers. Indeed, the sublime lays bare the fact that we cannot understand everything. As was pointed out above, the discomfort resulting from the lack of harmony between the powers of intuition (imagination) and reason is transformed into pleasure, not because the faculties are brought into harmony, as in the experience of beauty, but because of the very lack of harmony. It is this lack – this heterogeneous gap – that impels us to reflect. The question is whether this reflection makes us attentive to deficiencies in our cognitive powers. Or is the possibility of recognising the lack in our mind lost in the recognition of the superiority of mind in relation to nature? This is a question to which I will return in the last two sections of the chapter. Before turning to this question of the sublime, however, I shall look more closely at Lash's interpretation of Kant with regard to the singular subject and the possibility of communities based on difference. In Lash's text, it is not the sublime experience but rather the experience of beauty that is the linchpin of communities based on difference. As Lash sees it, the singular subjectivity is realised only through the aesthetic object. The aesthetic object is characterised by its finality, that is, by not being a means to an end. And qua finality, the aesthetic object serves as an ontological 'ground' out of which singularity is rendered possible. In Lash's view, it is this groundless 'ground' that forms the basis for 'communities-in-difference'.

The achievement of Kant's aesthetic critique

In order to approach the conditions for community based on difference, I will call attention to the relationship between the singular subject and the aesthetic object in Lash's text. First, however, I shall give a brief review of Kant's main criteria for the universal validity of the judgement of taste, since this backdrop is crucial to both Lash's and my own argument. The main concept in Kant's analysis of the judgement of taste is 'nature's subjective purposiveness' (*Zweckmäßigkeit*) or nature's purposiveness for our power of judgement (see [1790] 1987: V:181–186). Kant conceives of nature as an arena for human projects. Nature lends itself to being judged by us, the human subjects. According to Kant (ibid.: V:184), reflective judgement must think of nature as a purposive unity, as a heuristic principle, which means that reflective judgement gives guidance to our studies of nature. When we study nature with the aid of reflective judgement, we must assume that there is an order in nature as if nature was purposive in light of certain uppermost purposes, although we are not able to prove or state with certainty that nature displays such an order. We must simply proceed on this basis, because without an assumption of a natural order, reflective judgement would be rendered impossible. Particularities – nature's empirical particular laws – would not be conceivable as mutually bonded in a greater unity, as some universal, and this would preclude us from searching for a rule, a concept or a law. Writes Kant (ibid.: VI:187): 'I think of nature as harmonizing, in the diversity of its particular laws, with our need to find universal principles [*Allgemeinheit der Prinzipien*] for them, we must, as far as our insight goes, judge this harmony as contingent, yet as also indispensable for the needs of our understanding – hence as a purposiveness by which nature harmonizes with our aim, though only insofar as this is directed to cognition.'

The aesthetic purposiveness enables us to conceive for ourselves the harmony between an object (whether a product of nature or of art) and our cognitive powers or faculties (imagination and understanding). It is this harmony that makes us feel pleasure in aesthetic judgements – in judgements of beauty: '[W]hen we discover that two or more heterogeneous empirical laws of nature can be unified under a principle that comprises them both, the discovery does give rise to a quite noticeable pleasure' (Kant [1790] 1987: VI:187). When such a feeling of pleasure occurs, Kant notes, we can assume that a harmony exists. That is to say, the purposive harmony of an object with the mutual relation of the cognitive powers is a condition for empirical cognition (ibid.: VII:191). And as a condition for cognition, it must be presupposed as a requirement for all empirical judgement and cognition. 'The attainment of an aim [*Absicht*] is always connected with the feeling of pleasure; and if the condition of reaching the aim is an a priori presentation – as, in this case, it is a principle of reflective judgement as such – then [there is] a basis that determines the feeling of pleasure a priori and validity for everyone. And the feeling of pleasure is determined a priori and validly for everyone merely because we refer the object to the cognitive power' (ibid.: VI:187).

Because the principle of purposiveness is a precondition for the application of reflective judgement and is not diverted from experience, it is a priori. And because judgement gives itself this principle, it is of a subjective character. As mentioned above, this means that reflective judgement is universal and yet subjective. Espen Hammer (1995: 19) notes that the experience of beauty is, in Kant's philosophy, an awareness of an original pre-conceptual relationship of harmony to the world, which determinative judgement normally shrouds by subjecting it to conceptual subsuming constraints. It is a non-conceptual awareness of the order of nature. And precisely because aesthetic judgement lacks certain concepts about the purposes that objects serve, it is what Kant terms 'purposiveness without a purpose' (*Zweckmäßigkeit ohne Zweck*) (Third Moment of Judgement of Taste, concerning relation): '*Beauty* is an object's form of *purposiveness* insofar as it is perceived in the object *without the presentation of a purpose*' ([1790] 1987: §17:236). The feeling of pleasure involved in the experience of beautiful objects must be ascribed to a facilitated play of the powers of imagination and understanding (ibid.: §9:219) – experienced as purposive without purpose. In other words, in the experience of beauty, we cannot express through concepts that an object has some determined purpose. Nevertheless, its form remains purposive for our cognitive powers or faculties. We feel that beauty bears witness to something that can never be expressed through concepts – an original harmony of subject and object (Hammer 1995: 26).

This relationship between subject and object leads to another of Kant's preconditions for claiming that something is beautiful, namely, the fact that a linking that determines a judgement of taste is devoid of all interest (Kant [1790] 1987: §2:204–205) (First Moment of Judgement, concerning quality). According to Kant (ibid.: §2:205), the judgement of taste can have no purpose outside of itself: 'In order to play the judge in matters of taste, we must not be in the least biased in favor of the thing's existence but must be wholly indifferent about it.' Indeed, in Kant's philosophy, an interest is much more than utilitarian advantage. As Lash (1999: 212) makes clear, an interest can comprise any end outside of the object. To be disinterested in our contemplation of the aesthetic object amounts to being rule-seeking subjects. Moreover, to be disinterested means that the subjects are oriented towards the internal finality of the object, whereupon we treat the objects as 'internal goods' (ibid.). This leads back to Kant's concept of 'purposiveness without purpose'. Lash (ibid.: 213) explains: 'If our estimation – as either producers or receivers – of the object comes about through some other end than that finality which is integral to the object, then we cannot speak of aesthetic judgement. In fact we cannot speak of the faculty of judgement at all, and something else is at work. And the statements rising from it would not be universally valid.... Thus beauty is the form of a finality in an object apart from representations of an end: what Kant famously called *Zweckmäßigkeit ohne Zweck*.'

It seems that Lash wishes to group together the third and the first moments (concerning relation and quality, respectively) in Kant's analytic of the beautiful. This is probably due to the fact that Lash aims to establish a link between the singular subject and the final object. Above all, he seems to be concerned with the quality moment, that is, the subject's orientation towards the aesthetic object's internal finality. From his statement about the subject's orientation towards the finality in the object, Lash (1999) infers that singular subjectivity needs help not from above but from 'below'; singular subjectivity needs guidance from a 'ground', but this 'ground' is ungrounded, as it were (see ibid.: 211–212). The 'ground' is not grounded in any external point of reference because there are no metaphysical externalities or any other foundational references implied. Lash notes that in Kant, the 'ground' is to be found in the finality of the aesthetic object (cf. 'purposiveness without purpose'). This is, in Lash's view, the great achievement of Kant's aesthetic critique (ibid.: 212).

Community based on difference

Why is the non-instrumental character of the aesthetic object so important to Lash? And what is it that makes him preoccupied with the relationship between the singular subject and the aesthetic object? It is because this peculiar relationship touches upon a crucial matter with respect to difference and community.

The following quote might be clarifying: 'The ... ungrounded ground ... must centrally address the question of how we can have community while at the same time leaving space for difference. Perhaps we can open up this problem in this context. The notion of difference is crucially based on the idea of not a universal, but a singular, subjectivity.... We are singular only in our difference and self-difference.... The idea of reflective judgement in which the singularity of the subject is dependent on the internality of goods [aesthetic objects] thus at least begins to open up possibilities ... of how communities-in-difference may be possible' (Lash 1999: 214). In order to open up for community based on difference, Lash asserts, we need to emphasise the self-difference of the singular subject. Moreover, the singular subject must be conceived in relation to the object's finality. With respect to the latter, Lash employs the ancient term *poesis*, which refers to the non-instrumental relationship between subject and object. As opposed to instrumental reason or strategic rationality (*theorein*), characterised by a theoretical attitude towards the object (and a determinate, universal subject), *poesis* entails a disinterested, immediate 'I–It' relationship (ibid.: 199, 221). As Lash sees it, the aesthetic object opens up for existential meaning between subjectivity and freedom – between subjectivity and being. He amplifies: 'This is what Gillian Rose meant by the "broken middle". That is, what we have been calling the ground in this book is clearly the "middle". The middle is between subjectivity and freedom, subjectivity and being. The middle here is never a means (or an instrumentality), always a finality' (ibid.: 221).

The non-instrumental object is not confined to art, however; it can just as well be language, 'place' in the built environment, and so on. Regardless of its different manifestations, the non-instrumental object is, according to Lash (1999), of paramount importance for our freedom, reflexivity and existential meaning. Without the non-instrumental object as a ground, medium or middle, he argues, freedom, reflexivity and existential meaning are not possible. He moves on to suggest that when the middle becomes a utilitarian or instrumental means, we are back in *theorein*, wherein the subject is determinate (ibid.: 222). However, as he also notes, reflexivity is meaningless in the absence of sociality in a community, that is, in the absence of a situated intersubjectivity: *praxis*. When *praxis* is concerned, the 'ground' denotes situated intersubjectivity. In *praxis*, Lash reasons, singular subjectivity relates not to a 'thou' but to what is already an 'I–thou' relationship – to what is already a situated and, in principle, historical intersubjectivity (ibid.: 222). The 'I–thou' constitutes, in other words, an internal relationship (which is a significant element of Martin Buber's dialogic philosophy), in which 'thou' is constitutive of 'I'. In line with Jean-Luc Nancy (2000), we may assert that their existence is essentially co-existence. In a similar vein, Judith Butler (2004a, 2004b, 2005, 2009) emphasises the subject's lack of interiority and calls attention to the subject's primary co-existence with others. She links this primary sociality of the subject with vulnerability associated with grieving and loss. The experience of grieving and loss might evoke a sense of community by exposing the interdependency of the subjects. The subjects are exposed to a lack in terms of unknowingness, whereby one becomes a stranger to oneself. Or, in Lash's words, the subject is exposed as self-different, as opposed to unified and whole. This is indeed an experience of groundlessness. And in Lash's (1999: 222) view, no groundlessness is possible, no escape from determinacy is likely, without some sort of community as 'ground' and middle.

Arguing with Gillian Rose (1992) (as in the quotation above on the 'broken middle'), Lash (1999) maintains that the ground of *praxis* can be found in law, although more as an expression of community than as abstract laws. It can be found in *agape* – that is, in Christian love – and in Georg Simmel's concept of 'sociability'. The ground of *praxis* can also be found in Émile Durkheim's idea of 'collective representation' and in Hans-Georg Gadamer's notion of 'collective memory' (ibid.: 222). Lash is particularly informed by Gadamer's philosophy, in so far as Gadamer, too, is informed by Kant's Third Critique. It is Gadamer's interpretation of the relationship between nature and culture that seems to attract Lash's attention. Since this is also a crucial issue with respect to my argument, I shall elaborate on this in some detail.

Survival and transcendence

In order to grasp the concept of 'collective memory', we have to call attention to Gadamer's (1975) major work, *Truth and Method* (*Wahrheit und Method*). In this book, Gadamer develops his concept of the 'hermeneutical circle', informed by Arnold Gehlen's human anthropology. Gadamer is principally concerned with the aspect of Gehlen's anthropology that pertains to our lack of instincts (freedom/autonomy). According to Gehlen ([1940] 1988), the culture-making capacity of the human being is due to an instinctual deficiency that is being compensated for by a human will – a will to power. The term 'will to power' denotes an attempt to endow the constant stream of creation with finality – an attempt to give the stream of creation a form (cf. Schmidt and Kristensen 1986: 18). The will to power reveals itself in all human relations, in cognitive processes and in social processes. In the book *The Will to Power* ([1901] 1967), which is a selection of Nietzsche's posthumously collected notes, the doctrine of 'will to power' is related to a compensation for a lack in our instincts through the development of categories. According to Nietzsche, we apply our subsuming and logical power in order to survive and thrive. As Gadamer emphasises, we compensate for the non-determination in our instincts (*Instinktarmut*) through 'retaining what threatens to pass away'. We are, as such, 'permanence-retaining animals' (cited in Lash 1999: 226).

Gadamer holds that we first retain permanence in play or games. Lash amplifies that play entails the retention of permanence in its rules, in the identity to a pattern and in the fact that others must play along. Accordingly, the permanence is not just for oneself over time, but also for others, who occupy different spaces (Lash 1999: 227). Contrary to work, however, play involves an excess of purpose – of pragmatic purpose. This decisive element in Gadamer's hermeneutics clearly underscores that representation is rendered possible through activities that go beyond pragmatic purpose. Whereas work primarily involves determinative judgement, play involves self-rule-giving activity. The latter is by Gadamer termed 'transcendence', which requires moving beyond logic and calculation, moving beyond the pragmatic purpose of survival that humans – qua permanence-retaining animals – share with other species (see ibid.). It is this permanence-retaining capacity that Gadamer terms 'collective memory'. We may sum up Lash's argument as follows. Drawing on the logical categories, collective memory permits us to survive through our empirical will (to power), on the one hand. On the other hand, our permanence-retaining capacity enables us to do far more than merely survive. Representation allows for a certain degree of transcendence of determinative judgement, that is, transcendence of nature. And it is this transcendence, in turn, that allows us to define ourselves as finite creatures and to recognise our singularity or finitude.[9] Lash (ibid.: 227) maintains that the human capacity for transcendence is a necessary supplement to any adequate concept of reflective judgement. Without it, there is a deficit of reflexivity, and we would be unaware of our finitude.

To sum up and explicate, the interplay between survival and transcendence rests on the duality in the human capacity to retain permanence: the human being's logical faculty and empirical will (to power), on the one hand, and its capacity to transcend, on the other. According to Gadamer, play represents transcendence, inasmuch as play, in contrast to determinative judgement, is an aesthetic experience that implies a non-determinative anticipation. Lash (1999: 228) notes that we experience by performing a continuous hermeneutic movement guided by anticipation of the whole. The particular represents itself as a fragment of being that promises to make itself whole. However, qua non-determinate meaning, the particular can never make itself whole; the anticipated and unrealised whole constitutes a horizon that cannot be attained. As we saw in connection with the modern metaphysics of purity in Chapter 1, the end-goal would dissolve at the very moment we reached it: the symbolic order would implode into nothingness. In a similar vein, the hermeneutical reflective experience would evaporate into determinative judgement and pure method. The hermeneutical circle is, in other words, only operable as long as it cannot approach a full picture of the whole (see ibid.).

However, as we saw in the preceding chapters, the autonomous subject is sometimes sacrificed to a higher cause. When inscribed into a totalitarian utopian narrative, the subject is divested of its autonomy and transformed into an infinite, universal substance. This utopian aspiration could perhaps be depicted as a transcendence of immanence, since the concrete subject, on a symbolic level, moves beyond the aspects of life that link humans to the natural world. Yet, following Gadamer, Lash does not connect the concept of transcendence with this kind of yearning for infinity. On the contrary, by linking transcendence to play, he draws a vital distinction between transcendence and totalitarian determinism (which is characteristic of utopian aspirations). Some communities, he states, are based on instrumental determinism, which envisions people as a whole. Examples of this kind of determinism are humanity, the body and blood of Christ, and the proletariat. As Lash (1999: 245) sees it, these are foundational grounds wherein death itself is the constitutive limit for community. Death, too, might be fashioned into infinite substance, as in nationalism: 'It [death] too is worked or fashioned into infinite substance, in Christian salvation or the future of the proletariat, or of mankind. This is most apparent in nationalism, in which we die not as finite relational beings but for an infinite national substance, a thousand year Reich' (ibid.). According to Lash, the determinism in which the subject functions as a universal substance renders meaningful community impossible. When humans are seen as infinite substance, he argues, they are closed in on themselves and closed off from one another. Referring to Nancy's (1991) book *The Inoperative Community*, Lash (1999) contends that individuals can form communities only to the extent that they are not self-identical. Community is possible only through the regions of ourselves that do not fall under the universalism that lies in identity and self-identity. This is a community beyond metaphysical ideas of unity or identity. We cannot be complete as is God, Lash maintains (ibid.: 243). Rather, it is in our moments of self-difference that we form communities (ibid.: 237).

With a view to the preceding chapters, we may now suggest that identity and self-identity signify a denial of human lack. Lash (1999: 242) illustrates this point by referring to Hegel's master-slave dynamics, in which the master reduces the 'other' – the slave – to an image of himself. By contrast, a community based on difference entails living with lack, living with self-difference and aporetic subjectivity. As pointed out above, it involves breaking with any idea that purports to be a replacement for God, be it lost innocence (in the past) or a utopian end-goal (in the future).

The sublime

Thus far, I have subscribed to Lash's reading of Kant and his argument for difference-based community. However, we may question whether Lash's interpretation is too narrowly focused on the portions that support his Gadamer-informed argument. In my view, Lash (1999: 197) does rightfully point out that judgement has not yet fully descended into life. Yet he maintains that the universal subject and the idea of a metaphysical externality are replaced by the singular subject and finite object, which he conceives as a precondition for meaningful communities. I fully agree with Lash's assertion that a community based on difference entails living with lack. However, as I have suggested above, I do not believe that Kant's Third Critique brings us in this direction (nor does Gadamer) – at least, not as far as Lash seems to think. This statement of mine can be explained in relation to Kant's writings on the sublime, which Lash does not fully integrate in his discussion of the Third Critique.

As I see it, it is Kant's distinction between nature and culture that gives rise to the problem that I want to pinpoint. As I made clear in the preceding chapter, the modern configuration establishes a dichotomy between nature and culture. According to Dumont (1986), this dichotomy implies that the objective world is created of separate unities or substances in the image of the individual subject: *Naturwille* is subordinate to *Kürwille*. The human being qua a cultural being is regarded as autonomous in relation to nature; nevertheless, nature poses a threat to culture in cases where nature cannot be subjected to the human will. This is what happens in the sublime experience, when natural forces are overwhelming and prevail, so to speak, vis-à-vis the cultural, human powers. That being said, the sublime does not pose a threat in a pathological sense. If we take a closer look at Kant's delineation of the sublime, it becomes evident that the overwhelming experience is not literally devastating; it does not threaten to dissolve the cultural order. As has been pointed out above, the sublime does not undermine the subject's sovereignty in relation to nature. On the contrary, the sublime experience reaffirms human sovereignty and thus entrenches our independence from nature.

With regard to this, I posed the question as to whether the sublime experience also enables us to recognise our lack as finite beings, given that the sublime feeling results from the lack of harmony between our faculties or cognitive powers, that is, from our lack of omniscience. According to Lash, reflective judgement exceeds our logical capacity and empirical will to power due to the fact that human beings have the ability to transcend.[10] To emphasise that transcendence reveals our finitude, Lash (1999: 227) speaks of 'transcendence in finitude'. Taking into account Kant's discussion on the sublime, however, there are reasons to believe that Kant's philosophy might just as well take us in the opposite direction. In the following, I endeavour to illuminate Kant's concept of the supersensible so as to substantiate this point. I intend to show that the supersensible in Kant's philosophy invokes the universal subject, rather than pointing to the singular subject. Eventually, I argue, Kant (re)turns to God as the final guiding principle for human culture. To elaborate on this, I will draw on Carlos Wiggen's reading of Kant.

In the second part of the Third Critique, the critique of teleological judgement, Kant addresses the question of whether we can positively identify a deeper ground for what exists – an origin of nature. The answer seems to be both yes and no. According to Wiggen (1998: 50), Kant is of the opinion that we must assume that God is the origin of being, although this divine dimension, which cannot be grasped by our senses, cannot be positively determined. Nevertheless, Kant seems to believe that a divine dimension exists, because it would be wrong to assume that such a dimension does *not* exist. As Wiggen (ibid.) notes, Kant must reject a dogmatic scepticism, since it is irreconcilable with morality, whereas a sceptic belief (*Zweifelsglaube*) is reconcilable. If we do not posit God's existence, we will go straight towards the abyss. As Kant ([1790] 1987: §75:399–400) puts it: 'There is a God. But in fact the proposition entitles us human beings only to this restricted formula: The purposiveness that we must presuppose even for cognizing the inner possibility of many natural things is quite unthinkable to us and is beyond our grasp unless we think of it, and of the world as such, as a product of an intelligent cause (a God).'

The impossibility of a positive identification of the original ground or intelligent cause (God) arises from the fact that reason is inadequate, signalling a lack in our cognitive powers. We cannot explain the fact that we exist.[11] In this regard, Kant cuts off the notion of a positively determinable, operative God in nature, in favour of a sceptical belief. According to Wiggen (1998: 51), Kant demonstrates that a religious attitude can be nothing but a formal objection to atheism and its consequences (which are the dissolution of morality). Hence, Kant needs to posit something else, something more tenable, in place of the ousted figment – namely, the idea of freedom.

Freedom is an idea of reason that can be put into practice and experienced, and it is the basis for a society grounded in reason. On that account, Kant makes the concept of freedom superior to the dogmatic-metaphysical narratives that focus on God. But according to Wiggen (1998: 52), Kant has managed to tone this down in order not to end up with atheism. In fact, it seems that atheism for Kant is a greater evil than preserving the concept of God. In any event, Kant winds up with a recommendation to think of the final aim of all objects' existence (*Dasein*) as divinity. Wiggen refers to this as Kant's 'authentic standpoint', and it is Kant's concept of nature that leads him to this standpoint. According to Wiggen (ibid.), Kant has a dual view of nature. On the one hand, he thinks that nature can be depicted as regularities. On the other, he conceives of these regularities as contingent or, at the very least, of relative duration. These processes break against one another, and nature is eventually associated with chaos and coercion. Nature is thus considered to be the negative counterpart to freedom.

As noted above, it is this opposition between culture/freedom and nature that constitutes the basis for Kant's description of the aesthetic object. The aesthetic object is characterised by being non-purposive (*Zweckmäßigkeit ohne Zweck*), in contrast to nature, which is to say that the object of art is finite (cf. *poesis*). According to Wiggen (1998: 55), it is reasonable to assume that Kant wants to see aesthetic pleasure – the experience of beauty – as an inexplicable aspect of the human mind. At any rate, it seems evident that this quality or capacity is something uniquely human, belonging under the concept of freedom rather than the concept of nature (ibid.). As also noted above, however, the aesthetic emerges not only as beauty but also as the experience of the sublime. In this experience, we are confronted with the kind of nature in which mighty and devastating forces are unleashed – forces that assail human freedom by overwhelming us. The sublime feeling is evoked by those aspects of nature that do not correspond with, but rather diverge from, our mental categories and principles. Accordingly, the sublime signifies the potential fall of culture. Nevertheless, as suggested above, Kant's concept of the sublime seems to preclude him from acknowledging the sublime experience as a source of critique of our belief in, or aspiration towards, a godlike omniscience (our logical capacity and empirical will to power). Instead, Kant ([1790] 1987) submits that the overwhelming experience of nature gives rise to a concurrent experience of an unlimited ability in ourselves, namely, the supersensible: 'The *quality* of the feeling of the sublime consists in its being a feeling, accompanying an object, of displeasure about our aesthetic power of judging, yet of a displeasure that we present at the same time as purposive. What makes this possible is that the subject's own inability uncovers in him the consciousness of an unlimited ability which is also his, and that the mind can judge this ability aesthetically only by that inability' (ibid.: §27:259).

As was remarked above, the overwhelming impression of nature gives rise to a reaction whereby we envision the supersensible, morality and God, which makes the previous observation (of nature) seem small. The overwhelming impression or experience is thereby reduced to a triviality. Even if we should become victims of natural forces, the latter could never eradicate humanity and its mind. In other words, our striving for infinite progress, and in our reason a claim to absolute totality, is in Kant's Third Critique comprised in the concept of the supersensible substratum. What happens, according to Wiggen (1998: 59), is that this brings out the reflective judgement's striving for (the experience of) that infinite dimension – the home of the spirit. The experience of the sublime makes us strive for the absolute whole, the larger unity, which we normally call God. We could conceive of this movement from the abyss to the supersensible as a movement from the singular towards the universal subject.[12] Above all, it seems to testify to the duality of the modern subject: its concurrent autonomous and universal nature. As pointed out in Chapter 1, in modern ideology, the universal element tends to be incorporated into the autonomous subject.[13] With a view to the above, we may call this turn in

Kant's Third Critique a denial of lack (or heterogeneity), a move towards an omnipotent power. We might also characterise it as a homogenising of the heterogeneous. Accordingly, the Third Critique contributes to the conflation of modern and non-modern configurations that was delineated in Chapter 2 by way of adhering to a metaphysical, holistic element.

As for the possibility of a community based on difference, it seems plausible to claim that the encounter with the abyss, which opens up before us when we had hoped to find certainty, is a common (in the sense of widespread) human experience. If most people experience this from time to time, we might assume that such experience gives rise to – at least potentially – a feeling of sympathy among people. As such, this experience may constitute a sense of community prior to the question of what interest people have in one another. According to Wiggen (1998), such a community precedes the citizenship that can be extracted from the categorical imperative. As long as the community springs directly out of reflective judgement, it is more original than the legal community of citizens and people with shared interests (ibid.: 60). In my view, however, this kind of community, which is devoid of interests or purposes, is undermined by Kant's concept of the supersensible. The supersensible, in its striving towards omniscience or totality, leaves little room for self-difference, human lack and aporetic subjectivity.

Pathological ugliness

In the following, I maintain that Kant's philosophy does not provide sufficient grounds for envisioning a community based on difference, and I intend to push this argument one step further by elucidating what for Kant counts as pathological. Thus far, we have seen that beauty evokes a feeling of pleasure. Furthermore, we have seen that the sublime is associated with negative pleasure. The issue that remains to be elucidated is what, in Kant's view, is considered to be absolutely *not* pleasurable. What is it that gives rise to the feeling of disgust? If we take a look at Kant's Third Critique ([1790] 1987: §48), the feeling of disgust is evoked by the so-called ugliness (*Häßlichkeit*). Significantly, ugliness that arouses disgust is depicted by Kant as threatening by way of disintegrating the very voluntariness on which the aesthetic experience is grounded or dependent, namely, disinterestedness. Through the lack of aesthetic distance, Eliassen (2000: 15) notes, ugliness is like a negative mirror image of beauty with regard to both reflection and experience.

In contrast, due to the supersensible, the sublime is not depicted by Kant as a crisis. He is able to overcome the 'crisis' that follows from the break with culture by calling on reason, which, unlike understanding, is able to think without concepts. Eliassen (2000: 16) contends that reason manages to comprehend the incomprehensible through the pure and supersensible form of the ideas. On that account, the sublime does not pose a threat to culture in a pathological sense. Rather, it re-establishes culture based on reason. Ugliness that arouses disgust, on the other hand, cannot be contained in any idea because it evades human reason. In this respect, nature triumphantly overcomes culture, and the ugly is constituted as a pathological disorder. Ugliness collapses the subject's distance to the empirical world, as it were, which means that it makes both conceptuality and commonality disappear (ibid.: 15). This lack of conceptuality is indeed the trait of the sublime. However, as already mentioned, this experience does not cause any crisis, due to reason's ability to think without concepts (see ibid.: 16). With regard to the distinction between the sublime and the ugly, we may sum up the argument as follows. Ugliness is that in nature which we cannot comprehend; it refers to that which can neither become a part of us nor be sublimated by means of supersensible ideas. As such, the ugly reminds us of our limitations as natural beings, which means that the sovereignty of the human mind is revealed as limited or inadequate. So, instead of pleasure, Eliassen (ibid.) notes, ugliness creates a feeling of instant disgust in us. It makes us act 'naturally', that is, spontaneously and unfreely. With respect to the dynamics between purity and impurity, Eliassen contends: 'Kant's depiction of beauty thus presupposes an aesthetic of purity in which objects are limited to the representational and appropriable. On a general level, one could say that Kant belongs to a tradition in which pure is synonymous with assimilable. The impure, on the other hand, plagues the subject by resisting subordination' (ibid.: 17–18; my translation).

It is worth noting, however, that ugliness qua pathological impurity is of secondary character; its existence is diverted in an ontological sense (Eliassen 1995: 19). In response to Kant's Third Critique, Eliassen wonders if it is possible to conceive of an aesthetic of the impure that is primary rather than secondary: 'Perhaps it would be possible to conceive of the impure not as secondary or supplementary, but as original' (ibid.: 20). Would it be possible to conceive of the heterogeneous as preceding the homogeneous – of difference prior to identity? If so, Eliassen suggests, the heterogeneous might be regarded as an opportunity rather than a threat (ibid.: 21). His suggestion as to how this could be accomplished seems to be in line with Lash's argument. It is a matter of thinking of heterogeneity as such. Eliassen elaborates:

> In order for this to occur ... it is probably required that it [the aesthetic] lets go of the autonomy of the subject as a justification and telos, in favour of an acceptance of the object's and the subject's mutual constitution.... It would ... be a matter of getting a view of the concept's productive character, how the theory appears not only as a means by which to form the world, but also as a means to *de*form it.... The theory is thus brought out of the confines that its old judgemental task assigned it: to make judgements. Both the starting point and the outcome of the theory must

therefore accept its impurity; its task must thus be less to reduce and determine – to correct perception – and more to multiply, enrich, indeed to *deform* it. (ibid.: 22; my translation)

It is this conceptualisation of heterogeneity and difference that is the topic of Chapter 4. The question at issue is whether we can understand the lack in our mental powers as a condition of possibility for community rather than as a threat to it. I will analyse this question primarily through the philosophy of Lyotard, in so far as his philosophy comprises a critical development of Kant's Third Critique, in which the sublime, and not the beautiful, is at the centre of attention.

Chapter 4

Consequences of Heterogeneity

※

What interests us in this chapter is Lash's assertion that Kant's aesthetical judgement has not yet fully descended into life. The question is how it can be conceived to do so. How can we understand the heterogeneous – in terms of lack of totality and, in the human mind, a lack of omniscience – as a condition for community based on difference? In what way does the *aporia* between the singular and the general form the basis for community? I shall approach these questions through Lyotard's philosophy, informed by Kant's concept of the sublime. It must be noted, however, that Lyotard's concept of the sublime does not include the supersensible, nor does Lyotard's philosophy implicate any 'authentic standpoint'. Lyotard does not, as does Kant, homogenise the heterogeneous. On the contrary, he assigns heterogeneity a primary status. Difference is considered to be prior to identity, and the logic of identity – indeed, the metaphysics of purity – is thereby defied. Lyotard disavows any idea of external courses, foundational grounds, metaphysical elements or forces that serve to legitimate particular social orders. The lack in our mental powers is not depicted in terms of an abyss to be overcome. Rather, in accordance with recent forms of affirmative deconstruction, Lyotard conceives of the human lack as the condition of possibility for knowledge, critical reflection and new constitutions. In this respect, heterogeneity might also open up the possibility for community based on difference.

Modernism revisited, or, rewriting modernity

In order to elaborate on Lyotard's understanding of heterogeneity, I will give an account of his overall philosophical framework. It is the relationship between the modern and the postmodern conditions that constitutes this framework.

However, the modern and the postmodern are not regarded by Lyotard (1991: 25) as epochs or directions of style, in accordance with the modern obsession with periodisation. Rather, they are perceived to be two gestures, forces or energies in an ongoing contest. As we shall see, the modern is conceived as a consolidating and stabilising force, while the postmodern is considered to be a destabilising factor that renews the modern. It is essential to note that, for Lyotard (1992a), the prefix 'post' does not signify a movement of 'comeback', 'flashback' or 'feedback', that is, a movement of repetition. Rather, 'post' is defined as 'a procedure in "ana-": a procedure of analysis, anamnesis, anagogy and anamorphosis' (ibid.: 93). According to Lyotard, 'post' indicates something like a conversion – a new direction from the previous one – and he concedes that this idea of a linear chronology is in itself distinctly 'modern'. As for modernity, he writes: 'The very idea of modernity is closely correlated with the principle that it is both possible and necessary to break with tradition and institute absolutely new ways of living and thinking' (ibid.: 90).

Significantly, the relationship between the modern and the postmodern is not one of dialectics. Contrary to other major contributors in the field of continental philosophy, notably critical theory, Lyotard (1984, 1992a) does not think that societal modernisation or rationalisation leads to a negative dialectical reaction in terms of cultural counter-movements. He is sceptical of dialectical reasoning because the revolutionary 'new' simply reproduces the former order in new forms: the 'new' is nothing but a reflection of what it negates. This seems to be the real scandal of dialectics, which resembles the problem of opposition described in Chapter 1.[1] Lyotard's defiance of the logic of opposition arises from the proposition that what we overcome or criticise is imprinted in our alternative perspective (cf. Spivak 1985, 1988). As will be elaborated on below, Lyotard attends to this deconstruction of oppositional thinking in conjunction with another pivotal trait of affirmative deconstruction: thinking from difference rather than from identity. As long as difference or heterogeneity is conceived as prior to identity, difference cannot possibly be defined in contrast to identity – as its negation – because that would be tantamount to turning difference into (a new) identity. Lyotard aims to show that difference qua opposition of identity ignores or suppresses heterogeneity. Contrary to such reductionism, Lyotard insists on a relation of difference between the modern and the postmodern, which allows for several possibilities. The fact that something is not black does not mean that it has to be white (cf. Dumont 1986). It can be imbued with an infinite number of potential intermediate values. Lyotard is concerned with the way in which prevailing norms can be relocated in small portions. Hence, his philosophy is relegated to a strategy of rewriting by way of displacement.[2]

In his (re)writing, Lyotard is particularly preoccupied with the avant-gardes in the modernist movement, which he depicts as a revitalising force in relation to the basic principles of modern society, that is, its 'mode' in the Latin sense of the word. This is not a perspective particular to Lyotard alone, however, since modernism is generally perceived to be a cultural counter-movement to the modern societal order. What is peculiar to Lyotard, aside from the fact that he does not conceive of modernism as a *dialectical* counter-movement, is that he thinks the modernist movement is in constant danger of losing its subversive power by allowing itself to be bureaucratised and commercialised (1984: 76–77). In the state of looseness, modernism needs to be revitalised, he asserts, and it is postmodernism that reminds modernism of its subversive power. Lyotard (1991) conceives of the relation between the modernist avant-gardes and the postmodern rewriting of modernism as critical and inclusive – as a relation of displacement. Postmodernism is the productive power that reinstates modernism and gives it meaning. Based on the proposition that what we criticise will be imprinted in the new position, although not in terms of dialectical reflection of the old, Lyotard (ibid.: 79) maintains that the postmodern is part of the modern: 'It [the postmodern] is undoubtedly part of the modern. All that has been received, if only yesterday (*modo, modo,* Petronius used to say), must be suspected' (cf. Lyotard 1992a: 21). He moves on to suggest that things become modern by becoming 'post' something. For instance, Cézanne is post-Impressionist and Duchamp is post-Cubist. In this respect, postmodernism is modernism not at its end but at its beginning, and that beginning is recurrent: 'A work can become modern only if it is first postmodern. Postmodernism thus understood is not modernism at its end but in the nascent state, and this state is constant' (Lyotard 1984: 79; cf. Lyotard 1992a: 22).

The postmodern is that aspect of the modern that signifies the unpresentable in the presentation; it reminds us of the fact that the unpresentable exists. Because our powers of representation are limited, there may be things that cannot be represented, things that can neither be seen nor made visible. This is the postmodern aspect of modernism, which opens up to the non-determined, the aporetic gaps or lacks. In brief, postmodernism testifies to the lack, which Lyotard (1984: 81) formulates in the following manner: 'The postmodern would be that which, in the modern, puts forward the unpresentable in presentation itself; that which denies itself the solace of good forms, the consensus of taste which would make it possible to share collectively the nostalgia for the unattainable; that which searches for new presentations, not in order to enjoy them but in order to impart a stronger sense of the unpresentable.' To Lyotard, therefore, postmodernism is characterised by experimentation, which disavows the comfort and solace of realism and representational art. In Lyotard's view, modern painting, which avoids figuration or representation, enables us to see only by making it impossible to see; it will please only by causing pain. He contends that one recognises the avant-garde axioms in painting inasmuch as they devote themselves to making an allusion to the unpresentable by means of visual representations (ibid.: 78). And he moves on to suggest that the modern avant-gardes are perpetually flushing out artifices of presentation which make it possible to subordinate thought to the gaze and to turn it away from the unpresentable (ibid.: 79).

Two 'modes'

Writes Lyotard (1984: 78): 'I shall call modern the art which devotes its "little technical expertise" (*son "petit technique"*), as Diderot used to say, to present the fact that the unpresentable exists. To make visible that there is something which can be conceived and which can neither be seen nor made visible: this is what is at stake in modern painting.' What, then, is the difference between modern and postmodern art? In Lyotard's delineation of modern art, it may well appear that the two are identical. In order to recognise the difference between modernism and postmodernism, we have to take into consideration the distinction that Lyotard draws between two 'modes' concerning the relation between the 'presentable' and the 'conceivable'. He states that, on the one hand, '[t]he emphasis can be placed on the powerlessness of the faculty of presentation, on the nostalgia for presence felt by the human subject, on the obscure and futile will which inhabits him in spite of everything' (ibid.: 79). On the other hand, the emphasis can be placed on the power of sensibility or imagination, 'on its "inhumanity" so to speak (it was the quality Apollinaire demanded of modern artists), since it is not the business of our understanding whether or not human sensibility or imagination can match what it conceives' (ibid.: 79–80).

Lyotard illustrates the two different 'modes' by referring to well-known names from the history of the avant-gardes. On the former side, that of melancholia/nostalgia, he assigns a place for, among others, the German Expressionists, whereas Braque and Picasso are assigned a place on the latter, the *novatio* side. Other examples include Chirico on the one side and Duchamp on the other. The nuance that distinguishes these two 'modes' may be infinitesimal. In fact, they often co-exist in the same piece and, as such, are almost inseparable. Nevertheless, as Lyotard (1984: 80) sees it, 'they testify to a difference ... between regret and assay'. He maintains that the postmodern is that which searches for new presentations, not in order to enjoy them, but in order to impart a stronger sense of the unpresentable (ibid.: 81). In this regard, the works that are created by a postmodern artist are not, in principle, governed by established rules, and we cannot judge them according to determinative judgement. We cannot apply familiar categories to the text or work of art, Lyotard asserts (ibid.), as these are the rules and categories that are sought for by the work of art itself. The artist or author works without the constraints of rules in order to formulate the rules of what 'will have been done'. In this respect, Lyotard's conception of the postmodern resonates with Kant's aesthetic judgement, although, as we shall see later on, in the case of Lyotard's philosophy, the judgement has descended into life.

Against this backdrop, we may infer that the postmodern is the gesture that rediscovers and criticises lost or displaced fragments of history which have disappeared in (modern) generalisations, meta-narratives and all-encompassing interpretations. The postmodern creates renewal and innovative openings before 'modern' consensus, understanding or culture integrates these openings in its narrative or system of order. That is why, Lyotard (1984: 81) contends, the postmodern comes before the modern: '*Post modern* would have to be understood according to the paradox of the future (*post*) anterior (*modo*).' And that is why the postmodern in art is a displacement in relation to modernist avant-garde art. Tore Eriksen (1995: 250; my translation) offers the following clarification regarding the relationship between modernism and postmodernism: 'He [Lyotard] is not interested in their [the avant-gardes'] respective "answers" to the banal question: "What is a painting?" Rather, what interests him is the way in which they enquire and work, that is, the problem of form. They work abstractly or minimalistically – *ex minimis*. They gradually remove elements so as to arrive at the final and most fundamental. Lyotard's displacement consists of the fact that he adheres to the way in which they interrogate, the procedural course of action or the form of representation, but he disavows the concrete, substantial answers that they provide.'

Why is Lyotard not interested in the substantial answers arrived at by the avant-gardes? The reason seems to be, according to Eriksen (1995: 250), that the avant-gardes believed that they, one by one, had reached the ultimate ground. Through the quest for a final foundation, they attempted to represent the unpresentable. Lyotard replies that the foundational discourse must remain unattained, albeit, like Kant, he does not deny that the quest for foundations is necessary. Contrary to Kant, however, he contends that the quest for a firm ground is infinitely inconclusive and complex. Every new experiment is merely the conquering of a new and greater limit.[3] In this respect, art is a series of small narratives that are not directed towards a meta-language. Nor does art deliver the promise of revealing a new truth. On the contrary, art seeks to testify to an event to which no truth can be assigned (see ibid.) – an event that cannot be made the object of conceptual representation (Readings 1991: 74). The event denotes pure activity, a purely productive process.[4]

Heterogeneous condition of judgement

Although Lyotard is preoccupied with art, notably avant-garde art, his delineation of modern and postmodern aesthetics also pertains to the question of knowledge. How can we have knowledge of something that cannot be known, something that is beyond representation? What is the condition for knowledge in the context of postmodernism? Lyotard's philosophy concerns the role of knowledge in the encounter with aporetic gaps, that is, the heterogeneous, distinctive or singular cases that refuse being subsumed under familiar categories. This bears strong resemblance to Kant's Third Critique, particularly when it comes to the conditions of possibility for aesthetic judgement. The crux of the matter is how we can proceed from the singular case to the general without guidance from the understanding's pre-existent principles. It is interesting to note that Lyotard situates Kant's aesthetics on the breach between the modern and the postmodern condition. The aesthetic is modern in so far as reflective judgement is an experimental vantage point for reconciliation between the singular and the universal. And it is postmodern by way of demonstrating the impossible in this attempt (see Eriksen 1990: 43). The postmodern condition is the necessary but never attained endeavour to bring the unpresentable to presentation. According to Eriksen (ibid.: 46), postmodern thinking entails coming to terms with the idea of that which is not yet being thought but which we can nevertheless know something about, and which therefore is the condition for judging per se.

In accordance with Kant's philosophy, judgement involves the bridging of gaps between radical heterogeneity. The process of reconciliation is a process of forgetting. This may sound counter-intuitive to the extent that one associates determinative judgement and knowledge production with enlightenment – laying something bare and bringing it into light. But in line with his philosophy of difference, we could argue that conceptualisation signals forgetting in so far as we can know something only by forgetting something else. The order of things – conceptualisation, knowledge, representation, and so on – results from a process in which heterogeneity is ignored or suppressed. That which is brought forth is always represented at the expense of something else. As such, the excluded difference or otherness is not absent; it does not disappear, as it were. It is a remainder, a residual category that calls into question and destabilises social categories, and yet it is the heterogeneous condition for judgement and knowledge. The prior heterogeneity allows for representation by virtue of being its constitutive otherness. It is the residual imprint of the symbolic order.

For Lyotard, the process of ordering – the process in which the judgement attempts to reconcile the singular and the universal – necessitates the transition to the analytic of the sublime. In Chapter 3, we saw that the sublime in Kant's philosophy gives rise to his 'authentic standpoint' in terms of the supersensible.[5] If we juxtapose Lyotard and Kant on this issue, we may ask why Lyotard does not arrive at a similar standpoint. In my view, this is because Lyotard comes to terms with the sublime qua unbridgeable gap or an indeterminate 'now'. To him, the sublime does not display any superiority of the human mind. On the contrary, it reveals the lack in our mental powers and in our knowledge. As Kasper

Nefer Olsen (1989: 112) remarks, the 'unhappy' consciousness that characterises modernity is rooted in this trail-blazing 'now'. 'Here and now' we become aware of our vain attempt to bring the unpresentable to presentation. In the absence of totality or History as a universal horizon, the 'now' emerges in its full critical indeterminacy; it emerges as a pure event. Alluding to Barnett Newman's essay 'The Sublime is Now' from 1948, Lyotard (1991: 90) states that the 'now' is what consciousness cannot formulate and even what consciousness forgets in order to constitute itself. He goes on to suggest that the sublime 'now' involves the feeling that nothing might happen: the nothingness now (ibid.: 92).

In his book *Lessons on the Analytic of the Sublime*, Lyotard (1994) notes that the sublime appears to be 'contra-final' (*sweckwidrig*). It is a negative aesthetic, inasmuch as it introduces an aesthetic without nature (ibid.: 53f.). Contrary to Kant, Lyotard maintains that the sublime does not serve to restore the balance between nature and culture/freedom by way of displaying human superiority to nature. Nor will teleology make use of the results of the analysis of the sublime feeling, since the sublime is like lightning. Writes Lyotard (ibid.: 54–55): 'Nature, or what is left of it, quantity, serves only to provide the bad contact that creates the spark. The teleological machine explodes. The "leading" that nature with its vital lead was supposed to provide for thinking in a movement toward its final illumination cannot take place. The beautiful contributed to the Enlightenment.... But the sublime is sudden blazing, and without future.'

After the sublime

Modern art is, from the very beginning, conditioned by the relationship between the beautiful and the sublime, the latter being its impetus. But as mentioned above, the character of the event (in its critical immediacy) is always set aside and forgotten in the cumulative and teleological process of ordering. As was also pointed out, the sublime is a 'now' – or, more properly stated, 'now' is the sublime, which knocks consciousness out of play for a moment. As such, this moment *is* the sublime: the fact that *this* occurs prior to any possible determination of *what* occurs (Nefer Olsen 1989: 112). The sublime feeling bears witness to the fact that an 'excess' has 'touched' the mind, more than it is able to handle (Lyotard 1990: 32). The sublime is, as we have seen in connection with Kant's Third Critique, the experience of a transgression of limits. In the sublime, we experience that something has exceeded our cognitive powers.[6] The sublime signifies a breach in the flow of time that the imagination – the faculty that synthesises the heterogeneous – normally ensures. When the imagination fails in its attempt to synthesise, an abyss ensues, experienced as a shock.

It is this shocking experience that concerns Lyotard. In order to explain how the experience of the abyss evolves, he borrows the term *Nachträglichkeit* from Freud's psychology. In Lyotard's (1990: 15) philosophy, *Nachträglichkeit* implies two things: (1) a double blow that is constitutively asymmetrical, and (2) a temporality that has nothing to do with what the phenomenology of consciousness can thematise. He elaborates: 'The first blow ... strikes the apparatus without observable internal effect, without affecting it. It is a shock without affect. With the second blow there takes place an affect without shock: I buy something in a store, anxiety crushes me, I flee, but nothing had really happened. The energy dispersed in the affective cloud condenses, gets organized, brings on an action, commands a flight without a "real" motive. And it is this flight, the feeling that accompanies it, which informs consciousness *that* there is something, without being able to tell *what* it is ... The essence of the event: that there is "comes before" what there is' (ibid.: 16). Lyotard maintains that postmodern art cannot 'be' sublime, because it cannot present the unpresentable. All it can present is that it cannot present it. In so far as the event is beyond our powers of representation, we cannot possibly think it through in language or in art.[7] And yet we must try to find representations for it, which, of course, alludes to a paradox. Lyotard notes: 'When the sublime is "there" (where?), the mind is not there. As long as the mind is there, there is no sublime' (ibid.: 32). The sublime feeling is incompatible with time. Any rationalising of the sublime will inevitably be a post-rationalisation, because it will lag behind in relation to the sublime moment. What we can represent as the sublime, as 'it happens', is always something other than the sublime. It is 'it happened' – something that took place 'after the sublime'.[8]

Through the sublime feeling we are faced with 'the forgotten', that which is excluded in modern totalising orders, also referred to by Lyotard as 'the Thing' (*la Chose*) (a term he borrows from Jacques Lacan).[9] 'The Thing' defies both images and words. It designates that which cannot be represented without being missed, without being forgotten anew. As was noted above, representation entails effacement from memory, and as I suggested in the previous section, this might occur to us as a somewhat paradoxical process of enlightenment. Lyotard (1990: 26) notes: 'Whenever one represents, one inscribes in memory, and this might seem a good defence against forgetting. It is, I believe, just the opposite. Only that which has been inscribed can, in the current sense of the term, be forgotten, because it could be effaced.... One *must*, certainly, inscribe in words, in images. One cannot escape the necessity of representing.... But it is one thing to do it in view of saving the memory, and quite another to try to preserve the remainder, the unforgettable forgotten, in writing.'

With regard to the discussion in the preceding chapters, we now come to realise that forgetting because of memory denotes assimilation. The process of forgetting is a process of ordering whereby 'the Thing' is incorporated into a History or a totality. In his foreword to Lyotard's book *Heidegger and 'the jews'*, David Carroll remarks that Lyotard questions 'the limitations of all historicisms and "monumental" or memorializing histories that "forget" by having too certain – too definite, too representative, too narrativized (too anecdotal) a "memory"' (in Lyotard 1990: xiii). According to Lyotard, no one can pretend to be a witness to and truthful reporter of – or to be 'equal' to – the sublime affection without being rendered guilty of falsification and imposture through this very pretension (ibid.: 45). Suffice it to say, art cannot be sublime; it can only 'make' sublime.

Aporia and event

According to Lyotard (1990: 47), art cannot bear witness to the sublime, only to the *aporia* of art and to its pain. Another way of putting this would be that the sublime concerns the *aporia* between the singular and the general/universal. As remarked in Chapter 3, *aporia* signifies an unsolvable problem, one that has neither an opening nor an exit. *Aporia* signifies the impossible – the insoluble antinomy or the indeterminable event – which cannot be anything in itself, because it does not allow itself to be grasped as substance. The event is indeterminable in its lack of essence. To the extent that we try to determine the event, for instance, by trying to categorise it as something 'impure', we unwittingly reduce the unknowable to something 'pure' and known. In subsuming the unknown under a rule or a jurisdiction, we judge from something known. What was initially an event is then transformed into a situated entity, an identity. The event, however, is long gone.

What is crucial in this context is the fact that the heterogeneous is prior to the homogeneous. It is this ontologisation of heterogeneity that allows Lyotard to conceive of the ordering process as a process of forgetting. In the preceding chapters, we saw that the impetus behind the dynamics of purity-impurity is the exclusion of the heterogeneous. In this chapter, we have seen that the ordering process is a condition for conceptualisation, knowledge or representation, because we can know something only by excluding – forgetting – something else. Any categorisation, conceptualisation or identification is predicated upon heterogeneity. In this respect, *aporia* signifies a radical alterity in terms of a constitutive limit; it is a limit of thought that cannot be transgressed but nevertheless *is* transgressed (Priest 1995: 3-4). *Aporia* is ignored, and the heterogeneous is assimilated into an order. Carroll (in Lyotard 1990: xiii) remarks: 'For Lyotard, all critical thinking is indebted to this radical alterity, without ever being able to think it as such. It is an otherness in terms of which thought confronts its own limitations and is displaced and opened to what it is not. It is an otherness that all dogmatic thought strives either to incorporate into itself or to deny, repress or finally exclude and eliminate.'

In a commentary on Kant's conception of a priori conditions (which must be unconditioned in order to be a priori), Lyotard (1994: 56) notes that 'if critical examination can establish them as such, it must be able to see the nothingness of the conditions that is "behind" them.... All thought is a being put into relation – a "synthesis", in the language of Kant. Thus, when thinking reaches the absolute, the relation reaches the without-relation, for the absolute is without relation'. But how can the without-relation be 'present' to relation? In Lyotard's view, it can only be 'present' as disavowed (as metaphysical entity), as forbidden (as illusion). He maintains: 'This disavowal, which is constitutive of critical thinking, is the avowal of its own fury. It forbids itself the absolute, much as it still wants it. The consequence for thought is a kind of spasm.... The significance of this "appendage" thus significantly exceeds the exploration of an aesthetic feeling. It exposes the "state" of critical thought when it reaches its extreme limit – a spasmodic state' (ibid.). Every decision or judgement about limits has to try to pass through the ordeal of undecidability, of *aporia*. What Lyotard's philosophy encourages us to do with respect to this is to reflect not so much upon *what* happens, but on the fact *that* it happens, with *that* – 'the Thing' – being what is forgotten in the (re)production of the order of things.

Simulacrum

Gilles Deleuze ([1969] 1990) approaches this topic from a slightly different albeit related angle in his book *The Logic of Sense*. His point of departure is Plato's duality between the 'thing' in itself (the Idea) and its images – the original and the copy, the model and the simulacrum. For Plato, it is crucial to distinguish the authentic from the inauthentic, the true pretender from the false pretender. The true pretender appeals to a foundation that serves as a standard by which various pretenders can be judged. As such, the foundation refers to that which possesses something in a primary way (*en premier*), that is, the Idea's superior identity. Moreover, it establishes a hierarchy of all sorts of degrees of possessors – a hierarchy that culminates in the one who possesses no more than a simulacrum (ibid.: 255). As Deleuze makes clear, the Platonic 'model' is the Same, that which possesses in a primary way, whereas the 'copy' is the Similar, the pretender who possesses in a secondary way. An exemplary 'similitude' corresponds to the model or pure identity of the original, while the counterpart termed 'imitative' corresponds to the copy's 'resemblance' (ibid.: 259). Simulacrum, for its part, presupposes neither the Same nor the Similar. According to Deleuze, simulacrum constitutes the only Same (the Same of that which differs) and the only resemblance, the resemblance of the unmatched (ibid.: 265). Yet simulacrum is not simply a false copy. Simulacrum calls into question the very notations of model/original and copy. While the copies are secondary possessors – well-founded pretenders that are guaranteed by resemblance – simulacra are false pretenders, based on dissimilarity. Deleuze points out that the simulacra imply an essential perversion or deviation (ibid.). On that account, the Platonic motivation was to repress simulacra, preventing them from climbing to the surface.

From this, we could draw some parallels to the dynamics of purity and impurity. In the words of Deleuze ([1969] 1990), God created the human being in his image and resemblance, but through sin the human lost the resemblance while maintaining the image. We have become simulacra, Deleuze states, alluding to the concept's demonic character (ibid.: 257). As already mentioned, simulacrum signifies a disparity or a radical difference, and by reason of this we cannot define it in relation to a model imposed on the copies – a model of the Same from which the copies' resemblance derives. If simulacrum still has a model, it is another model, a model of the 'other' (*l'Autre*) (ibid.: 258). Deleuze's argument is aptly summarised in the following passage (ibid.: 258–259):

> [T]he simulacrum implies huge dimensions, depths, and distances that the observer cannot master.... In short, there is in the simulacrum a becoming-mad, or a becoming unlimited, as in the *Philebus* where 'more and less are always going a point further', a becoming always other, a becoming subversive of the depths, able to evade the equal, the limit, the Same, or the Similar: always more and less at once, but never equal. To impose a limit on this becoming, to order it according to the same, to render it similar – and, for that part which remains rebellious, to repress it as deeply as possible, to shut it up in a cavern at the bottom of the Ocean – such is the aim of Platonism in its will to bring about the triumph of icons over simulacra.

With this in mind, and with a view to the preceding chapters, we may now (re)turn to the issue of totalitarianism. As we have seen from the above discussion, totalitarianism entails ignoring or suppressing the *aporia* in an attempt to establish normative communitas, such as ethnic or national identities. With regard to the latter, we could say that nationalism is that which binds a state to the collective will to power of a people (cf. Dumont 1986: 121). It is a will to ignore aporetic difference and suppress simulacra. As Lyotard points out in several of his books (e.g. 1984, 1988, 1992a), the suppression of heterogeneity invokes a totalitarian horizon in terms of an imagined collective subject.[10] With respect to modern ideology and individuality, Dumont (1986: 130) contends: '[T]he nation – as found, say, in Western Europe in the nineteenth century – is the sociopolitical group corresponding to the ideology of the Individual. It is thus two things in one: a collection of individuals and, at the same time, a collective individual, an individual on the level of groups, facing other nations-individuals.' Totalitarianism could be conceived as an attempt to re-establish a unity of people – a unitary people – in response to the modern social divisions and the dissolution of foundations and identity (see Lefort 1986).

If we recall the ethnocentric fallacy – the conflation between the ideal and the real – that was treated in Chapter 1, we may suggest that ignoring heterogeneity between the singular/autonomous and the general/universal allows for a given culture to be identified with humanity per se. Arguably, denying the *aporia* has totalising consequences, even as it is expressive of the whole of humanity. This is a paradox on which Dumont, among others, has written extensively. Dumont's (1986) paradigmatic example is the way in which Fichte identifies Germanness with universality. Fichte establishes a hierarchy among peoples in the name of the very value of universalism (ibid.: 123). In this way, the German nation becomes the exemplary example of humanity, a perfect incorporation of a universal idea. In his comparison of German and French ideology, with a view to the relationship between nation and humanity, Dumont concludes (ibid.: 131), in line with my argument advanced in Chapter 1: 'We observe that the old ethnocentricism or sociocentricism which exalts *us* and disparages *others* did survive in the modern era, but in two different ways: the Germans saw themselves, and tried to impose themselves, as superior *qua* Germans, while the French consciously postulated only the superiority of the universalist culture, but identified with it so naively that they looked on themselves as the educators of mankind.' With regard to the French case, Roland Barthes ([1957] 1993: 140) asserts that the whole of France is steeped in this anonymous ideology. As he sees it, there is a conflation of the unwritten civic norms, the nation and the universal identity of Man. Practised on a national scale, norms of the bourgeoisie are experienced as the evident laws of a natural order.

Bonding without bonds

Both Dumont and Barthes, each in their own way, suggest that national communities are founded on an imagined original identity – an imagined 'common being', to paraphrase Benedict Anderson (1983). The question that was raised by Lash, which becomes fully pertinent here, is whether it is possible to envisage a community of equal human beings that does not emanate from identity. Is it possible to be together without 'common being'? Is it possible, however paradoxical it might be, to be bonded without bonds? The condition of possibility for a community of equals, as emphasised by Lash, is the unconditional or unconditioned character of the relationship between humans. It requires an immediate, reciprocal and equal 'I–thou' relationship, in line with Wiggen's (1998) envisioning of a community prior to any interest people might have for one another. In his book *Aporias*, Jacques Derrida (1993; cf. Derrida 2000) describes unconditional relations in terms of waiting for the 'other' without expectations – without ideas and images (cf. simulacrum). This requires an unconditional openness towards the 'other', towards the event.

In reference to the concept of the *arrivant*, Derrida (1993: 33) writes that the word can mean 'he or she who comes, coming to be where s/he was not expected, where one was awaiting him or her without waiting for him or her, without expecting *it* (*s'y attendre*), without knowing what or whom to expect, what or whom I am waiting for – and such is hospitality itself, hospitality toward the event.' As this passage suggests, Derrida is concerned with the *arrivant* par excellence, the *arrivant* who does not yet have a name or an identity. And because he or she does not yet have an identity, his or her destination is equally de-identified. The absolute *arrivant* is not an invader or an occupier, since invasion presupposes some self-identity for the aggressor and for the victim. Nor is the *arrivant* a legislator or the discoverer of a promised land, since he or she exceeds the order of any determinable promise (ibid.: 34). According to Derrida, the *arrivant* surprises the host, who is not yet a host or an inviting power in such a manner that the host's own identity may be called into question. This process, whereby the host becomes foreign to herself/himself, is akin to Lash's (1999) depiction of self-difference. It is this self-difference that allows for openness towards the unknown, the forgotten.

Within Derrida's philosophy, fighting for – and thereby becoming aware of – one's identity allows for a potential openness towards other identities. The decisive factor is whether one can wait long enough in a state of indeterminacy before judging, before closing off and lapsing into identity politics. Is it feasible to hope for an unconditional and unconditioned encounter with 'others'? Can we wait for the 'others' without expectations? Lyotard (1990: 39–40) is not overly optimistic:

> Today, hatred comes softly as integration ... into a permissive collectivity in the name of the 'respect for differences' ... between the 'ethnocultural' components of what remains of the old modern nations. The modern version of the Catholic church can lend itself to this show of tolerance. One has to keep in mind here that 'catholicism' means to militate according to totality and in view of it, and that *tollere* and *aufheben* connote, at the same time, the suppression as well as the elevation of what one tolerates. Keep in mind above all that tolerant permissiveness with regard to the aforementioned differences is required ... by the total mobilization of energies (Jünger) in all possible and imaginable forms, which is the moving principle and the sufficient reason for that which takes on form ... around us and in us, under the names (or pseudonyms) of developed, or administered, or postmodern, or technoscientific society.

It is the goal of 'development', Lyotard maintains, that nothing happens for which one is not prepared. As he sees it, the only things that happen are those things that are supposed to help the system 'optimize its performances'. And that which has happened must be kept under control. It is not only necessary to represent, but one must also calculate; one must estimate in advance the represented quanta and the quanta of the representatives (ibid.: 40; see also Lyotard 1991). One must plan, as in the case of planned pluralism (cf. Adorno and Horkheimer [1944] 1997).

Nefer Olsen (1989: 119) comments that far from letting the ideal of the political subject's 'enlightenment' come true, the computerisation of society is to Lyotard a gigantic machinery of repression, capable of absorbing the sublime in art and the event in politics. Lyotard makes us aware of the fact that the naturalisation of the event is immanent to the very logical basis of techno-scientific society. We can only think of the event as not-yet-happened (no data are given), or as already happened, that is, as already inscribed in the given (the already presupposed). Nefer Olsen (ibid.: 120) remarks that between these two poles nothing happens, by definition. Nothing can happen without having already happened. The event is reduced to an experience in which the forgetting is already setting in – and forgets itself – at that very moment (see Lyotard 1991: 105–106). But despite this pessimism, the heterogeneous is still the condition of possibility for knowledge production. Lyotard retains this attitude with regard not only to aesthetics, but also to ethics, politics and science. The postmodern condition is a general condition of curiosity; it is the impetus for philosophical critique, experimentation and displacement. It is principally in his philosophy of language that Lyotard addresses the heterogeneous condition for knowledge. Hence, we shall now direct attention to his ontologisation of heterogeneity in language. This, in turn, will shed light on the question of whether difference-based community is possible.

Two types of difference, two kinds of conflict

The above discussion suggests that if we are to form community on the basis of difference rather than identity, the experience of the heterogeneous cannot be reduced to a pragmatic or trivial incident. Lyotard's philosophy of language serves to develop this argument. At the same time, his philosophy of difference sheds a new light on crucial aspects of the dilemma between equality and distinctiveness. The crux of the matter is whether cultural distinctiveness should be accentuated or ignored. The first strategy (of accentuation) seems to run counter to the latter strategy (of disregard). Or perhaps the problem is more complex than that, refusing the oppositional logic of the multicultural dilemma of interaction.

In Chapter 1, the disregard of difference was linked with the problem of opposition. There I addressed this issue as a matter of assimilation. To the extent that the 'others' do not express their distinctiveness, I argued, it will result in a self-effacing homogenising with the majority. This will be the case as long as cultural differences are deconstructed theoretically but continue to flourish on an empirical level. However, deconstruction is not tantamount to assimilation. One lesson we may learn from Lyotard's philosophy of language is that deconstruction of difference results in a politics of assimilation only to the extent that we discount heterogeneity as being prior to identity, that is, to the extent that we presuppose an original identity. If we take the identity to be original, then we are likely to universalise a particular standard of judgement and reduce differences to instances of the Same (which translates into ethnocentrism). If, however, we proceed from the assumption that difference is prior to identity, such a unifying project would immediately be called into question. From the latter perspective, the dilemma between the deconstruction of identity categories, on the one hand, and the accentuation of distinctiveness, on the other, can be depicted as a tension between difference qua unpresentable heterogeneity (the otherness cannot be expressed in the existing idioms) and difference as representable (the 'others' can have a voice, and difference can be expressed). Within philosophies of difference, one normally distinguishes between ontological difference and 'ontic' difference. Whereas ontological difference is unpresentable or non-identifiable, 'ontic' difference denotes distinct categories that already exist and circulate in society and in language. Whereas ontological difference is prior to social classification, 'ontic' difference constitutes our system of social classification, our social or cultural order.

In order to look more closely at the relationship between the two concepts of difference, I shall elaborate on the aspects of Lyotard's philosophy of language that are most relevant to the issue at hand. I will focus primarily on his core concept, 'the differend', which, contrary to 'litigation', refers to an irresolvable conflict. In the preface of his main work, *The Differend*, Lyotard (1988: xi) explains the difference between the two types of conflict: 'As distinguished from a litigation, a differend [*différend*] would be a case of conflict, between (at least) two parties, that cannot be equitably resolved for lack of a rule of judgment applicable to both arguments. One side's legitimacy does not imply the other's lack of legitimacy. However, applying a single rule of judgment to both in order to settle their differend as though it were merely a litigation would wrong (at least) one of them (and both of them if neither side admits this rule).' 'The differend' is an irresolvable conflict based on irreconcilable premises for judgement. Any attempt to solve the conflict will be an act of injustice to at least one of the parties. This can be formulated as a dilemma: 'Either you are the victim of a wrong, or you are not. If you are not, you are deceived (or lying) in testifying that you are. If you are, since you can bear witness to this wrong, it is not a wrong, and you are deceived (or lying) in testifying that you are the victim of a wrong' (ibid.: §8). A wrong is distinguished from a damage by the fact that a damage can be rectified and put right, whereas a wrong, since it results from one being judged according to another system of rules or jurisdiction, cannot be rectified in the same manner. As already mentioned, any attempt at compensating for the wrong is likely to intensify it. According to Lyotard (ibid. §13), 'the differend' is signalled by the inability to prove, due to the lack of a universal rule of judgement. He amplifies: '[T]he damages you complain about never took place, and your testimony is false; or else they took place, and since you are able to testify to them, it is not a wrong that has been done to you, but merely a damage, and your testimony is still false' (ibid.: §7).

One of the first examples of 'the differend' that Lyotard (1988) brings forward in his book relates to ideological-political totalitarianism. 'Either the Ibanskian witness is not a communist, or else he is. If he is, he has no need to testify that Ibanskian society is communist, since he admits that the communist authorities are the only ones competent to effectuate the establishment procedures for the reality of the communist character of that society' (ibid. §4). However, if Ibanskian does not defer to the authorities, he ceases to be a communist. This is the case in so far as the state 'knows no reality other than the established one, and it holds the monopoly on procedures for the establishment of reality' (ibid.).

After the events of September 11 in 2001, it seems reasonable to depict the conflict between the United States and the other NATO countries, on the one hand, and Muslim allied groups, on the other, as a 'differend'. We may ask whether the US, with the support of NATO, actually carried out a reprisal in attacking Afghanistan, or whether the conflict was irresolvable, given that it was not between two states, but between a country and an international Muslim network. Furthermore, there are reasons to believe that the US intensified the wrong when disregarding international law. For instance, by defining the prisoners held at Guantanamo Bay as 'unlawful combatants' rather than 'prisoners of war', the US circumvented its commitment to the Geneva Conventions, enabling the government to try the prisoners in a sequestered military court behind closed doors and without the possibility of appeal. As has been pointed out by several commentators, the accused were then deprived of their rights and, accordingly, their humanness (e.g. Butler 2004b).

In this context we may recall Arendt's (1973: 300) assertion that a man who is nothing but a man has lost the very qualities that make it possible for other people to treat him as a fellow man. For the purpose of our present discussion, we may emphasise that the wrong from which these people suffer cannot be put right due to the inability to prove. In this respect, Lyotard's concept of 'the differend' is akin to Giorgio Agamben's (1998, 2005) concept of the 'state of exception'. The prisoners find themselves in a state of exception in which the law applies by no longer applying. That is to say, they find themselves within a jurisdiction that – in a sovereign manner – banishes them. They are assimilated or incorporated by the law, and yet they are simultaneously excluded from the domain of civil rights. Agamben (1998: 25) maintains that the concept of exception refers to that which cannot be included in the whole of which it is a member and cannot be a member of the whole in which it is always already included. That is why the relation of exception is a relation of ban; it is a kind of relation to the non-relational (ibid.: 29). Writes Agamben (ibid.: 19): 'To refer to something, a rule must both presuppose and yet still establish a relation with what is outside relation (the nonrelational). The relation of exception thus simply expresses the originary formal structure of the juridical relation. In this sense, the sovereign decision on the exception is the originary juridico-political structure on the basis of which what is included in the juridical order and what is excluded from it acquire their meaning.'

Stripped of social and political rights, the prisoners are turned into naked life (*homo sacer*), or, to use Arendt's (1973) term, they are 'civil dead'. These and more recent examples concerning the 'war on terror' conform to the judicial terminology that characterises the examples in *The Differend*, while the book is otherwise philosophical. Lyotard (1988) establishes a direct link between discursive heterogeneity and social and political conflicts based on the assumption that there can be no appeal to a pre-discursive reality. In this sense, his linguistic concept of difference forms the basis for conceptualising culturally incompatible differences. Cultural difference does not, however, signify 'culture' in an identitarian sense. On the contrary, cultural difference designates that which is being excluded by such identity categories, notably, universalised or naturalised categories; it points to the unknowability of 'others'. As Lyotard (ibid.) sees it, 'the differend' qua heterogeneity between rules of judgement originates in language. It arises from the heterogeneity of phrases, which in turn lays the basis for heterogeneous 'genres of discourse'. This suggests that 'the differend' operates on the socio-cultural level, but it nevertheless signifies an unpresentable difference – a non-identity – on the discursive level. Significantly, it is on the basis of the heterogeneity of phrases (sentences) that Lyotard establishes his concept of 'the differend'. I shall not elaborate on his philosophy of language in detail, however. I shall restrict myself to delineating the aspects of Lyotard's philosophy that concern the ontologisation of heterogeneity.

Discursive conflicts

In Lyotard's vocabulary, a genre of discourse is defined by its purposive logic. Every genre of discourse constitutes a unique – and hence different – purposive logic. Or, to put it another way, different genres of discourse are characterised by their unique purposive logics, and, as such, they are agonistic with respect to their purpose. As Lyotard (1988) sees it, language is a zone of conflict between different genres of discourse that fight about the linkage of heterogeneous phrases. Qua purposive logics, genres of discourse purport to appropriate or possess phrases, as it were; the purpose of all genres is to reduce the heterogeneity (of phrases) that constitutes them. According to Lyotard, '[a] phrase, which links and which is to be linked, is always a *pagus*, a border zone where genres of discourse enter into a conflict over the mode of linking' (ibid.: §218). The war in language, he contends, arises from the very happening of phrases, since every phrase threatens the continuity between the phrase that happens and those that precede it (ibid.: §229). The conflict is thus caused by the question 'How to link (phrases)?' or 'Which phrase follows?'. Due to the fact that only one phrase happens at a time, every linkage between one phrase and the next is respectively a 'victory' and a 'loss'. In other words, every time a phrase happens, one genre of discourse has defeated all the others, which, for their part, 'remain neglected, forgotten, or repressed' (see ibid.: §§184, 188). As Lyotard points out, there are as many different ways of winning as there are genres (ibid.: §186).[11]

When a conflict arises between heterogeneous phrases *within* a genre of discourse, the genre's own rules regulate the conflict. This kind of conflict is by Lyotard termed 'litigation' (1988: §13). As indicated above, litigations are solvable conflicts in the sense that the parties recognise the same rules or laws. But whenever there is a conflict *between* genres of discourse, there are no common rules that can regulate the conflict. The conflict is irresolvable in the sense that there is no regulatory basis or forum for appeal that can indicate the right means by which to link from a given phrase (see ibid.: §43). The only way to 'resolve' the conflict between heterogeneous genres of discourse is to impose silence on the other genres of discourse, which in fact happens every time a phrase is linked to another. However, the victory is not final, since no phrases exist without linkage. The conflict is thus constant or recurrent. At the same time, it is *de facto* always settled, in so far as linkage has always already happened. We are no longer confronted with an irresolvable conflict, because it has been imperceptibly 'reduced' to a solvable conflict; 'the differend' has resolved into 'litigation'. Accordingly, there is a 'differend' behind every linkage of phrases, an irresolvable conflict that is compensated for and forgotten in language, hidden by pragmatics. Or, to be more accurate, the underlying heterogeneity in language is hidden by the way in which we use the language. Against this backdrop, we realise that genres of discourse do nothing more than shift 'the differend' from the level of regimens to that of ends (ibid.: §40).[12]

As I pointed out above, Lyotard's concept of heterogeneity is very much informed by Kant's heterogeneous faculties (*Fakultäten*). In *The Differend*, Lyotard endeavours to revisit our cognitive powers and their various conditions. By allowing genres of discourse to replace Kant's conception of faculties/powers, Lyotard (1988: 118–127) depicts the *aporia* between understanding (the theoretical) and reason (the practical) as a 'differend' between the cognitive and the ethical genres of discourse. He aims to draw a substantial distinction between the various genres of discourse, akin to Kant's distinction between the theoretical, the practical and the ethical spheres of justification.[13] Just as Kant is unable to found practical reason in reason itself, Lyotard maintains that a genre of discourse cannot justify itself. For instance, the technical (performativity's) genre cannot comprise its own legitimising basis by explaining how its criteria for judgement (effective/ineffective) are true, sound or just. Lyotard adheres to

Kant's division of spheres precisely because it does not allow for conclusions; at the most, it allows for analogising (see Sejten 1989: 93). For example, we may establish an analogous relationship between the beautiful and the good, the beautiful being a symbol of the morally good. Similarly, the causality-idea of understanding can be employed 'as if' it belonged to the ethical sphere. With respect to the latter, the notion of an analogy with the laws of nature serves as an idea for practical reason (see Lyotard 1988: 130–135).[14]

However, as our discussion reveals, Lyotard parts with Kant on essential points. Notwithstanding his adherence to Kant's incommensurable relationship between the faculties (articulated as a 'differend' between genres of discourse) and his endorsement of Kant's notion of the sublime as an experience of the abyss between the cognitive powers, Lyotard does not eventually homogenise the heterogeneous by depicting the sublime as stabilising and consolidating. Distinct from Kant, Lyotard conceives of the heterogeneity of the sublime as a destabilising and problematising force. In order to emphasise the significance of this shift in relation to Kant, I will now draw attention to the consequences of heterogeneity in language with respect to the dynamics between 'us' and the 'others' on the socio-cultural level. My main focus will be on the injustice that befalls the 'others' when faced with an irresolvable conflict.

Consequences of heterogeneity

In Lyotard's philosophy, 'the differend' denotes an irresolvable conflict between genres of discourse. However, 'the differend' is not confined to language, as if language was a system of signs isolated from practice. As Lyotard's ideological-political and juridical terminology and examples indicate, 'the differend' is by no means an idiosyncratic concept pertaining to semantics. We have seen that 'the differend' is signalled by the inability to prove, due to the lack of a universal rule of judgement (Lyotard 1988: §13). To be more precise, 'the differend' occurs when the 'regulation' of the conflict that opposes the parties is done in the idiom of one of the parties, while the wrong suffered by the other is not signified in that idiom (ibid.: §12). In this respect, the wrong is a consequence of 'the differend'. A wrong results from the fact that the rules of the genre of discourse by which one judges are not those of the judged genre or genres of discourse (ibid.: xi). As Lyotard makes clear, a wrong is a damage 'accompanied by the loss of the means to prove the damage', for example, 'if the victim is deprived of life, or of all his or her liberties, or of the freedom to make his or her ideas or opinions public, or simply of the right to testify to the damage, or even more simply if the testifying phrase is itself deprived of authority' (ibid.: §7).

Lyotard is particularly concerned with the Jews who were held in concentration camps during the Second World War. What concerns him is their inability to bear witness to what happened there. Even those who survived the Holocaust lost the means by which to prove the damages. Lyotard is, of course, neither the first nor the last to address this issue. One of the first to deal with the inadequacy of accounts given by Holocaust survivors is Primo Levi, who was himself imprisoned in Auschwitz during the war. In his last book, *The Drowned and the Saved*, Levi (1989) forcefully articulates the paradox of testimony, 40 years after the Holocaust. Those who did not survive cannot testify to what happened, he states, and those who survived are among the privileged – the exceptions – and cannot bear witness on behalf of the dead. Pointing out the gap between what is told and what cannot be told – between the drowned and the saved – he infers that the survivors are not the true witnesses.[15] In a similar manner, although not from a first-hand perspective, Arendt (1973: 444) contends that '[t]here are no parallels to the life in the concentration camps. Its horror can never be fully embraced by the imagination for the very reason that it stands outside of life and death. It can never be fully reported for the very reason that the survivor returns to the world of the living, which makes it impossible for him to believe fully in his own past experiences. It is as though he had a story to tell of another planet'. If the survivors testify in their own idioms as victims, they would not be able to impart the wrong that has been done to them. And if they speak in the language of the jurisdiction, there would be no way of recognising the wrong. The only sign that remains is silence. According to Lyotard (1988), silence is the very characteristic of a wrong – of a 'differend'. As such, the 'silence of the survivors [of the Holocaust] does not necessarily testify in favor of the non-existence of gas chambers'. On the contrary, their silence can just as well be conceived as a result of the fact that they cannot express through language what happened to them. In line with Arendt, Lyotard (ibid.: §§26–27) argues that one could conceive of the gas chambers as an 'inexpressible absurdity'.

Given the philosophical premises on which Lyotard bases this argument, it is evident that silence is associated with the concept of *aporia*. Silence signals an unbridgeable gap between the singular/heterogeneous and the general/universal. It testifies to an event that has happened, something that cannot be synthesised by or subsumed under a universal rule or a general concept. The concept of the event denotes something that cannot be expressed in language, something that cannot be represented in existing idioms. What is more, there is a link between silence (following from a wrong) and totalitarianism in Lyotard's philosophy. To Lyotard (1988: §7), totalitarianism is an outcome of ignoring 'the differend' between genres of discourse. Or, to be more precise, totalitarianism issues from the conflation of the true and the just, that is, from disregarding the incommensurability between the descriptive statement and the prescriptive statement. Empirically speaking, the problem of totalitarianism occurs when a descriptive statement or an utterance of truth is employed to advance an admonition or an imperative as to how one ought to act or live. Either one can proceed from a model of society (the social aspect) with which the prescriptive can correspond, for example, the egalitarian society, in which case one's practices are measured up against the idea of society (cf. Dumont's concept of value-ideas). Or one can proceed from a social consensus as the basis for the determination of a law – that is, from the will of a collective subject, a 'we'. In the latter case, the law is what the people want, and what the people want is the law (Readings 1991: 111). In his dialogue with Jean-Loup Thébaud in *Just Gaming*, Lyotard depicts the latter form of totalitarianism or self-determination in terms of a demand to decide justice as society's knowledge about itself (Lyotard and Thébaud 1985). The law is then the knowledge or the will of a universal subject, which means that there is a transition from this description to the prescriptive of just courses of action; the prescriptive is derived from the descriptive. The link between silence (following from a wrong) and totalitarianism then becomes obvious social order or political ideology that lays claim to justice, equality, humanity or democracy is totalitarian, inasmuch as the embodiment of equality, justice, humanity, and so on does not acknowledge alternative standards of judgement. As was suggested in Chapter 1, the totalitarian aspect of modern political ideologies is connected to the fact that they allow little room for testifying to unequal, unjust or inhuman treatment. Their claim to truth and justice makes it virtually impossible to testify to a wrong. Such testimony would easily be dismissed as 'anti-egalitarian', 'inhumane', etc. Against this backdrop, Lyotard's assertion that there is no just society makes perfect sense (ibid.: 25). Societies that purport to represent the law are immediately unjust by way of silencing oppositional voices (see Readings 1991: 111; cf. Butler 2004b).

Totalitarianism in practice

It we recall the argument in the Introduction, we may now interpolate that judging the practices of the 'others' on the basis of 'our' standards/ideals is not only a comparative fallacy with regard to levels of analysis. Above all, provided that the conflict is 'regulated' in the idiom of the majority, it displays a disregard for heterogeneity. The policy documents that served to illustrate the social democratic politics of integration revealed that practices such as arranged marriages and polygamy are considered to be inhibitive of equal rights concerning gender equality and individual freedom. Likewise, non-Christian practices, such as circumcision of men, are treated by politicians as a health issue, in accordance with the prevailing conventional norms. As long as the wrong suffered by the 'others' cannot be expressed in this idiom, however, the conflict cannot be solved justly, and the 'others' are put to silence. In the subsequent chapters, we saw that ethnocentric totalitarianism originates from an erroneous inference from the particular to the universal, associated with the fact that the *aporia* between the singular/heterogeneous and the universal/general is ignored. Along the same line, the *aporia* between 'is' and 'ought' is ignored. 'Our' practices – 'the way we do things here' – are constituted as a normative standard, allowing for a specific cultural order to be perceived as universal and its standard of judgement as universally valid. Ignoring 'the differend' eventually leads to the paradoxical situation in which the ideal of equality brings about injustice for the 'others'. The more general conclusion I want to draw from this is that ethnocentrism amounts to disregarding 'the differend'. Or, to be more precise, ethnocentrism ensues from the fact that 'the differend' is trivialised and forgotten in pragmatics (in both a linguistic and a political sense). The consequence is, as I have emphasised above, that the 'others' are coerced into silence and thus are not able to articulate their complaints about what they experience as unjust treatment. On the contrary, their complaints are likely to exacerbate the problem by perpetuating 'the differend'. Their cultural difference would be exposed to a judging authority whose mission is to conduct the prevailing standard, and the inferior position of the 'others' would eventually be reaffirmed. Alternatively, the 'others' could be left to their own devices, that is, left to their own jurisdiction, as an act of cultural relativism. However, as long as the parties co-exist under conditions whereby the one party constitutes a majority, the conflict is inevitable and irresolvable.

I could draw on several examples from the media, including the 'war on terror', to illustrate 'the differend' and the injustice that ensues.[16] However, in addition to the examples above, I shall restrict myself to mentioning a rather humble case that attracted the attention of the Norwegian media some years ago. It all started when a couple who married at the Islamic Cultural Centre in the city of Bergen was permitted to include a so-called bridal gift (*mahr* in Arabic) in their marriage contract – an amount of money or certain objects which the man gives to the woman when they marry (or they can agree on a postponed gift). The bridal gift is the woman's property throughout the marriage, whereas the man possesses the rest of the estate. When this practice became publicly known through the local media, the county governor immediately criticised it on the grounds that such a cultural or religious practice is 'out of place' with regard to the Norwegian marriage institution. He was of the opinion that the marriage practice breaks with the principle of individual equality, as opposed to the dominant Protestant marriage practice, which putatively promotes individual equality. In this way, the Western and Christian conventional norms were universalised and linked with human equality. What is more, the county governor obviously took the gift to the bride to be a 'dowry'. Dowries are gifts from the wife's side of the family to the bride and normally include things that the bride will need in her marital life. However, dowries are not agreed upon by contract. So by mistaking a bridal gift for a dowry, the governor made an error of category. Or, to put it differently, his judgements were made on erroneous premises.[17] As such, the example alludes to 'the differend'.

As long as the majority conflates bridal gifts with dowries, the Islamic Cultural Centre loses the means by which to defend itself. Alternatively, the centre could appeal the decision by claiming that dowries are not against the law, but that would be a complaint in conformity with the county governor's definition of terms. Accordingly, it would not be an expression of the injustice that the centre suffers. Rather, it would be a complaint about the governor's opinion and his interpretation of the law. The centre faces a dilemma in terms of a 'double bind'.[18] Either the wrong that the centre complained about did not take place, which means that the testimony is false, or it did in fact take place. And since the centre is able to testify to it, it is not a wrong that has been done but only a damage, and the testimony is still false (see Lyotard 1988: §7). In the absence of universal rules of judgement, no tribunal will be able to judge justly for both parties. According to Lyotard, political action must consist of testifying that the two sides cannot be brought together (ibid.: §22–24).

New idioms

It is the feeling of the sublime that allows us to testify to 'the differend'. In line with Kant, Lyotard describes the sublime as a link between two opposing feelings. On the one hand, the sublime feeling indicates a presence beyond our capacity to comprehend and represent, and we feel pain because we realise that no action is the correct one. The feeling is accompanied by an impulse to recoil from the unknown. On the other hand, we experience a feeling of pleasure, associated with the creative impulse to act, which impels us to proceed and follow up on the feeling. The sublime calls for a reaction by which we seek to talk about the event, that is, to bear witness to the event ('it happens'). It is a testimony for the unpresentable or non-identical, a testimony for that which no longer is ('it happened'). According to Lyotard, the feeling of the sublime makes us aware of the fact that 'something' occurs beyond representation and comprehension; it makes us conscious of the *aporia* between the singular event and its conceptual representation. However, even though the feeling demands a reaction, it gives no clue as to what that action should be. The feeling happens independently of any realisation of meaning; it comes out of the blue, so to speak. The demand for action takes place with the initial presentation brought forth by a phrase ('it happens'), whereas the reaction takes place with the linkage of phrases ('it happened'); it takes place with the representation of the presentation. On that account, each phrase has the potential to demand our attention through the feeling of the sublime, but our explanation of what exactly called for us to react cannot fit the initial feeling (Williams 1998: 85–87).

As for the gap between the demand and the reaction, the task of bearing witness to 'the differend' must involve searching for new idioms in order for the wrong to find an expression and for the plaintiff to cease being a victim (Lyotard 1988: §21). This requires new rules for the formation and linking of phrases: 'A lot of searching must be done to find new rules for forming and linking phrases that are able to express the differend disclosed by the feeling ["One cannot find the words"], unless one wants this differend to be smothered right away in a litigation and for the alarm sounded by the feeling to have been useless. What is at stake in a literature, in a philosophy, in a politics perhaps, is to bear witness to differends by finding idioms for them' (ibid.: §22).

We have seen that the 'fate' of the postmodern condition is the necessary but never successful attempt to bring the unpresentable to presentation, to give the non-identical an identity, and it is the feeling of the sublime that expresses this incomprehensibility and hence unpresentability. It signifies that *something* happens (*dass etwass geschieht*) that cannot be managed or formulated, or rather that *it* happens (*dass es geschieht*) – an occurrence that 'precedes' the question pertaining to *what* happens (Lyotard 1991: 90). In this respect, the feeling of the sublime is not a basis for the resolution of conflicts. Rather, it directs our attention towards the *aporia* or 'the differend' per se. It is crucial to recognise this double role of the sublime: it is associated both with specific 'differends' and with 'the differend' in general. Without the prospect of more than one irresolvable conflict, it is always possible to sacrifice the specific 'differend' on the altar of totalitarian order – and thereby forget (about) it. However, due to his ontologisation of heterogeneity, Lyotard (1984: 5) defies this trivialisation and the attendant homogenisation of conflicts. He refutes philosophies, systems and practices that proceed from the premise that there is only one correct means by which to nurture dialogue, only one correct way by which to understand and eventually resolve conflicts, as the consensus does violence to the heterogeneity in language.

At this juncture, we should look more closely at the relationship between the heterogeneity in language and cultural difference. There is a continual oscillation between discursive heterogeneity/conflict and socio-cultural heterogeneity/conflict in Lyotard's (1988) philosophy. As for the discursive level, he suggests that the multiplicity of stakes, on a par with the multiplicity of genres of discourse, turns every linkage into a 'victory' of one of them over the others, resulting in excluded possibilities. The genres of discourse limit the possibilities of linking by inscribing each and every phrase into the pursuit of certain stakes. 'In this sense, a phrase that comes along is put into play within a conflict between genres of discourse. And this conflict is a differend, since the success (or the validation) proper to one genre is not the one proper to others' (ibid.: §184). The next moment, in regard to the socio-cultural level, Lyotard (ibid.: §141) asserts: 'The social is implicated in the universe of a phrase and the political in its mode of linking.... The civil war of "language" with itself is what is always at play in one as in the other. The only difference lies in the manner of instituting the litigations to regulate the differends.' We may ask, then, how this 'link' between the ontology of phrases and the socio-cultural level of irresolvable conflicts comes about. Is the transition from one level to the other really that straightforward? Are we faced with the same kind of exclusions in both cases? It seems to me that two possibilities arise. Either the transition from one level to the next is problematic because there are two diverging concepts of 'the differend' involved, or there is not really a transition between levels but rather a conflation of language and the social world, which allows for discursive heterogeneity and socio-cultural heterogeneity to converge in a single concept of 'the differend'. These statements warrant an explanation, so I will briefly expand on them in the following.

Where language is concerned, Lyotard's concept of 'the differend' seems to coincide with the rather commonplace assumption within continental philosophy that we approach the world through language, which means that there will always be things that evade our concepts. The gap between words and things is generally referred to as 'the crisis in language'. If we then turn to the socio-cultural level and look at how Lyotard (1988) treats the problem of irresolvable conflicts, we see that his concept of 'the differend' does not simply signify a lack in our ability to grasp 'the real' world conceptually. Especially when addressing the impossibility of bearing witness to the horror in Auschwitz, it is evident that Lyotard wants to pinpoint something more than a lack of words, that is, something more than the impossibility of adequately describing this devastating experience. In this case, 'the differend' signifies an absolute breakdown of language as such. It signals a disruption or an abyss in language that gives rise to a sublime feeling. As pointed out above, however, this is not a sublime experience that makes us aware of human superiority vis-à-vis nature. Rather, it is an instance of the sublime with an ugly touch, so to speak. Unlike Kant, Lyotard does not seem to need a concept of 'ugliness' to designate the absolute breakdown of categories, as the concept of the sublime will suffice. The sublime denotes an insurmountable gap, not simply between words and things, but, significantly, between damages and the ability to bear witness to them. We are faced with human desolation in conjunction with a demand to find new idioms: 'In the differend, something "asks" to be put into phrases, and suffers from the wrong of not being able to be put into phrases right away' (ibid.: §23). The decisive question, then, is whether there are two concepts of 'the differend' involved in Lyotard's philosophy – the one signifying a 'crisis in language', the other signifying a human crisis (and possibly a crisis in the category 'human'). Or does 'the differend' in language translate into socio-cultural wrongs, *tout court*? Put differently, are the exclusions that occur due to neglected, forgotten or repressed possibilities of linking compatible with the exclusions that arise from the impossibility of phrasing a wrong?

At first sight, this might look like a question that pertains to the transition from the ontological level to the ontic level, in so far as the ontology of phrases (prior heterogeneity in language) is juxtaposed with irreconcilable conflicts on the socio-cultural level of empirical experience and identity. And the question does indeed concern the aporetic relationship between non-identity and identity, but this should not be confused with a corresponding split between levels (i.e. a level of non-identity pertaining to the ontology of language as opposed to a socio-cultural level of identity). Although Lyotard does not say much about this issue, I think it is fair to posit – with respect to the problem at hand – that his concept of 'the differend' is the same but different. There certainly is dissimilarity between excluded or forgotten possibilities in language, on the one hand, and exclusions by way of silences on the socio-cultural level, on the other. And yet the concept of 'the differend' seems to be the same. In both cases, it denotes the impossibility of 'right' linking (*aporia*/deadlock), combined with a demand to link – 'one has to link', 'one must search for new idioms' – signalled by the feeling that 'one cannot find words' (see Lyotard 1988: §22). In this regard, there are not two different concepts of 'the differend' at play in Lyotard's philosophy. Rather, we may say that there is an inherent tension in the very concept, and this feature distinguishes Lyotard's philosophy from less radical approaches to 'the crisis in language'. The 'crisis' could easily be reduced to a problem of mapping the world properly due to a conceptual deficiency. This would not be to defy the possibility of finding the 'right' words, however; it would merely be an acknowledgement of the inadequacy of our systems of language and knowledge. As mentioned earlier, Lyotard does not allow for such a trivialisation or homogenisation of heterogeneity. As he sees it, our account of the world is not incomplete because we lack the right conceptual tools, but because every conceptualisation leaves out – excludes – something, a remainder or residual heterogeneity. And it is this heterogeneous exclusion, in turn, that calls upon phrases, that 'asks' to be put into phrases.

It is nevertheless somewhat unclear in Lyotard's philosophy whether the demand for new idioms entails identity formation. Does the search for new idioms mean that the 'others' should be given a voice and hence an identity? If so, we are confronted with a paradox, or at the very least a dilemma – one that characterises philosophies of difference in general. The crux of the matter is that the 'others' can overcome their (ethnical) silence only by being identified as different from 'us'. But as I pointed out in Chapter 1, such recognition implies a homogenisation whereby the 'others' are reduced to negative mirror images of 'our' identity. The 'others' are, in other words, reduced to instances of the Same. If, on the other hand, the otherness of the 'others' remains silent in its ineffable difference, the practical result would most probably be a self-effacing homogenisation with 'us' – a complete assimilation into the prevailing order. So the question is whether Lyotard's philosophy provides us with a feasible solution to this antinomy. Does it enable us to loosen this knot in order to escape this deadlock?

Apparently, the feeling of the sublime implies a disturbance of established ways of understanding, so that the subsequent reaction marks a break with the established methods. The established identities are then displaced, including the relationship between 'us' and the 'others'. But does this mean that the 'others' must have an identity in order not to remain silent? Or does it mean that the 'others' must remain silent in their difference? Are we able to displace something/someone without giving it/them an identity? Lyotard seems to agree with both alternatives, or, put another way, he seems to dissolve the problem as presented. From the outset, both 'we' and the 'others', in an empirical or ontic sense, have an identity. This identity is subsequently displaced, whereupon we discover that both 'our' identity and the identity of the 'others' arise from a process of forgetting. Lyotard's philosophy suggests that the displacement of existent identities might make us attentive to silences, to particular 'differends' and 'the differend' in general. The strategy of deconstruction has the potential to make us aware of the fact that any existent identity exists at the expense of something else. And since it is this openness towards the undefined and unidentifiable otherness that is the very reason for demanding new means by which to speak of the unidentifiable, the *aporia* between the unidentifiable and the identifiable is no longer a paradox that prevents us from proceeding – on the contrary, it is the very condition for proceeding onwards. The aim, then, is not to give the silenced 'others' an identity or a voice, because that would be to betray silence in terms of identifying the unidentifiable otherness. The challenge is to displace established identities, while keeping in mind that there will always remain an irreducible residue, something that cannot be articulated. Below, I will expand on this strategy of displacement by reference to my argument in Chapter 3 concerning Lash's 'ground'. However, contrary to Lash, whose point of departure is the beautiful in Kant's Third Critique, I shall proceed from the feeling of the sublime, as defined by Lyotard.

Non-determinative judgement

With regard to the sublime in Lyotard's philosophy, the feeling of pleasure accompanies the demand for new idioms, whereas pain accompanies the acknowledgement that there is no solution to be found within the existing medium. Lyotard directs our attention towards the shock and the doubt produced by the sublime. The sublime in art entails a creative break with nostalgic longing for absolute forms of values – a break with rules and conventions. Lyotard designates both modern and postmodern art as sublime; however, it is only the postmodern (aspect of) art that is the real sublime. This is due to the fact that the postmodern sublime does not admit the possibility of a time without breaks and events. Lyotard's insistence on the postmodern as the foremost point of any modern movement can therefore not be conceived as a modern dynamics of liminality and communitas. Rather, the postmodern must pertain to a different logic – a logic of displacement – in which something unknown is produced: new rules and new genres of discourse.[19] This is what displacement is all about. Lyotard (1984: 81) amplifies: 'Here, then, lies the difference: modern aesthetics is an aesthetic of the sublime, though a nostalgic one. It allows the unpresentable to be put forward only as the missing contents; but the form, because of its recognizable consistency, continues to offer to the reader or viewer matter for solace and pleasure. Yet these sentiments do not constitute the real sublime sentiment, which is in an intrinsic combination of pleasure and pain: the pleasure that reason should exceed all presentation, the pain that imagination or sensibility should not be equal to the concept.'

It is only the postmodern sublime that testifies to the unpresentable, regardless of whether we react to art or other spheres. It is only the postmodern sublime that senses an opening for (or possibilities for) new meanings. In other words, it is only the postmodern sublime that makes us search for new idioms. But how do we know what to look for and where to look? As noted above, the feeling of the sublime comes without any form of indication of direction. But what about Lyotard's philosophy? Does it offer us any kind of signpost? Lyotard's philosophy encourages us to search for the non-determinative, reflecting laws that allow the event to be presented in its difference/singularity, rather than being repressed through representation. In that sense, Lyotard's philosophy leads us in a specific direction: away from the belief in absolute forms and values, away from absolute identities and purity – in brief, away from homogeneity and towards heterogeneity. He maintains that the 'unhappy' awareness of the unpresentable – the indeterminable 'now' of the event – is the condition of possibility for judgement and knowledge. The event is the condition for proceeding onwards and for calling into question established 'truths'. In this regard, Lyotard introduces the abyss between presentation (event) and representation as, to use the language of Lash, a 'groundless ground' for thought and action. It is an unpresentable ground against which meaning and truth are defined and constituted.

The fact that Lyotard makes difference/heterogeneity primary in relation to the identical, without thereby turning difference into a new identity or ultimate foundation (for communication), does not, however, mean that he leads us in a specific *empirical* direction. He does not tell us how to judge. Given the primacy of heterogeneity, he cannot positively decide how to judge, or how to judge justly. All Lyotard can do is to remind us that any judgement, any categorisation of something/someone – indeed, any formation of identity – is an act of ignoring heterogeneity, a process of forgetting. Accordingly, he holds that justice is an idea that cannot be made into a norm. A just judgement would be to respect the non-decisional character of justice by not prejudging it (see Readings 1991: 127). However, even though we cannot make the correct judgement or the correct linking of phrases, we have to link; we have to make judgements. And the only criterion is the non-determinative idea of justice: the demand for a linkage that can testify to the event.

The issue of non-formalised justice is discussed by other philosophers as well. For instance, Derrida argues that there is no justice except to the degree that some event is possible, which, qua event, exceeds calculations, rules, programmes, anticipations, and so forth. As Derrida (1992: 27) sees it, justice is the experience of absolute alterity and, as such, is unpresentable. At the same time, however, it is the chance of the event and the conditions of history. He contends that justice obstructs the horizon of knowledge, arguing that a horizon, in terms of a regulative idea or in any other meaning of the word, is both the opening and the limit that define an infinite progress or a period of waiting. But justice does not wait. A just decision is always required immediately – 'right away' (ibid.: 26). And even if it did give itself all the time to consider the facts about the matter, Derrida explains, the moment of decision, as such, always remains a finite moment of urgency and precipitation. The moment of decision 'always marks the interruption of the jurido- or ethico- or politico-cognitive deliberation that precedes it, that *must* precede it' (ibid.). The question remains, however, as to whether this philosophy of difference eases the problem of opposition. Is the emphasis of continual displacement or perpetual deferment of established rules or identities, including the relationship between 'us' and the 'others', a sufficient ground for exceeding the logic of opposition that characterises modern ideology? This question *can* be taken to be an empirical issue. To the extent that we consider it to be a philosophical/theoretical question, however, we need to look more closely at Lyotard's response to this problem for discussion and to determine its implication with respect to the subject.

In Chapter 1, we saw that there are several 'solutions' to the problem of ethnocentrism pertaining to the relationship between 'us' and the 'others'. However, as I pointed out, they all seem to presume a notion of an inclusive humanity and a dual subjectivity. The underlying assumption seems to be that human beings are simultaneously identical (universal) and unique (autonomous). Whereas the first position – the universal dimension – nourishes ethnocentrism, the latter tends to prompt cultural relativism. Taken together, they comprise a multicultural dilemma between equal dignity and distinctiveness. Lyotard's philosophy, for its part, appears to move beyond the duality of ethnocentrism and cultural relativism. One reason for this is his defiance of the modern notion of universal subjectivity (incorporated into the autonomous subject). His ontologisation of heterogeneity forecloses the possibility of an identity common to all humankind. In line with Derrida and others, Lyotard deconstructs the Western humanist subject, and he calls into question totalitarian ideas of purity, universality and identity as guiding principles in history and society. The 'death' of the universal subject is in Lyotard's philosophy implicated by his concept of language, that is, by the peculiar relationship between human beings and language. As the above discussion has suggested, human beings cannot be detached from language. If we follow Lyotard, we have to disavow the notion of human existence *in abstractum*. Accordingly, we have to defy the sovereignty of the subject. Within the framework of the philosophy of difference, the subject cannot possibly be self-sufficient or self-contained, let alone self-identical. By the same token, we must defy the possibility of pure identities and generative principles. We may infer that subjectivity and identity are essentially self-different, and that foundations are fundamentally contingent (e.g. Lyotard 1990: 45).

This argument can be held against commentators who dismiss incommensurability. Among these is Donald Davidson (1984), whose assertion is that a common ground for comparison must exist in order to state that something is heterogeneous and thus incomparable. Davidson's well-known objection to incommensurability in some ways parallels Dumont's argument that every ideology is relative in relation to the others. According to Dumont, a comparison of values is possible only between two systems taken as wholes. As noted in Chapter 2, Dumont (1986) takes as his point of departure a holistic hierarchical model in which 'encompassing of the contrary' is a pivotal element. Different/distinct identities are considered to be encompassed by the identical or the whole, suggesting that differences are hierarchically subordinate to the whole. Likewise, the self-referencing unified subject – the universal subject – is assumed to have the empirical self and non-self subordinated to it. The non-self is contained within the self, and the non-self is, at the same time, the opposite of the self (ibid.: 125). Within a holistic model such as this, identity includes difference. It is worth noting, however, that Dumont's argument does not resonate with the assertion that identity is predicated upon difference or otherness. When holism is concerned, identity subsumes difference by way of encompassing. In this respect, identity is, as is the subject, granted a universal status. Hence, Dumont's objection to the thesis of incommensurability seems to assume a universal unity, which Lyotard rigorously refutes (including the non-modern unity between 'is' and 'ought').

To conclude this argument, it is the heterogeneity in language that, according to Lyotard, renders self-difference or singular subjectivity possible. In accordance with Lash (1999), it seems reasonable to suggest that language, due to its non-determinative and contingent nature, constitutes a 'groundless ground'. Furthermore, we have seen that language is non-instrumental and that humans are in an immediate 'I–thou' relationship with language, which alludes to Lash's delineation of *poesis* (as opposed to *theorein*). In a similar vein, Lyotard's philosophy suggests that there is a reciprocal correlation between language and humans, language being intrinsic to our being, as it were. Given this reciprocal relationship, language renders possible existential meaning between subjectivity and being, which in turn points to Lash's depiction of *praxis* – the situated intersubjectivity or the sociality of a collectivity.

Sharing the impossibility of sharing

We are now in the position to infer what Lyotard's philosophy implies with regard to community based on difference. The most important insight is perhaps that his philosophy invites us to think of community without a delimited identity, essence or foundation. The mythological notion of a unified 'people' is radically called into question. As noted by Carroll (1990: xxiii), the 'people' must be conceived as a perpetual exodus, both from themselves and from the Law to which they attempt to respond but to which they can never adequately react (cf. Derrida 1992). This argument corresponds with my critical remarks regarding the totalitarian elements of modern political ideologies.

Community, then, is an ongoing and open practice that can never be realised or materialised in terms of fixed boundaries (see Agamben 1993). It is a bonding without bonds, originating from a non-trivial experience of the heterogeneous – the indefinable, non-shareable and unpresentable singular – prior to the interest that people might have in one another. In the words of Derrida (1992), community calls for an unconditional openness towards the *arrivants*. It means that we have to wait for the 'others' without expectations, without ideas and images. According to Lyotard (1990: 91), it is the experience of sharing the non-shareable that links people together. That is why a community based on difference challenges the communal boundary and confounds the logic of the border. It 'unworks' the metaphysical horizon pertaining to dominant notions of community, disrupting the totalising and exclusionary myth of national, racial or religious unity. It is, as such, a paradoxical community – a community without community ('nous tous désormais') (Nancy 2000: 40).

In his delineation of the limits for what can be communicated and hence shared, Lyotard, as does Lash, refers to Nancy: 'In Nancy's problematic, the "Being-toward-death" signals the impossibility for the singularities of sharing more than the impossibility of sharing. One takes part in death, one does not share it. It is the limit of what can be communicated. What one calls community resides in the forgetting of this impossible "communication", in an operation of self-constitution … which engenders, tautogorically, the community as a work (of itself), as an "immanent" power of which the community is the always reiterated act. And Nancy concludes that only an "unfashioned community" would be respectful of this unshareable that disperses the singularities but, at the same time, "exposes" one to the other' (Lyotard 1990: 91). As the quotation suggests, the language of communication implies distance, but it also binds us together. Most importantly, the communication is non-instrumental; it is 'purposiveness without purpose' (cf. Kant's Third Critique).

As pointed out in Chapter 3, a community based on metaphysical ideas of unity or identity, on the other hand, would be a community in which the subjects are universal substances, closed in on themselves and closed off from one another. It would be a community that represses or eliminates the heterogeneous, whereby difference is turned into an instance of the Same. The latter alludes to the logic of opposition, which appertains to the multicultural dilemma. To the extent that community is perceived as normative communitas, differences are precluded from serving openness towards the 'others' and from contributing to a critical questioning of the prevailing rules and categories. The prospect of being exposed to the otherness of the 'others' – of being receptive to silences and 'remembering' the forgotten, which Lyotard regards as the very condition for community based on difference – is thus rendered impossible. Victor Seidler (1998: 111) notes that modernity is questioned precisely for this reason, that is, because of its insistence on turning difference – the 'other' – into an instance of the Same. Within the framework of the dilemma between equality and distinctiveness, the possibility for a community based on difference is limited by the fact that the 'others' are identified and recognised in opposition to 'our' identity. This reductionism occurs through a mechanism of assimilation and culturalisation/subordination that discursively reproduces both 'us' and the 'others' and hence results in the problem of opposition. It seems reasonable to conclude, therefore, that the multicultural dilemma comprises a reductive totality whereby dialogue is reduced to monologue and difference is suppressed in the name of some unitary notion of the 'human' (see ibid.). Lyotard's philosophy of difference, adherent to a strategy of displacement, serves to unravel this problem of opposition – and the concurrent universalisation of 'our' identity – on a philosophical/theoretical level. How this problem can best be handled on a practical-political level, however, is an entirely different matter.

Chapter 5

Conditions for Dialogue

※

Proceeding from 'the differend', this chapter will shed light on a key issue pertaining to multicultural dialogue. One question to be pursued is how 'the differend' is manifested in the relation between 'us' and the 'others'. Another question is how we can establish a multicultural dialogue that breaks with the oppositional logic of the multicultural dilemma. I will take as my starting point the totalitarianism of truth with which much social and political theory is imbued, arguing that a totalitarianism of truth allows little room for incommensurability. As we saw in the preceding chapters, a totalitarian horizon does not allow for incompatible evaluative standards. In this chapter, I will focus more directly on the conditions for dialogue so as to envision a cultural encounter that does not involve the assimilation and culturalisation/subordination of 'others'. As suggested in Chapter 4, a non-totalitarian concept of dialogue might prove difficult unless we manage to establish a critical distance to our own criteria of judgement.

Arguing with Hans Herbert Kögler (1999), I will attempt to show that notwithstanding Gadamer's anti-totalitarian stance, his hermeneutics comprises a truth-oriented totalitarianism on which his concept of dialogue is based. In line with Kögler, I argue that Gadamer's approach to dialogue entails a prejudgement, which results either in a total assimilation of the 'others', in cases where the dialogue is considered to be successful, or in assimilation combined with culturalisation, often accompanied by individualisation, in cases where the dialogue is seen as unsuccessful. As we shall see, Gadamer (1975) conceives of language as a productive dialogue in which substantially different views confront one another and merge in a new and deeper insight. Specific perspectives unite in a single interpretation, which becomes identical with the subject matter (ibid.: 398, 403). What seems to be implied here is a teleology that prevents interpretation from being a matter of critique, that is, a matter of critically dissociating our own horizon from that of 'others'. On the contrary, in Gadamer's view, dialogue is a matter of fusing horizons, of fusing all relevant perspectives concerning the subject matter into a new, true insight. The question I want to pose is whether this translates into assimilation, whereby differences are reduced to instances of the Same.

Subsequently, I will elaborate on how we could feasibly attain a reflective, critical distance to our evaluative standards. I endeavour to show that an abstract distance, based on universalisation of 'our' rationality, is not appropriate with regard to multicultural dialogue. In order to illustrate the problems of abstraction, pertaining to rational discourse, I will use Jürgen Habermas's discourse ethics as a point of reference. I then juxtapose Habermas's discourse ethics with Gadamer's hermeneutics, which is characterised by a lack of distance. As I attempt to show, however, their perspectives appear to converge in a totalitarianism of truth, which does not allow for the critical distance required in multicultural dialogue. It is my contention that a feasible multicultural dialogue is premised upon a critical distance that does not abstract from the practical level of the 'good life'. Hence, a critical distance is not to be confused with an abstract distance of rational discourse. As for abstract distance, the question of justice is addressed exclusively in relation to moral laws, norms or principles. A critical distance, on the other hand, does not confine the question of justice to deliberations of right and wrong. The question to be pursued, then, is whether issues concerning the 'good life' can possess an aspect of equality and justice without resolving into universal rationality. This question is of vital importance if we are to avoid prejudgement and totalitarianism. The final issue that will be addressed is how dialogue might be organised in order to resist totalitarianism.

Totalitarianism of truth

In his book *The Power of Dialogue*, Kögler (1999) opposes Gadamer's concept of dialogue, arguing that Gadamer (con)fuses understanding of meaning with the act of judging. As Kögler sees it, identifying a common theme does not guarantee a shared view of the subject matter. On the contrary, we may agree in identifying a common theme or subject matter while acknowledging that certain concepts, valuations and views necessarily exclude one another. Kögler contends that the rules and standards of one language game or context would be contrary to the rules of another, precisely because both relate to a common subject matter. He refers to Charles Taylor's analogy of 'sport and games' to illustrate his point. Chess and soccer are simply different in the fact that they do not oppose or conflict with each other with regard to the specific moves allowable within each context of rules. Soccer and handball, on the other hand, allow for incommensurable moves with respect to a common point of reference – the ball (ibid.: 70–71). Kögler goes on to argue: 'The movement from a prior understanding about the experience of another's meaning to a new and deeper substantive view could be guaranteed only if both interlocutors were to belong to a context in which already-shared criteria, procedures, and resources were available for resolving disagreement. Only then could we expect each disagreement to be forged into a new unity' (ibid.: 71).

However, if the context of meaning is set by symbolic structures that are entirely different from our own, we will not, according to Kögler (1999), be able to go directly to the subject matter in such a manner that 'the truth' will reveal itself. The evaluative standards will differ from one another in such a way that we will be faced with incommensurable perspectives on 'the truth' (ibid.). In taking this stance, Kögler apparently invokes relativism with respect to evaluative standards. However, this is not to be confused with classical cultural relativism (as outlined in the Introduction to this volume). Rather, it should be seen as an argument for incommensurability. Kögler states quite explicitly that Donald Davidson is wrong in his disclaimer of incommensurability. As we saw in the preceding chapter, Davidson (1984) defies the thesis of incommensurability, suggesting that the possibility of understanding another's meaning precludes the likelihood of radically divergent evaluative standards (cf. Dumont 1986). Kögler (1999), for his part, insists on distinguishing between understanding and judging. He contends that the semantic presupposition of identical meaning by no means decides the epistemological question of a common standard of truth. On the contrary, cases of incommensurability depend on a mutual understanding between the participants (ibid.: 161). Drawing on Rorty, Foucault, Bernstein and others, Kögler maintains that it is a mistake to equate incommensurability with untranslatability when incommensurability concerns epistemological orientations, that is, criteria of judgement.[1] He asserts that necessary conceptual bridgeheads do not guarantee a symbolic unity of meaning. Rather, they allow irreconcilable differences in world view to appear (ibid.: 163–165).

We may infer from Kögler's argument that in order to avoid doing injustice to the 'others' in a dialogic encounter, we have to take into account the distance between the underlying symbolic structures of the parties involved. Alluding to Lyotard's concept of 'the differend', attention should be directed to the ontological differences that separate the parties. With Gadamer's truth- and content-oriented perspective as a starting point, however, one is likely to ignore the fact that evaluative standards are irreconcilable. 'The differend' is likely to be repressed through a process of assimilation in which the distance between the majority and the 'others' collapses. The following quotation from Kögler (1999: 168) underlines the danger of incorporation: 'I take the idea of a universal context of judgment to be a methodologically dangerous position, because it invites an ethnocentric attitude with regard to our own standards of evaluation, especially if they are hypostatized into essentialist criteria of truth and moral adequacy.'

The corresponding side of assimilation is contextual explanation or objectification of the 'others', which is akin to the concept of culturalisation. Significantly, when a dialogic model that equates understanding with evaluative consensus is confronted with radically divergent symbolic orders (which renders consensus impossible), it often leads to a contextual explanation. Writes Kögler (1999: 140–141): 'Gadamer's model gets caught up in the dichotomy between an ultimately affirmative understanding of truth (i.e., the ascription of the others' meaning to one's own ontological premises) and an external context explanation. Either we understand something as true within the fusion of horizons, or we explain it through contextual circumstances.' In such cases, the utterances and actions of the 'others' are explained in light of psychological, cultural or social factors, whereas 'our' statements are not objectified in a similar manner. By being the subjects of contextual explanation (culturalisation and/or individualisation), the 'others' are likely to be depicted as exceptions that prove the rule. And to the extent that the 'others' are seen from a cultural relativist point of view and recognised as being distinctive, they tend to be depicted as a self-related totality. In neither case does one allow oneself to become engaged in the claims that they put forward. Due to the objectifying attitude, Kögler argues, we do not take their assertions seriously – assertions that could challenge our own symbolic order. Instead of opening ourselves to the truth claims of the 'others', we keep them at a safe distance (see ibid.: 146).

Contingent foundations

Kögler (1999) develops his argument in the following manner. If there is no distinction between understanding meaning and comprehending truth – or, methodologically speaking, if we do not introduce the dimension of symbolic order between the meaning of a statement and its truth value – then we only seem to foreground our orientations, while in truth we reintroduce them untouched on the side of the 'others'. Through this dialogic pseudo-openness, understanding the 'others' becomes a circular process, imprisoned within one's own horizon of meaning. It follows that neither self-critique nor radical innovation is possible (ibid.: 143). On the contrary, substantial agreement on basic assumptions, in terms of a commonality of a shared truth, becomes the very criterion for accepting and recognising the 'others'. Kögler maintains that we recognise the 'others' as rational subjects to the degree that they are rational in the way that we are ourselves (ibid.: 148; cf. Brown 2006).

In summary, Gadamer's '*strong* concept of understanding' requires that 'understanding goes hand in hand with comprehending truth' (Kögler 1999: 201). Rationality and truth are brought so closely together that 'what can count as rational "for them" must be what "we ourselves" take to be true' (ibid.). When the 'others' are reduced to a mirror image of 'us', they do not pose a threat to the coherent unity of our own understanding of being (ibid.: 147). The imperative of truth is, in other words, a totality in which radical difference or irresolvable conflict is nothing other than an explanation for what goes wrong when the parties fail to agree on the truth. Kögler moves on to suggest that as long as we judge or evaluate immediately in the process of interpretation, that is, as long as understanding of meaning and judgement are concurrent, we cannot avoid relating specific utterances and actions of the 'others' to 'shared and assumed conceptions and practices of our own background' (ibid.: 156). We relate the particular of the 'others' to the general of our own. If we are to avoid this fallacy of comparison, it seems necessary to abstain from totalising. According to Kögler, '[a]n accretion of meaning, which alters and extends what we take to be true, is possible only if *a totalizing equivalence* is not established between the disclosure of (the others') meaning and (our own) conceptions of what is true' (ibid.: 143).

In accordance with Lyotard's perspective, Kögler (1999) points out that a non-totalising perspective defies higher-order theories of history, that is, grand narratives or utopias, founded on continuity. Such narratives, he argues, make the historical-cultural world become the metaphysical complement of a self-identical subject. In addition, he contends, historical meaning is not to be referred back (in a search for the origin) to a pure experience. And finally, a non-totalising perspective excludes the particular discourses from possessing their actual or authentic meaning in some 'unsaid' that is inherent in them (ibid.: 204–205). Kögler asserts, as does Lyotard, that we cannot relate our conceptualisation of the world to a dimension behind or beyond language – to an external point of reference. Similarly, MacIntyre (1988: 382) points out that the paradigmatic uses – the conceptualisations – of key expressions in a society are inseparably related to the legitimating genealogies of that society.

It is against this background of an 'unbroken attitude toward truth' that Kögler (1999: 202) insists on explicating the underlying conception patterns and their ontological premises. Only then can we distance ourselves from our own horizon. This requires a far weaker concept of understanding than that of Gadamer – one that necessitates the formal positing of a common world or subject matter as a reference point for dialogue (cf. 'the ball' in the example above) (ibid.: 201–202). However, as indicated above, the identification of a subject matter is by no means the same as a commonality of evaluative standard (ibid.: 155). Kögler's point is that we can disclose the particularity and the contingency of our own concepts and evaluative standards by being attentive to other evaluative standards and different symbolic orders. When we discover that our frame of reference is inadequate in the interaction with the 'others', we might become aware of the limitations, inconsequences and poverty of resources of our own world view (see MacIntyre 1988: 387–388). Kögler (1999: 212) maintains that the interpretive process can bring into relief the experience of intelligible difference. Accordingly, alterity or difference is at the fore in his 'critical hermeneutics': 'In this "critical hermeneutics," we do not attempt interpretively to remove alterity but rather seek to employ alterity productively toward a *different experience of ourselves*. This productive use arises from the fact that only in the experience of a foreign or unfamiliar order do we recognize this *as* a symbolic order' (ibid.).

The conclusion we may draw from this, reflecting back on Lyotard's philosophy, is that incommensurable idioms do not prevent us from taking a common subject matter as a point of departure. Incommensurability precludes only a common standard of judgement with respect to these subjects. When understood as productive heterogeneity, incommensurability is a condition for critical reflection. It signifies a thought-provoking gap, which makes us aware of our limitations. But at the same time, it makes us proceed and search for new idioms. On the one hand, the dialogic encounter makes the parties aware of the aporetic gap between them. On the other hand, when disclosing the particularities and contingencies of each party's own concepts and standards, the encounter constitutes a dialogue within which difference is not reduced to an instance of the Same.

It must be noted, however, that being attentive to other evaluative standards and different symbolic orders is not tantamount to context sensitivity, nor can it be equated with personal sensitivity training. Needless to say, words cannot gain meaning apart from the context in which they are applied, but the term 'context sensitivity' is normally deployed by researchers who endeavour – in a responsible way – to give an account of people's lived experience and real lives, as opposed to the prevailing order of power and domination. It often seems to be the case that context sensitivity, when used as a means to give a true account of people's lives, is predicated upon the apprehension of an unproblematic material reality, devoid of power, as if a socially constructed world of power relations was imposed on actual conditions in the world – the so-called real world (Brown 1995: 35ff.; Butler 1992; Scott 1992). The context sensitivity is thus likely to imply context explanation, as described above, and inasmuch as it invokes an authentic standpoint, it tends to obscure more than it reveals when it comes to the contingency of foundations and evaluative standards. Combined with a notion of an ethical virtue that make us behave sensitively towards and empower the 'others', we might argue that a context-sensitive approach runs the risk of reinstituting fixed metaphysical referents – ultimate foundations – and eventually of engendering the assimilation and culturalisation/subordination of the 'others' (see Egeland and Gressgård 2007).

Power, domination and resistance

Informed by Foucault, Kögler (1999) draws a vital distinction between domination and other power relations. He conceives of power relations as strategically oriented relations between individuals or social agents who seek to act on and thereby influence the action, thought and perception of others. What defines a relationship of power, Kögler notes, is exactly this indirect efficacy of actors working on the experience of other actors, like an action upon an action (ibid.: 233). When one exercises power, he maintains, one governs subjects. However, as long as it is the subject's substantial freedom that is the target of power exertion, the exercise of power actually presupposes a non-determined subject. Moreover, power relations are in principle reversible, which means that they are not ontologically determining structures or causalities (ibid.: 235). As Kögler sees it, the analysis of power has to determine to what extent the tendency towards a negation of the freedom built into the power relation has actually taken precedence, that is, the degree to which reversibility has been temporarily revoked.

Kögler (1999) is particularly preoccupied with domination. He defines domination as an operative power relationship that is no longer capable of being made fluid by the agents. Power relations become relations of domination, he notes, whenever freedom is eliminated. Whereas power relations presuppose free subjects that are involved in 'open and fair' struggles, domination entails determinate patterns of thinking, acting and perceiving that have been 'crystallized into fixed positionalities' (ibid.: 236). A pressing question is how these relations of domination have been able to stabilise themselves. What allows these structures of dominance to be consolidated? In accordance with my argument concerning the will to power, Kögler contends that it is our synthesising capacity, always already founded in the symbolic order (in the holistic character of our world disclosure), that stabilises relations of domination. However, such structures need power practices and technologies to reproduce themselves. Hence, they also always carry the potential for a restructuring of the established order (ibid.: 237f.). The critical task of analysis is to lay bare and unmask processes of normalisation that turn individuals into dominated subjects. This means, according to Kögler, that we must fill the 'vacuum of freedom' that the power technologies attempt to fill completely, but are never capable of entirely occupying because of the 'mutual interdependence of power and freedom' (ibid.: 238f.). In the language of Lyotard (1988, 1990), it is the prior heterogeneity that prevents power technologies from filling the vacuum of freedom completely. From his point of view, domination could be seen as a totalitarian attempt at ignoring the heterogeneity that forms the basis of ordering processes.[2]

To the extent that something qualifies as a power practice, Kögler (1999) suggests, it is ascertained as such by the way it stands in a relationship to the self-understanding of the individuals and to their conception of a 'good life'. The crux of the matter is whether or not the individuals '*suffer* under the given conditions' (ibid.: 241f.). Since the 'good life' cannot be grounded philosophically in a universally binding manner, power cannot be detached from the specific ideas and expectations that constitute an acceptable existence for the individual. For that reason, Kögler maintains, it is crucial to clarify what is being struggled for and what is being rejected (ibid.: 242f.). Significantly, both power and individuality are situated in a symbolic order, so that the notion of an abstract, universal subjectivity has to be defied, alongside the notion of total or absolute power (ibid.: 246). Resistance is thus not a matter of revolutionary struggles energised by a utopian end-goal; rather, it pertains to social and cultural identity. As Kögler sees it, the objective of resistance is to 'unfold a positive picture of one's own identity', freed from earlier, domination-laden connotations (ibid.: 244). In this struggle, he argues, 'the central task for the individuals or social groups in question is to define and to unfold their identity – indeed, in a symbolic as well as a material sense' (ibid.: 243).

To summarise, we have seen that Kögler – contrary to perspectives that call for context sensitivity on the basis of so-called lived experience and real life (often accompanied by ideology critique in order to reveal the authentic truth about the dominated subjects) – advocates relativism in terms of contingency and incommensurability with respect to standards of truth. Accordingly, he suggests a power critique that necessitates a break with the immediate self-understanding of the agents. In his view, a critique of dominating structures necessitates a critical distance to one's own truth claims, which can be achieved through a hermeneutical experience of 'others' – of other epochs or cultures.

Proximity and distance

In order to avoid prejudging, we have to disavow universal (universalised) standards of rationality, but it is equally important to distance ourselves from our particular standards of truth. In short, we need to search for a critical distance that is neither strictly abstract nor particular. One alternative could be found in the literature on ethics. To the extent that ethics is considered to be grounded in practice, practical ethics provides us with a concept of justice that might correspond to Lyotard's notion of judgement without criteria. As long as his concept of justice is separated from 'truth', it does not presuppose an ultimate foundation in terms of an original whole or a telos. On the contrary, justice is conceived as a non-determinative idea, which evades representation or conceptualisation. As long as we regard justice as a non-determinative idea, we cannot, in a cognitive manner, know or live up to the idea of a law or a norm. We cannot pre-cognise what justice is, and in this respect, justice is a matter of judging on a case-by-case basis (see Readings 1991: 109).

In the discussion above, we saw that Kögler (1999), in his critical-hermeneutical model of dialogue, draws attention to the suffering of the 'others'. He calls upon a human capacity to engage with – and show an interest in – co-others, based on a proximity to their suffering. This moral capacity not only involves an understanding of the situation of the 'others', but also requires of us that we undertake a critically distanced interpretation of their situation. This seems to correspond with Kögler's critique of Gadamer's totalitarianism of truth, alluding to the pragmatic philosophy of Wittgenstein. In *Philosophical Investigations* Wittgenstein ([1953] 1968: §297) states: 'Pity, one may say, is a form of conviction that someone else is in pain.' A pragmatic approach to ethical conduct runs counter to (moral) philosophies that advocate a total identification with the sufferer. If we were to identify totally with the sufferer, we should become sufferers ourselves, as if we were able to experience the same suffering. If we defy this possibility, however, we may claim that pity or compassion requires a particular distance between 'us' and the 'other(s)', that is, a distance between the subject and the addressee(s). It is this peculiar critical distance that I shall examine below.

As I mentioned above, Gadamer's model of dialogue concerns the criteria for the 'good life'. And, as I also mentioned, his concept of dialogue presupposes a consensus with regard to evaluative standards. Gadamer's concept of dialogue aims at consensus on the basis of a common truth. That is to say, understanding of meaning and evaluation of validity concur in the process of interpretation. However, to the extent that understanding and interpretation converge in a single unit, dialogue is characterised by a lack of distance to our standards of judgement. As I see it, it is Gadamer's concept of language that is the source of his totalitarianism of truth. In his book *Truth and Method*, Gadamer (1975) conceives of verbal utterances as an artistic, aesthetic activity, suggesting that it is when the linguistic dimension of understanding is explicitly expressed that the juncture between understanding and interpretation takes place. Interpretation is conceived as the verbal or lingual expression of what we have understood. This means that interpretation is somehow internal to understanding. According to Gadamer, the interpretation simply makes understanding explicit (ibid.: 398). Understanding and interpretation are connected in such a manner that verbal expression *is* understanding; we cannot possibly understand without interpreting. In Gadamer's view, therefore, understanding something is to make it one's own, and there is no other way of making it one's own than through language (verbal expression). Understanding includes interpretation through conversation, through dialogue (ibid.).

Kögler (1999) calls into question this model of dialogue because as long as understanding and interpretation concur, the utterances of the interlocutor will have to be related to concepts and practices in our own background. The pressing question is how we can theoretically assert a distance between understanding and interpretation without lapsing into a theory in which interpretation is totally abstracted from understanding. If we take into consideration Kögler's argument, we may respond by stating that our understanding of the identities of the 'others' and their conceptualisations of the 'good life' presupposes a proximity to the situation. At the same time, however, a disclosure of the ontological premises on which the symbolic orders are based – and a concurrent disclosure of the structures of domination – presupposes a break with the immediate self-understanding of the agents. The break involves a critical distance to the concepts that are being used in order to describe reality. In other words, proximity and distance need to be inextricably intertwined if a critical distance is to be attained. Likewise, a critical distance between the parties is of vital importance for the dialogue. In this respect, the dialogic encounter involves two types of distance, which comprise two aspects of a feasible multicultural dialogue: a distance to one's own self-understanding, including one's own criteria of judgement, and a distance between understanding and interpretation. The latter translates into a distance between the parties involved in the cultural encounter. In the following, I shall look more closely at this critical distance, which can be found in practical ethics. My point of departure will be the concept of 'moral performance', as defined by Arne Johan Vetlesen and Per Nortvedt (1994).[3]

Vetlesen and Nortvedt (1994) take 'moral performance' to be a sequence that consists of three elements: perception, judgement and action. Perception logically precedes judgement, which in turn logically precedes action. According to Vetlesen and Nortvedt, both perception and judgement depend on our emotional capacity for empathy and our cognitive powers of interpretation, deliberation, abstraction and imagination. Moral perception, they argue, is to 'see' what is morally significant in a given situation, and that sets in motion the deliberating activity of moral judgement. In this context, the faculty of judgement refers to the more exact interpretation of the nature of a given situation, and it enables us to assess deliberately the correct options for relating to, and possibly intervening in, the situation (ibid.: 64f.).

The first element in the sequence of moral performance – perception – determines whether we notice that the welfare of others is at stake in a given situation. According to Vetlesen (1994: 8, 17), the ability to perceive has its source in human receptivity, that is, in our capacity 'to be alert to', 'to become aware of' or 'to be attentive to' – in brief, in our capacity to see ourselves as 'addressed' by a situation or incident. Needless to say, this entails openness towards others. Vetlesen notes that this openness towards others is not passive but active, and yet it is not something that the subject self-consciously 'does', 'produces' or 'brings about' (ibid.: 17). As he sees it, it is a matter of emotional-cognitive openness towards the world and all that we encounter in it (as opposed to pseudo-openness). From a practical-ethical point of view, being is constituted by receptivity, and understanding is conceived as a mode of being, a way of being in the world. Hence, understanding is not a matter of gaining access to the human and moral phenomena that we encounter in a detached and disinterested way, like cognitive knowledge. Knowledge is indeed involved in our deliberation of whether or not the welfare of others is at stake, but it is gained only to the extent that we are involved in the present situation, to the extent that we have a (non-instrumental) interest in what occurs. According to Vetlesen and Nortvedt (1994: 67), the notion of disinterested access to the world is a fiction when moral phenomena are concerned, because only by being involved in the situation can we gain access to the welfare of others.

As Vetlesen (1994: 4) sees it, it is moral emotions that anchor us to the particular moral circumstance, to the aspect of a situation that addresses us immediately, to the here and now. Entering into the moral domain involves identifying a situation as carrying moral significance in the first place, none of which would come about, Vetlesen argues, without the basic emotional faculty of empathy (understood as an emotionally based sensitivity to the situation of others) (ibid.: 4; cf. Vetlesen and Nortvedt 1994: 68).[4] To summarise, it is our feelings that provide and shape the setting for judgement and action. Our emotional abilities sensitise us to – and help us see – that a phenomenon or situation carries moral relevance (Vetlesen 1994: 334). Subsequently, the faculty of judgement enables us to examine the extent to which, and in which cases, moral emotions meet the demands that we must impose for moral validity. In this respect, the faculty of judgement occupies itself with the interpretation and deliberation of the welfare of the affected parties in a specific situation. This transition from perception (the initial intuitive and empathy-based access into the situation) to judgement (the more concentrated interpretation and deliberation of the situation's particular nature) seems to correspond with the transition from understanding to evaluation that I described above.

The 'good life' and justice

Vetlesen and Nortvedt (1994) consider altruistic emotions – empathy, compassion, caring and sympathy – to be essential to moral conduct. In their view, these emotions are the more concrete expressions and manifestations of the faculty of empathy (ibid.: 92). Altruistic emotions are different from non-rational affections in that they have a rational aspect. According to Lawrence Blum (1980), feelings differ with respect to the rationality and intentionality that they possess. Some feelings 'interpret the world' in terms of our personal antipathies and sympathies, while others, such as compassion, are directed towards the particular situation that a fellow human being might be in, as well as the special needs that he or she may have. As Vetlesen (1994: 79) notes, by reference to Blum, compassion may counter-balance moods and inclinations that are self-interested. The central aspect of compassion is the situation in which the sufferer finds her- or himself. It is the very situation that engages us and guides our involvement, which means that our engagement cannot be strictly personal. We have to keep a certain distance to the other persons involved in the situation (Vetlesen and Nortvedt 1994: 106).

This critical distance enables us to go in and out of the situation, depending on what it demands. In accordance with Wittgenstein's account of suffering, Vetlesen and Nortvedt (1994) point out that the power of imagination enables us to understand others' feelings without feeling the same thing ourselves – without becoming sufferers ourselves. There is an interplay of emotional and cognitive powers so that one's empathy is led towards the object with the aid of the imagination (ibid.: 59). This seems to resonate with Kögler's (1999) assertion that the dialogic encounter enables us to take on the role of other people without making the 'others' similar to 'us'. In an analogous vein, although in a different context, MacIntyre (1988: 395) states: 'To possess the concepts of an alien culture ... informed by ... imagination, differs in important ways from possessing the concepts which are genuinely one's own.' Vetlesen (1994) remarks that the power of imagination prevents empathy from being confined to the close at hand and the well known. The imagination enables the feeling of empathy to extend to situations in which the ethical I's addressee is not physically and/or psychologically close but foreign and distant. In the process of imagination, empathy is extended to include the 'others' who are outside of 'our' community. Vetlesen moves on to suggest that empathy is activated from an initially passive, non-participatory standpoint: we *become* activated through the imagination. Accordingly, there is a pre-existent distance between the subject and the addressee – between 'us' and the 'others' – with regard to empathy. It is this non-participatory distance that the imagination temporarily suspends (ibid.: 327).

The critical distance is not, however, restricted to some kind of moral domain of suffering. It can be identified in a number of everyday encounters. For instance, Roslyn Bologh's (1990: 213f.) approach to George Simmel's concept of 'sociability' seems to involve a similar distance. She defines sociability as an encounter whereby one's presence makes a positive difference in relation to others and affects them. The participants influence one another and show an interest without considering one another as a strategic means to an end (ibid.: 14). In accordance with Vetlesen and Nortvedt, Bologh's concept of interest is non-instrumental, denoting the promise to create a positive difference, whereby we acknowledge that we learn from what is between us. What is between us makes a difference for each and every one of us; it brings us together and keeps us apart (ibid.).

However, even though empathy extends beyond the proximate others, it can direct itself only towards selected others, who are then temporarily transformed into psychologically proximate others. As such, empathy-based ethics is not adequate when it comes to granting people equal rights (Vetlesen and Nortvedt 1994: 206). Empathy is surely essential to the deliberation of whether or not rights appear within the participants' horizon of awareness, but a compensatory political ethics is needed in order to justify equal rights. According to Vetlesen (1994), rights must be justified through the guidance of ethical norms and principles, abstracted from the immediate situation. That is to say, the issue of justice must be raised to a level abstracted from practice. However, provided that the compensatory norms and principles entail an abstract distance, it seems pertinent to ask whether or not justification is possible without doing injustice to the 'others'. Or, put differently, can issues concerning the 'good life' possess an aspect of equality and justice?

This question, which was posed at the outset of this chapter, touches upon a crucial matter with regard to the dilemma between equality and difference. Above we saw that a central issue in the debate on multiculturalism is whether recognition of cultural distinctiveness presupposes equality in terms of equal rights. Another way of putting this would be to ask whether matters of practical character concerning the 'good life' are inextricably linked to matters of right and wrong. Blum (1998) is among those who think so, and he criticises Taylor, among others, for ignoring the strong connection between matters of the 'good life', on the one hand, and matters of right and wrong, on the other. MacIntyre (1988) is another proponent for a non-abstract approach to the issue of justice. In his view, universal rationality cannot form the basis for judgement. Rather, we must address the question of justice grounded in a dialogic situation that respects the specific character and history of the traditions and individuals involved (ibid.: 398). These arguments are, to a certain extent, akin to Lyotard's contention that justice excludes totalising principles relating to a 'truth' or a representable order of things (a descriptive) (Lyotard and Thébaud 1985). If we accept that justice presupposes reflective judgement, in which we judge without criteria, then judgement must be grounded in situational practice.

Given that justice must be grounded in situational practice, it seems pertinent to ask whether justice entails a moral and cultural relativism and a corresponding strategy of 'maintenance of spheres' (cf. Introduction). Without going into detail, I want to reject such an allegation. Suffice it to say that Lyotard's concept of justice disavows the logic of identity upon which cultural relativism hinges. Likewise, his concept of justice disavows relativism – in terms of 'anything goes' – with regard to judgement. Reflective judgement does not translate into relativism in the sense that all judgements are equally valid. In so far as cultural relativism and moral relativism arise out of determinative judgement through its insistence upon the plural representability of law, Lyotard's conceptualisation of the non-determinative faculty of judgement rejects the relativistic insistence on equal validity. Proponents of cultural relativism and 'anything goes' do not question justice based on principles or laws per se. Rather, they merely multiply the concept (see Readings 1991: 25), or, as David Wood (2001: 373) puts it, they merely multiply 'the heads on the monster'. But how about seeing justice as a pure and simple individual matter? The condition by which the situational concept of justice avoids individualism is precisely the fact that it calls into question the liberal concept of individuality – and the corresponding concept of privacy – that allows for moral subjectivism. Situational justice requires a critical distance to our criteria of judgement so as to reveal the cultural or symbolic structures that constitute our evaluative standards. As I have suggested above, intersubjectivity is essential in this process.

Conventional and post-conventional norms

To elaborate on the question as to whether practical matters concerning the 'good life' are inextricably linked to matters of right and wrong, I shall now enquire into the relationship between the concept of the 'good life' and the concept of justice. I will draw on the distinction that Vetlesen (1994) makes, informed by Klaus Günther (1988), between conventional and post-conventional levels of norm validity. Whereas post-conventional morality concerns justification, conventional morality concerns the application of norms. Or, put differently, whereas questions concerning the validity and justification of norms call for a principal and context-free clarification, questions concerning the application of norms call for a situation-specific distinction (Vetlesen 1994: 285). In the latter case, the rules or norms that we use in a concrete situation do not transcend the context of the practice in which we participate, and the norm remains real. Within post-conventional ethics, on the other hand, the validity of the norms is clearly separated from actual situations or concrete social relations. Moral norms are seen as universal, theoretical principles, abstracted from contextual boundaries. It is precisely this gap between the real and the ideal, Vetlesen argues, that renders moral judgement possible; it is the awareness of this difference that gives ethics its critical potential (ibid.: 291). In this regard, Vetlesen's perspective is highly influenced by Habermas. They both hold that post-conventional ethics is based on the awareness of the principal difference between the ideal and the real community of communication (*Kommunikationsgemeinschaft*).

Principally, Habermas (1984) makes use of the concept 'post-conventional' to distinguish between liberal and traditional norms, or, to be more precise, to define devices that do not appeal to metaphysical authority. As such, the term 'post-conventional' is associated with the project of Enlightenment, denoting a non-divine universality, a universality of (secular) norms. By comparison, the term 'conventional' denotes the particularity of norms, sometimes associated with cultural autonomy and cultural relativism (cf. Barry 2001). When ethics is concerned, Habermas (1988, 1989, 1990, 1993) contends that only an ideal ethics can ensure a critical distance to moral norms embedded in social practices. In a similar vein, Vetlesen (1994: 291) asserts that the factual social validity of practice-embodied norms is questioned with regard to their rational validity. The aim of post-conventional ethics is to generate a rationally motivated consensus in conventional ethical matters. Habermas (1988) maintains that truth – the attainment of rational consensus – involves two types of norms: those of freedom and those of justice.[5] Proceeding from this, he establishes procedures for attaining rational consensus. What can be demonstrated as absolutely right, he argues, is only the discursive procedure. Consequently, he establishes an internal relationship between law and morality, in line with Kantian ethics. His central thesis is that proceduralised law and moral justification mutually implicate one another (ibid.: 243). Habermas is of the opinion that only theories of morality and justice developed in the Kantian tradition hold out the promise of an impartial process for the justification and assessment of principles (ibid.: 241). In this respect, he assigns to the discursive procedure the status of moral imperative.

Habermas's definition of truth – the attainment of rational consensus – leads Seyla Benhabib (1986: 286) to raise the question as to whether the meaning of truth is to be defined as rational consensus, or whether the attainment of rational consensus is a criterion of truth. This in turn raises the question of whether rational consensus should be understood as procedural, with no regard for the content of the reasons and evidence actually used in argumentations (ibid.). Although in his later works Habermas abandons the deductive relationship between the conditions of argumentation and the norms for communicative ethics, he retains the procedural aspect. He assumes that all participants in argumentation presuppose a certain ethical norm that they cannot deny without being self-contradictory. Benhabib's critical remarks concern this procedural aspect, which also leads back to Kögler's argument against a consensus of truth, in that it points to the absolute ground upon which Habermas's truth criteria are based.

Benhabib's (1986) question also points to another aspect of discourse ethics, namely, its abstract character. This abstract character suggests that ethical questions are completely detached from the concrete situations and issues concerning the 'good life'. That is to say, it suggests that ethical questions pertain exclusively to ethical principles. Three levels of abstraction are involved here: abstraction from given motivations, abstraction from the particular situation and abstraction from an established mode of life. It must be noted, however, that Habermas insists that ethics is in fact linked to practice. But by this he does not mean concrete practice. Rather, discourse ethics appertains to *ideal* practice. Habermas (1990) conceives of ethical principles as intended situations that have not yet come into being, which means that the situations are hypothetical. Accordingly, discourse ethics is not concerned with taking the role of others; instead, it assumes a third-party standpoint – the standpoint of an impartial judge. The individual who has done something wrong to concrete others must realise that he or she has also violated something impersonal or at least suprapersonal, namely, a generalised expectation that both parties hold (ibid.: 48). In this way, Habermas omits the emotional bonds that characterise the conventional level of face-to-face relations.[6]

Solidarity and truth

In the following, I aim to question both conventional and post-conventional ethics with respect to the critical distance needed in moral judgement. I allow Habermas to represent the post-conventional level of norm validity, whereas Gadamer represents the conventional level. By juxtaposing Habermas and Gadamer, I endeavour to elucidate the division between the real and the ideal concerning moral judgement. I take as my starting point their conceptualisations of solidarity, because, as I see it, solidarity is akin to the concept of pity or compassion that was discussed above. As such, it allows us to pinpoint the structure of distance that is involved in both conventional and post-conventional ethics. On that account, the controversy between Habermas and Gadamer might provide us with a better understanding of the distance that is needed in order to deal with questions of justice.

As indicated above, solidarity is often associated with emotions such as sympathy and compassion. For Habermas, however, solidarity is primarily a cognitive matter, based on rational discourse. The emotional aspect of moral performance, which forms the basis for sympathy and hence presupposes proximity, is not dealt with in his discourse ethics. This is probably due to the fact that Habermas does not distinguish between proximity and distance, or the concrete and the abstract, in the manner that we have seen above. Instead, Habermas (1990: 48) conceives of the individual person as a carrier (*Träger*) of the society to which she or he belongs. In this respect, he follows a pattern that closely approaches the subject configuration that pertains to modern ideologies. What we encounter in the concrete person is not only the particular, but also – at the same time – the general or universal.

Habermas (1989: 244) establishes an intimate connection between concern for the welfare of one's fellow humans and interest in the general welfare, asserting that each person must take responsibility for the other. However, in so far as Habermas focuses on the general expectations that all participants allegedly share, solidarity becomes an experience based on the assumption that – qua consociates – all human beings must have an interest in the integrity of their shared life context in the same way (ibid.). The interaction that generates solidarity is thus participatory from the outset. In other words, Habermas's concept of solidarity does not correspond to emotions such as compassion and sympathy, which presuppose that one's fellow humans are initially distant – before imagination temporarily suspends the physical and/or psychological distance between the subject and her or his addressee(s). As Vetlesen (1994: 327) notes, precisely because Habermas does *not* regard the experience of solidarity as extending beyond the established community, towards the distant and foreign 'others', his concept of solidarity serves to consolidate conformably the community. Whereas Habermas's concept of solidarity takes a pre-established *intra*-communal 'we' as its focus, Vetlesen understands solidarity to mean *inter*-communality, that is, a matter of producing an encompassing 'we' where there first existed a 'we' and a 'they' (ibid.: 328).

Gadamer's concept of solidarity is essentially different from that of Habermas's, and yet there seems to be an almost one-to-one correspondence between them when it comes to the assumption of an initial participation. To Gadamer (1975), solidarity denotes an original community – a prior solidarity between people that cannot be traced back to a contractual relationship. Contrary to Habermas, however, Gadamer does not ground his concept of solidarity on rational discourse. Rather, he suggests that rational discourse actually presupposes (a pre-established) solidarity. For Gadamer, solidarity is a precondition for understanding. Anyone who enters into a dialogue has already admitted that she or he considers the conditions of it as given, since we cannot go behind this consensual community and ask how the agreement was established and what sustains it over time (see Vetlesen 1988). Habermas, on the other hand, wants to establish this kind of common conversational foundation on a purely procedural basis, through rational discourse. As Vetlesen (ibid.: 33) notes, Habermas wants to subject the 'given' conditions of conversation to a kind of critical reflection which he claims Gadamer's hermeneutics evades. However, given the fact that Habermas assumes a preceding agreement, the manner in which he legitimises critical reflection closely approaches Gadamer's concept of solidarity. The decisive difference seems to be that Gadamer anchors the conversation's foundation in a (real) original community, while Habermas's concept is a formal (ideal) one, directed at the reflective transcendence of the pre-established agreement. Thus, whereas Habermas promotes a pretension for the universality of critical reflection, Gadamer defies the same possibility. Vetlesen (ibid.: 36) holds that Habermas pretends to be ideal by justifying the conditions of possibility, while Gadamer points out the impossibility of such an attempt. The problem with Gadamer's position is not that he assumes a prior solidarity, however. It is more that he seems to assume that, in addition to being the condition of possibility for understanding, solidarity is the condition for interpretation. As I have suggested above, it is the (con)fusion of understanding and interpretation that leads Gadamer towards a collapse of the critical distance to our evaluative standards.

Against this backdrop, it becomes clear that Gadamer's notion of a pre-established solidarity serves to reaffirm the totalitarianism of truth that was addressed above. The same seems to be true of Habermas. We have seen that his critical, evaluative distance, in its pure cognitivistic nature, is totally detached from the conventional level of norm validity. We may therefore infer that he ignores the real conditions of moral reflection, and this disavowal seems to prevent him from posing (relevant) questions of justice concerning the 'good life'. At the same time, Habermas's notion of an abstract distance is inextricably linked to a community's rational consensus – an agreement on certain norms – which amounts to a totalitarianism of truth. Above, we saw that Kögler criticises both Gadamer and Habermas for their 'unbroken attitude toward truth'. Kögler (1999: 161) summarises: 'My critique of Gadamer's (and Habermas's) truth-oriented model of understanding contends that, in situations involving incommensurable interpretive and evaluative premises, this model's "will to judgement" must always privilege the prejudgements of the interpreter.'

The question of whether a critical distance to our own criteria of judgement presupposes a universal rationality, or whether it is possible to establish a critical distance at a conventional level, is thereby largely interrogated, but not entirely. Thus far, I have suggested that a critical distance cannot be achieved by detaching moral issues totally from situational practices, that is, from the conventional level (Habermas), or by *not* distancing issues of justice from this level's pre-established consensus (Gadamer). In the next section, I will move on to suggest that a critical distance to our evaluative standards might be based on the structure that is characteristic of the feeling of sympathy, ensured by the power of imagination.

Critical distance

Informed by Nathan L. Tierney's (1994) book, *Imagination and Ethical Ideals*, I have argued elsewhere that a critical distance might be established at a conventional level (Gressgård 1997). In what follows, I shall outline the principal thread of my argument, which I start off by inquiring into the faculty of imagination. By virtue of being a cognitive, intellectual activity, imagination is associated with a critical distance. At the same time, however, it is associated with proximity by virtue of being based on experience, perception and emotions. According to Tierney (1994: 44), imagination is different from both conceptualisation (abstract thinking through general concepts) and mental imaging. It is also different from creativity or innovation.

As Tierney (1994: 45) sees it, the concept of imagination is related to Wittgenstein's concept of 'seeing-as'. 'Seeing-as' refers to a process by which we alter our perception and perspectives so as to have varying experiences of a single object. Proceeding from the idea that noticing an aspect is a matter of seeing a likeness, Wittgenstein develops the argument that 'seeing-as' is a special work of the imagination. For example, we may see a photograph as a representation of something; we may read a set of lines as a poem, and so on. For the purpose of our discussion, 'seeing-as' could mean seeing a person as one who is (or is not) worthy of respect (ibid.: 48). In a similar manner, Butler (2009) points to the aesthetic aspect of norms when, for example, the war in Afghanistan is 'seen as' defending women. And perhaps more interestingly, she seems to invoke a concept of 'seeing-as' when problematising gender perception whereby an ostensible reality is coupled with what is taken to be mere artifice, play, falsehood and illusion: 'If one thinks that one sees a man dressed as a woman or a woman dressed as a man, then one takes the first term of each of those perceptions as the "reality" of gender: the gender that is introduced through the simile lacks "reality", and is taken to constitute an illusory appearance' (Butler 1999: xxii). In this sense, 'seeing-as' serves to denaturalise the categories through which one sees. Tierney (1994) seems to conceive of this activity not as a matter of concluding but as a matter of analogising. He treats 'seeing-as' as a peculiar experience between perception and conceptual thought, with some examples being closer to one or the other (ibid.: 45). What distinguishes 'seeing-as' from perception is the presence of a certain element of control that seems to be lacking in ordinary perception. However, this element of control is not of the kind that we have over what we think, as distinguished from that over what we perceive. 'Seeing-as' remains pre-inferential, because it precedes what can be determined (ibid.: 46).

As Tierney (1994: 46–47) makes clear, the idea of controlled perception is an elusive one, since our traditional categories of experience normally lead us to treat control as something we exercise after perception is 'given'. There is a tendency to force cases of 'seeing-as' into the categories of either mistaken belief, or of make-believe and fantasy, that is, as perceptional error. What is imagined tends to be contrasted with what is true, and as a consequence of our habit of treating perception as passive (in accordance with the German term *Perzeption*), the analysis of mistaken belief could easily lead to the Cartesian conclusion that error is a misuse of judgement. However, as Tierney (ibid.: 47) also makes clear, perceptional error normally entails a belief, whereas 'seeing-as' does not. For example, we may see a tree as a person without a corresponding belief commitment. It is exactly the element of control at the level of perception that distinguishes 'seeing-as' from mistaken perception. It is the element of control that gives 'seeing-as' the genuine character of imagination.

Against this backdrop, Tierney (1994) maintains that 'seeing-as' is not simply a matter of the will exceeding the understanding – of differentiating the real from the unreal. Rather, it is a matter of distinguishing between the literal and the metaphorical (ibid.: 49). In a similar manner, Roger Scruton (1979) draws a distinction between literal perception and imagination. In the case of literal perception, where seeing is normally tantamount to believing, and where knowledge is the fundamental aim, we do not notice this 'choice'. Scruton maintains that what I see is inextricably entwined with what I believe, and that I have no control over my beliefs. If I can see the tree 'as' a face, while still believing it to be a tree, he moves on to suggest, I have stepped outside the realm of literal perception into that of the imagination (ibid.: 87).

If we now return to Tierney's account, we realise that seeing something *as* something is a more productive activity than simply seeing similarities. It is just as much a matter of seeing differences. In this respect, imagination denotes a critical activity – the activity of 'seeing' something as something distinct. Tierney (1994) remarks that the notion of seeing is wider than that of visualising. (It should be noted in this context that, contrary to *Perzeption*, the German term *Wahrnehmung* involves activity – active perception.) To see – in a broad sense – is to make certain kinds of interpretive distinctions in an object or in one's word (ibid.: 49). The power of imagination, understood as 'seeing-as', is hence a cognitive capacity, but it is nothing like rationalist reasoning in the Habermasian sense. The concept of 'seeing-as' does not fit into the post-conventional concept of rationality, but nevertheless it involves an abstraction. Arguing with T. E. Wilkerson (1973) and E. H. Gombrich (1969), Tierney (1994: 52f.) asserts that 'seeing-as' involves abstraction in the sense that we mentally construct a background (matrix) for our perception and interpretation. As indicated above, however, the process of abstraction is not detached from perception, from our situational positions. The concrete practices at the conventional level and the cognitive aspect of 'seeing-as' do not, therefore, correspond to the concept of ideal practice and the universal element pertaining to post-conventional theories. On the contrary, recalling Butler's account, 'seeing-as' could serve to subvert universalised or naturalised identity categories.

With this in mind, we could argue that a critical distance does not have to be legitimised – by abstract principles – on a post-conventional level of norm validity. The critical distance might as well be attained – through the imagination – on a conventional level. In other words, issues concerning right and wrong do not have to be treated on the basis of universal standards of judgement (Habermas). But neither do we need a pre-established consensus in order to treat issues of justice (Gadamer). The point that I have made in this section is that the power of imagination, notwithstanding its embeddedness in concrete situations, possesses an element of control, and it is this element of control that enables us to establish a distance to our evaluative standards. So, in line with Kögler's perspective, we may conclude that while understanding entails seeing similarities, evaluation/judgement, by virtue of being a critical activity, involves seeing differences (without any pre-established standards restraining the process). In this respect, the critical activity of evaluation is consonant with the ancient Greek term *krisis*, identified with the art of making distinctions, which is essential to judging (see Brown 2005: 5). Needless to say, critical distance is the condition for self-reflection and an open and reflective dialogue – a dialogue that does not proceed from a predetermined justice. As pointed out above, it is through dialogic openness towards the 'others' that our evaluative standards can be critically scrutinised.

Suppression of heterogeneity

In order to elaborate on the conditions for dialogic openness, I will now return to the concept of domination. Above, we saw that domination entails a substantive suppression of difference. One of my critical remarks suggested that domination is an impediment to multicultural dialogue. In *Foucault and Social Dialogue*, upon which I will base my argument in the remainder of this book, Christopher Falzon (1998) addresses this issue by investigating the problem of domination with respect to dialogue. I will draw on Falzon's argument to substantiate both Kögler's critical perspective and the subsequent discussion on ethics, while at the same time incorporating the most central insights from Lyotard's philosophy of displacement and my critical discussion of the dilemma between equality and distinctiveness. As I see it, Falzon's book supplements the above discussion, while at the same time linking the most important currents to yield a conclusion. Given the extensive interrogation of the conditions for dialogue throughout this book, the main issue that remains to be addressed is how resistance to totalitarianism might be organised. Before proceeding to this topic, I will first expand on how domination implies the suppression of difference or heterogeneity.

The suppression of heterogeneity seems to be a characteristic feature of societies in which integration implies planned pluralism and dialogue in accordance with pre-established evaluative standards. If we are to enter into an open and critical dialogue with another party, rather than defining heterogeneity in negation to a given identity, we have to conceive of it as a productive force. This is what Falzon (1998) emphasises by stating that the 'other' is truly other by virtue of being something genuinely new, unexpected, unpredictable – something that comes from 'outside'. In line with Kögler's argument, Falzon contends that the 'other' has independence from us and resists our efforts to impose ourselves upon it. It might even, in turn, influence, affect and transform us (ibid.: 33). Compared with Kögler, however, Falzon seems to go one step further in his account of otherness. In accordance with Lyotard, Derrida and Deleuze, Falzon articulates the experience of the new and the foreign in terms of a shock, an encounter with something that escapes our classificatory categories, something that is beyond the horizon of our experience. Like

Lyotard and Lash, he concedes that the shocking experience might nurture a foundationalist or totalitarian world view based on a nostalgic longing for metaphysical absolutes. However, this is only one way of reacting. The striving for infinity – in terms of an original or absolute whole – does not prevent heterogeneity from lying sub-surface like a volcano, as remarked on by Lyotard with respect to the sublime. The experience of a shock is likely to reveal the lack in our cognitive powers and to demonstrate the futility of our belief in absolute knowledge. It has the potential of making us realise that understanding and ground are not final or definitive; rather, they are contingent.

Falzon's perspective bears a strong resemblance to Kögler's (and Foucault's) assertion that domination occurs at the expense of a basic freedom. Likewise, it resonates with Lyotard's insistence on the fact that totalising processes of 'forgetting' take place on the basis of an underlying heterogeneity. By depicting the encounter with the 'other' as an open-ended dialogue, which can be brought to an end by silencing the 'other', Falzon clearly alludes to a prior heterogeneity. The dialogue is occluded when the radical difference and the basic freedom that serve as the condition of possibility for the social order are suppressed or ignored (as we have seen Gadamer and Habermas do on a conceptual level, which attains concrete social and political form in modern politics). In Falzon's (1998: 41) view, the silencing of the 'other' takes place to the extent that thinking – or human activity in general – overcomes the 'other' and falls into a solipsistic self-enclosure and sterile repetition (see also Adorno and Horkheimer [1944] 1997; Laclau and Mouffe 1985). In such a case, we are imprisoned and limited by our own ruling categories. In so far as thinking always involves imposing our categories on the 'other', for the purpose of creating order and meaning, such self-enclosure is of course a constant possibility. But the silencing of the 'other' is still a derivative, a secondary state. As has been pointed out earlier, the silencing of the 'others' presupposes the dialogic interplay that it arrests. In line with Lyotard and others, Falzon (1998: 41) maintains that self-enclosure – immanence – and the sterile repetition that characterises a totalitarian world view constitute a forgetting of the encounters with the 'other'. It is a forgetting of the dialogic interplay out of which ruling categories have emerged. This strongly suggests that the process of forgetting is always temporary.

As pointed out in Chapter 4, the concept of dialogue that is implied in a philosophy of difference contrasts radically with so-called historical, dialectical dialogue. Within a dialectical logic, dialogue is ostensibly open to otherness; however, because of its metaphysical grounding and its oppositional logic, it inevitably assimilates the 'others'. As has been illustrated above, grand narratives, like Hegelian dialectics, operate according to an oppositional logic whereby otherness is resolved into a negative and derivative mirror image. The interplay between the self and the 'other' is reduced to purity-impurity dynamics. Along these lines, in his book *Power/Knowledge*, Foucault (1980: 114–115) designates dialectic thinking as a way of avoiding the open and always hazardous reality of conflict by reducing it to a Hegelian skeleton (cf. the scandal of dialectics in Chapter 4). However, the problem is not the production of social or cultural forms as such, since this goes on constantly – and must go on in order for us to make the world intelligible. Rather, the problem is the absolutisation of particular forms and the consequent suppression of the otherness, transgression and innovation through which new forms arise (Foucault 1980: 49). In other words, the problem is not power but domination – the process whereby otherness is entirely overcome, mobile dialogue is arrested, and reversal and transformation are precluded. According to Falzon, it is in the context of establishing states of domination that metaphysical thinking ultimately finds its place (ibid.). Totalising metaphysical thought, in which we entirely subordinate the 'other' to our organising principles, takes a concrete social and political form, he notes, in those states of domination in which corporeal forces are brought into complete conformity (ibid.: 50).

Following Foucault, Falzon (1998: 50) associates domination with normalising power in terms of control and regulation based on categorisation and classification of human behaviour. Techniques of regulation contribute to normative categorisation in conformity with prevailing standards of evaluation. A main tactic for imposing and maintaining domination is to present the normative categories as universal, necessary and obligatory. Falzon (ibid.) remarks that the modern philosophical effort to impose a new order upon the world, grounded in an understanding of the human being as a metaphysical subject, is taken up in the demand of enlightenment for rational social governance – a disciplinary reorganisation of our social practices in accordance with norms that are founded on reason and human nature. Grounded on ultimate foundations, the aim is to create good citizens, as is the case in modern ideologies, including social-democratic policies of today. Through rational argumentation, differences are depicted as deviances that call for rehabilitation, and, as illustrated in the Introduction of this volume, these kinds of mechanisms are central aspects of liberal-democratic state policies.

Openness towards the forgotten

Notwithstanding the totalitarian dimension of social orders and state policies, the commission of a relatively constant injustice towards the 'others' is, as I have pointed out above, always a derivative, secondary state. Even though categorisation entails forgetting and disregarding radical difference, not even the most dominant forms of categorisation can, according to Falzon (1998: 52), suppress dialogue completely; no social ordering can be absolute or eternal. Exclusion of heterogeneity is a necessary condition for social ordering and identity formation, and yet it is not ultimately extinguished. The prior heterogeneity is a constant destabilising, dynamic force in relation to social forms. Both Falzon and Kögler are of the opinion that the process of dialogue continually challenges and transforms these forms. It is important to note, however, that the human capacity for transgression of social norms is not conceptualised by Falzon in terms of liberation. Rather, in accordance with Foucault's perspective, Falzon takes the human capacity for transgression of social norms to be a non-normative freedom. Freedom is not an ideal or an end-goal to be achieved by rising above historical circumstances and by establishing an ideal form of life (as in the modern ideologies). Indeed, freedom is already present within history (ibid.: 53). In line with Lyotard's delineation of the displacement between modernism and postmodernism, Falzon maintains that 'if the human material upon which power is exercised were not irreducibly resistant and capable of questioning the social order, history itself would be unthinkable. We might even say, perhaps perversely, that resistance or revolt is the transcendental condition of history, for it is that without which history cannot exist. Revolt is that which makes history as dialogue, dialogical change and transformation possible' (ibid.: 54).

Furthermore, Falzon (1998: 54) notes that resistance 'does not ground anything or establish limits of any sort. It is fundamental, but it does not found anything'. Similar to Lyotard's philosophy of displacement, resistance is depicted as a disturbance of existing forms of thought, which serves to open up the possibility of their transformation (ibid.: 55). Falzon goes on to suggest that resistance is an expression of other voices that have been buried under – and forgotten by – historically and dialogically emergent forms of domination, that is, totalising processes. On that account, resistance does not stand in need of any normative justification (ibid.: 88f.). But how can we know for sure that we are being genuinely open to 'others' and receptive to dialogue? The answer follows from the above argument: we cannot avoid being involved in dialogue. As Falzon notes, we continually encounter 'others', influence them, exert power over them – and at the same time we are influenced by them (ibid.: 89). We will continually be exposed to new challenges, shocks and surprises that destabilise and transform the social order. The true 'other' is that which we cannot assimilate because it escapes our control and illuminates the limits of our (will to) power. So to the extent that we find our prevailing categories being challenged and called into question, we are also in a position to be open to dialogue (ibid.: 90). And according to Falzon, this is not an epistemological challenge but a moral one (ibid.).

Up to this point, I have been arguing with Falzon, and his last statement appears to coincide with the connection I have made between relativism, in terms of incommensurability, and ethics pertaining to the question of justice. I have underlined the social ontology of the subject that concerns our capacity to be affected by and to take the role of one another, and I have engaged in a discussion about discourse ethics. On the basis of my above arguments, therefore, we might regard the shock – the experience of something evading representation – as an *ethical* demand to find new idioms. However, I have also emphasised the gap between 'is' and 'ought', which deters the possibility of concluding from the moral or ethical sphere to the sphere of truth and knowledge. As I argued in Chapter 4, we may indeed establish an analogy between the two domains with respect to judgement, which might prove fruitful. But that does not mean that the challenge of establishing multicultural dialogue is principally a matter of ethics.

Contrary to Falzon, and perhaps also at odds with Lyotard (to the degree that he advocates an ethics of otherness), I take the condition for dialogue to be an issue of knowledge, concerning representability and intelligibility. What I have described as the experience of lack in our cognitive powers, as in the case of the sublime, signifies a thought-provoking heterogeneity. The experience of the sublime is thought-provoking by virtue of being both obstructive and productive for our thinking and doing.[7] The discovery of the lack in our cognitive powers is experienced as a demand – with the aid of the imagination – to *understand* the 'others' before passing judgement. As such, understanding entails a postponement of judgement, a delay that is long enough to allow us to be affected by the 'others' and to reflect critically upon our otherwise uncontested evaluative standards of thought and action. Clearly, understanding is a matter of knowledge, but it does not imply a disinterested stance, as in post-conventional cognitive knowledge. Far from evoking omniscience (*theorein*) and the ideal of Enlightenment, it appertains to practice and intersubjectivity – thought *as* action. And yet there is a critical distance involved, due to the power of imagination. I have defined the imagination as a critical activity that accentuates differences without reducing them to negations of our identity. Through dialogue with 'others', I have argued, we can sense the possibility of new formations of meaning with the aid of the imagination. In accordance with Lyotard's philosophy, I take the new forms of meaning to be the effect of the dialogic displacement of the old ones. The most important element in this argument is not that dialogic displacement produces new – or alternative – forms of knowledge, since the production of knowledge inevitably involves determinative judgement. Rather, the decisive point is that the displacement renders us open to that which escapes determination, that which escapes our intelligibility. It must be noted, however, that the challenge of representation has – as my discussion has suggested – vast ethical consequences in regard to justice.[8]

Keeping this in mind, we may now return to Falzon's argument on the importance of openness towards otherness. In his treatment of dialogue, Falzon (1998: 90) draws, as does Kögler, a distinction between openness and pseudo-openness towards 'others'. Pseudo-openness entails a continuous domination of the 'others' by way of consumption; it implies a totalitarianism of truth in which we do not allow ourselves to be challenged, surprised or shocked by the new and unexpected. As Falzon (ibid.) notes, the encounter with the 'other' is already constrained so that the starting point can remain unchanged. The otherness of the 'others' is reduced to a consolidating impetus in oppositional purity-impurity dynamics or dialectics. That which is other is subordinated to the Absolute Subject (ibid.).

However, the opposite approach, which opposes ethnocentric universalism and historical totalitarianism in favour of cultural autonomy, is equally problematic with respect to multicultural dialogue. As long as one recognises cultural distinctiveness on the basis of a presumed essential nature of the 'others', arguing for protective collective rights for the sake of cultural preservation, the problem of domination is perpetuated. Radical cultural relativism clearly sacrifices dialogue in favour of identity politics and the consolidation of separate spheres. Falzon (1998: 93) maintains that the all-encompassing whole comprises a plurality of local unities, wholly governed by their own all-embracing form of thought and action, unable to communicate with one another. In the Introduction, we saw that cultural relativism denies the possibility of a common communicative universe. Moreover, in Chapter 4 we saw that cultural relativism implies determinative judgement through its insistence on the plural representability of law, which means that determinative judgement and dominant evaluative standards are not called into question. On the contrary, determinative judgement is multiplied. So instead of invoking universalised, ethnocentric norms, cultural relativism presupposes multiple communicative spheres defined by corresponding sets of norms, each and everyone characterised by determinative judgement and a holistic structure.

Neither ethnocentric universalism nor cultural relativism allows for an open and critical dialogue. Neither perspective conceives of social and cultural groups as dialogically constituted. In response to this, Falzon (1998: 93) emphasises that different social groups can and do influence one another. As already noted, we cannot escape the dialogical interactions in which we are affected and influenced by others. Neither individuals nor groups can have an essential nature or a universal identity. In line with my argument in the preceding chapters, Falzon (ibid.: 94) states that '[i]mposing categories upon the other is part of the process by which the other's meaning and nature are constituted, by which it comes historically to be what it is'. In this process, both the 'others' and 'we' are constituted, since any formation of identity, any determination, arises within and in relation to existing symbolic orders. In a dialogical situation, however – and this is a decisive point – the imposition of categories upon the 'others' is not a 'final understanding' of them. It is only the 'beginning of an open-ended process' (ibid.).

How to organise dialogic resistance

From the point of view of Falzon (1998: 96), resistance against totalitarianism necessitates a defiance of absolute, all-embracing forms of order. And in accordance with Lyotard, we may conceive of resistance as a strategy of displacement. Resistance involves the destabilisation of established norms and notions, including notions of 'us' and the 'others'. Yet as long as resistance resides in language as a non-identifiable remainder that destabilises the prevailing order from within, there is no privileged site from which to organise resistance. So how can we possibly organise resistance? If we proceed from Kögler's critical perspective, resistance against domination is a matter of comprehending the agents' self-understanding, their formation of identity and conceptualisations of the 'good life'. Correspondingly, resistance is also a matter of understanding people's suffering – suffering that is brought about by structures of domination. Thus, from the point of view of Kögler, the organisation of struggle against structures of domination both proceeds from and results in a firm cultural identity. As already mentioned, Kögler (1999: 243) posits that the central task for the individuals or social groups in question is to define and to unfold their identity – in a symbolic as well as a material sense. In comparison, Falzon takes the argument one step further in the direction of Lyotard and other philosophers of difference. In his conception of the encounter with the 'others', Falzon emphasises the shock, the unidentifiable aspect of the 'others' – the otherness of the 'others' – in line with Lyotard's conceptualisation of the sublime experience. Falzon seems to be concerned with non-identity, while Kögler's notion of resistance bears upon identity.

Falzon's focus on non-identity is consistent with the way in which he conjoins resistance and non-normative freedom. As noted above, Falzon (1998) holds that resistance does not establish limits of any sort. However, despite his assertion that freedom does not have any normative connotations and that resistance does not need to be justified, and despite the fact that he speaks of resistance in terms of openness towards the new and unexpected, which bears strong resemblance to Lyotard's call for attentiveness to the unarticulated/unspoken, Falzon, too, ends up arguing in favour of identity formation. In his view, we need 'to make it possible for otherness to reassert itself in forms of resistance and transgression', in the 'production of new forms of life and the revitalisation of culture' (ibid.: 96). Eventually, Falzon ends up advocating an organisation of resistance that brings together 'disparate energies into a concerted, organised whole' (ibid.). This constitutes a form of 'strategic essentialism', as defined by Spivak (1987: 205), involving a strategic use of essentialism in a scrupulously visible political interest (cf. Spivak 1993). By virtue of forming contingent alliances, strategic essentialists distinguish themselves from traditional groups or movements based on a metaphysical view of liberation and a universal human identity. Contingent alliances bear upon contingent foundations, as opposed to ultimate foundations (see Butler 1992; Laclau 1996). In this respect, strategic essentialism defies the possibility of grand narratives, such as a utopian form of life grounded in an inclusive humanity. According to Falzon (1998: 96), it is exactly these kinds of totalitarian ideas that resistance targets. Likewise, resistance targets fragmented and local struggles induced by the notion of essential group identities pertaining to cultural relativism. And it targets the liberal concept of the sovereign, self-sufficient autonomous subject.

However, in their (strategic) suppression of difference and dialogue, contingent alliances of resistance continually run the risk of accommodating to the notions and structures that they challenge. Unification and organisation, no matter how strategic they may be, entail identity formation, be it temporary or not. Falzon (1998) is, of course, aware of this danger, but he nevertheless seems to think that a temporary suppression of difference is necessary in order to establish a united, powerful front against domination. 'A group needs to put aside internal differences', he asserts, 'in order to be able to fight in a concerted and effective way and to bring about social change' (ibid.: 96). Against this backdrop, we may ask whether strategic essentialism is an acceptable solution with regard to the argument in this book. Is it possible to advocate political mobilisation as a means for social change in conjunction with attentiveness to otherness? Or is this an insoluble antinomy? This question alludes to the dilemma addressed in Chapter 4, pertaining to the gap between identity and non-identity. There I posed the question as to whether we are able to displace something/someone without giving it/him/her an identity. Drawing on Lyotard, I responded by pointing out that both 'we' and the 'others', in an empirical sense, have an identity, which is subsequently displaced, whereupon we discover that both 'our' identity and the identity of the 'others' arise from a process of forgetting/silencing.

In her article 'Can the Subaltern Speak?', Spivak (1988) addresses the problem of silencing by emphasising the role of colonialism in the production of the (post-)colonial subject. Her point is that the subaltern woman cannot speak, not because she does not have a voice, but because she is excluded from the channels of social mobility and the dialogic level of utterance that enable her to represent herself and be heard. (In this respect, the question 'can the subaltern speak?' alludes to the question of whether the 'others' can be recognised on their own terms and are entitled to discuss the very terms of recognition.) Spivak highlights the impossibility of representation and the danger of appropriating the 'other' by assimilation when speaking for subaltern groups. As long as speaking is a transaction between speaker and listener, the solution is not to give the subaltern woman a voice, but to allow her to speak for herself. However, the dilemma of representation does not prevent Spivak from using the power of language to articulate the experiences of subaltern women in her academic work. She alternates between deconstruction of dominant narratives of social change and political representation, on the one hand, and the demand to articulate the lives and histories of subaltern groups in order to give them a voice, on the other, a key aspect being strategic essentialism. By signalling the impossibility of universalisation while at the same time enabling a unifying strategy, strategic essentialism entails what Habermas (1987) takes to be a performative contradiction in the sense that there is a discrepancy between performance and proposition: we make use of essentialism to criticise essentialism, or we use language to question the operation of language.

Strategic essentialism could be seen as, alternately, a catachresis, an oxymoron or a deadlock. It might not prove to be an optimal strategy when it comes to addressing silenced otherness, as the danger of ignoring 'the differend', rather than bearing witness to it, is likely to occur. However, it is perhaps a feasible solution in a social world in which the systems of classification are an irrevocable empirical fact. A philosophical deconstruction of identity, including the concepts of inclusive humanity and group distinctiveness, will be to no avail as long as the identity markers continue to exist as signs of deviance from a given, universalised norm. A short-term strategy to affirm a political identity might turn out to be useful where resistance is concerned, in so far as it aims to expose the conventional character of the allegedly post-conventional norm – what Butler (1997: 91) calls 'the promising ambivalence of the norm'. Such a strategy allows for unconventional reuse – or misuse – of the universalised norm; it allows for a productive exploitation of the master's tools. This repetition of the norm does not consolidate an original term but instead displaces both the term itself and the framework within which it acquires its 'original' meaning. In this sense, performative contradiction is hardly a self-defeating enterprise; it can, in fact, function as a political self-displacing action of identity in an open-ended democratisation process (which suspends the need for final judgement) (see also Butler 2000).

Akin to the dialogic perspective outlined above, Butler advocates a strategy of 'cultural translation', a term that she borrows from Bhabha (1994). 'Cultural translation is … a process of yielding our most fundamental categories, that is, seeing how and why they break up, require resignification when they encounter the limits of an available episteme.… It is crucial to recognize that the notion of the human will only be built over time in and by the process of cultural translation, where it is not a translation between two languages that stay enclosed, distinct, unified. But rather *translation will compel each language to change in order to apprehend the other*' (Butler 2004a: 38). With reference to Spivak, Butler (2000) makes clear that translation always runs the risk of appropriation, and yet '[t]he First World intellectual cannot refrain from "representing" the subaltern' (ibid.: 36). This latter statement resembles, in a certain sense, the demand to search for new idioms in order to speak for the 'differend'. For Butler, cultural translation entails bringing into relief the non-convergence of discourses, which could be perceived as a testimony to the unspeakable. At the same time, cultural translation provides the unspeakable with an opportunity to speak for themselves by reusing or misusing the dominant terms, thereby displacing – through a performative contradiction – the dominant terms. In this sense, the displacements seem to go both ways, and that constitutes perhaps the dialogic dimension of cultural translation.

In order to avoid appropriation into the dominant discursive framework, it is of vital importance that the frame of intelligibility is challenged, although not from a standpoint external to the frame but from its own borders (see Butler 1997: 90). A post-conventional stance is then repudiated in favour of *un*conventional formulations of universality, rendering the universal claims more open to reformulation (Butler 2000: 40–41). It is important to note, however, that norms do not exist – with a given meaning – on a post-conventional, abstract level at the outset, before they are (un)conventionally applied and attributed (new) meaning. As our discussion has suggested, norms are always conventional in the sense that they emerge from a specific cultural location within which they acquire their meaning, although they might be universalised and taken to be post-conventional. Accordingly, the potential for critique and changes does not reside in an abstract distance that detaches us completely from practical life. A critical distance is established on a conventional level when the act of interpretation constitutes a reflective interruption of our ordinary understanding – our prevailing representations. Interpretation is parasitic on understanding, just as 'seeing-as' is parasitic on ordinary perception, the crucial element being the imagination. As we have seen, the imagination is our faculty of presentation, which allows us to posit new figures of the thinkable and to judge differently – in *praxis* (see Zerilli 2005).

If we now take into consideration this move from the impossibility of representing, signalling a subversive moment of radical difference, to the positive organisation of resistance through new representations, it is evident that the framework of multiculturalism is displaced accordingly. Claims to equality are not based on the idea of a unified subject and the Western ideal of equal dignity, but instead involve a 'new' universality by way of cultural translation. So what happens to the concept of cultural difference? Do we still need it? Evidently, neither Butler (2000) nor Spivak (1999) is concerned with recognition of cultural distinctiveness, which would, in their view, amount to a preservation of marginality. Rather, the subaltern needs to reach the dialogic level of utterance and claim enfranchisement, which belongs to the nature of equality (see Butler and Spivak 2007: 65). As already mentioned, however, equality presupposes difference, and cultural translation entails a dialogic relation that prevents differences from being assimilated. But do we still need a concept of *radical* difference?[9]

At this juncture, it is perhaps pertinent to reiterate an earlier point, outlined in Chapter 4, pertaining to the dynamic interplay between ontological and ontic difference. There we saw that primary, ontological heterogeneity is the condition of possibility for ontic differences in terms of social classifications. Through a process of exclusion, the ordering process constantly produces a heterogeneous outside – an irreducible residue that calls into question and displaces our ontic categories. Because we cannot avoid using unifying categories in order to make meaning, there will always be a process of forgetting, but there will also always be displacement. Societies cannot do without organising principles, regulating structures and identities, but these principles, regulations and identities are never fixed. The dynamics between the ontological and the ontic constitutes an endless play. Arguably, Lyotard does not deny that the quest for foundations is necessary; he only suggests that this quest is infinitely inconclusive and complex. We are in need of foundations to ground the social, but as the above discussion has suggested, these grounds are always contingent. Society will always be in search of a foundational ground, but the moment of ground and the moment of the actualisation of this ground, Oliver Marchart (2007: 8) argues, will never meet because of the unbridgeable chasm of the difference between these terms. Clearly, the radical gap between the ontological and the ontic constitutes the radical impossibility of ultimate grounds, and yet this gap also constitutes the possibility of grounds as present – their empirical 'existence' as ontic beings (ibid.: 15). The search for a foundational ground is thus both an indispensable and an impossible enterprise; it is a paradoxical enterprise (ibid.: 9, 175).

The conclusion I want to draw from this, in line with Marchart, is that the absence of an absolute, firm ground of society makes it necessary to institute contingent grounds. Order is necessary for meaning to arise, but it is not necessary that one particular social order should become dominant. Nor is it necessary that the process of ordering – the process of forgetting – should make us forget that the forgotten exists. Here it should become clear that we cannot view society as an 'objective' unity in terms of a 'complex whole' (Badiou 2005: 42; see also Lyotard 1984: 11ff.; 1988: §5), because no matter how complex that unity or whole may be, it alludes to an enveloping or encompassing totality by which particularities can be contained. Moreover, viewing society as a complex whole – an intelligible totality – invokes a notion of exhaustive knowledge pertaining to modelling and planning, which disavows the possibility of radical difference and incommensurability (see e.g. Adorno and Horkheimer [1944] 1997; Laclau and Mouffe 1985; Wood 2001: 373f.). I do not mean by this that all attempts to gain knowledge by way of mapping differences and politically planning for pluralism are in vain, but such efforts constantly run the risk of assimilating the unspeakable into existing norms of dominance by way of managing and regulating difference, often in the name of tolerance (see Brown 2006).

I want to end my argument with a passage from Falzon (1998: 98), just to remind us of the importance of not forgetting the forgotten within the discursive framework on which the discussion of equality and distinctiveness, including my own contribution, hinges: 'What resistance can usefully demand from dominant forms of cultural organisation in order to assist this struggle is not tolerance of one's difference, but rather that the dominant cultural forms be aware of their finitude and historicity, that they recognise that theirs is not the only way of proceeding, and thus that they be receptive to the possibility that there might be different ways of thinking and acting.'

Notes

Preface

1. The concept of 'path dependency' is, according to Favell (2001: 27), developed in organisational economics to describe apparently 'sub-optimal' behaviour by the market in its 'choice' of successful products competing against each other. However, the way in which Favell uses the term 'path dependency' (i.e. in the context of public policy) is not sustained by the power of historical legacies or traditions. To him, path dependency is not merely a question of habit or an irrational reproduction of inherited conventions; rather, it is a symptom of the contemporary political forces that are invested in the current status quo and the need to reaffirm continually the current framework.

2. In this context, the word 'values' denotes something that one holds to be worthy of aspiration and preservation in oneself, in addition to constituting a foundation for ethical judgement.

Introduction

1. In the debate on multiculturalism, ethnic groups and cultures are often equated. Members of an ethnic group are assumed to have common forms of cultural expression, life forms (habits, customs and concepts) as well as cultural products. (Culture also involves history, tradition and common fate.) However, the conflation of ethnic groups and cultures is questionable for several reasons. First of all, anthropologists have pointed out that ethnic identity is principally a trait of social organisation, rather than being an aspect of culture (see e.g. Barth 1969). The decisive element for the constitution of ethnic groups is delimitation and recruiting processes on the basis of cultural differences. Secondly, the equation of ethnicity and culture tends to obscure the internal differentiation within ethnic groups and cultural similarities across these groups (see e.g. Yuval-Davis 1997). This in turn gives rise to the question as to who shall be regarded as the legitimate bearers of the group's culture. In so-called identity politics, the representations of 'our culture' emerge as an argument for recognition and special rights. Hence, culture and ethnicity are constantly negotiated and transformed

in political processes in which people struggle in order to be the true representatives and bearers of 'a culture'. It is with these reservations that I use the term 'culture' in the following discussion.

2. Not all multiculturalists confine the questions of equality to individuals. See, for example, Lawrence Blum's (1998) critique of Charles Taylor's and Nancy Fraser's positions on this topic.

3. The term 'political action' is somewhat misleading with regard to the matter at hand, because it seems to refer to a practical-political level rather than an ideological level. In order to emphasise that the problem under discussion appertains to an ideological tension, in addition to involving practical-political action *on both sides* of the debate, I prefer to use the term 'ethnocentrism'.

4. The majority population is normally seen as representative of the universal, neutral human being, whereas ethnic minorities are regarded as products of their respective cultural groups. Culture is perceived to be something that the 'others' possess. We tend to believe that culture entails a kind of deviance, in contrast to a culturally neutral zone in which we place ourselves (see e.g. Brown 1995, 2006). Accordingly, the 'others' are characterised by their distinctiveness compared to the majority population.

5. In the aftermath of the murder of Fadime Shindal, a number of critical newspaper articles on forced marriage and honour killing appeared. Several national politicians emphasised the responsibility of Muslim leaders. For instance, the Minister of Local Government and Regional Development, Erna Solberg (Conservative), stated that the imams harm young Norwegian immigrants because, by their behaviour, they exacerbate the prejudices towards the Norwegian society. She claimed to be provoked, among other things, by the fact that the imams fan the flames of the prejudices that a portion of the male immigrants have against Norwegian women. To a very great degree, the imams overemphasise sex, she told the newspaper *Bergens Tidende* (6 February 2002). The following day, she publicly demanded that the immigrant community confront the practice of forced marriage. Even arranged marriages carry with them a germ of compulsion, she told the national newspaper *Dagbladet* (7 February 2002). In a similar vein, the leader of the Socialist Left Party, Kristin Halvorsen, expressed to *Dagbladet* that she wanted a thorough discussion of the rules and norms that are to apply to everyone who lives in Norway. She told the newspaper that both the Islamic Council and immigrant parents need to be frank about marriage practices. They must inform their children that the children themselves will decide whom they want to marry, she said (*Dagbladet*, 28 January 2002). That same day, in the same newspaper, the former Minister of Children and Family Affairs, Karita Bekkemellem Orheim (Labour), proposed a ban on marriage between cousins as part of a campaign against forced marriage (*Dagbladet*, 28 January 2002). The parliamentary leader for the Labour Party, Jens Stoltenberg, agreed to submit a bill that would require religious leaders to know the Norwegian language in order to get public grants for their congregations (*Aftenposten/NTB*, 3 March 2002). The Labour Party won a majority in the Parliament for this proposal. In addition, there was a majority vote for a proposal requiring immigrants to go through an obligatory introductory programme in Norwegian language and civics. Those who chose not to participate would not receive a permanent settlement permit in Norway (*Aftenposten*, 19 April 2002).

6. Ålund focuses on a Swedish policy document that is akin to the Norwegian policy documents. The report to the State Immigration Agency in Sweden is aimed at empowering young immigrants by strengthening their cultural identity with a view to integration. The objective is to prevent problems from occurring among these youngsters.

7. The tendency to speak about social inequality in individual terms is probably due to the liberal distinction between the private and the public spheres. The liberal principle of equal treatment of individuals gives rise to the idea that discrimination is the exception that proves the rule, rather than seeing discrimination based on markers of difference as the rule (Young 1990). As long as discriminatory treatment is viewed as applicable to isolated cases, the treatment is either individualised or culturalised (cf. Brown 2006). Measures against discrimination tend to ignore socio-economic mechanisms and institutional patterns that form the basis of social divisions.

8. It must be noted that subordination is not a problem per se. The problem of asymmetry – and the paradox of multiculturalism – arises out of a discursive framework within which subordination amounts to inequality. Young (1990: 200) points out that a widely held principle of justice in egalitarian societies is that positions and rewards should be distributed according to individual merit. Positions should be awarded to the most qualified individuals. However, since criteria for evaluation necessarily carry normative and cultural implications, the egalitarian principle serves to legitimise a hierarchical division of labour in the societies that assume the equal moral and political worth of all persons (ibid.: 205). For instance, the criteria carry assumptions about ways of life, styles of behaviour and values that derive from and reflect the experiences of the privileged groups who design and implement them. Since the ideology of impartiality leads evaluators to deny the particularity of these standards, Young maintains, groups with different experiences, values and ways of life are evaluated as falling short. This is why Young speaks of the 'myth of merit'.

Chapter 1: Dual Subjectivity and the Metaphysics of Purity

1. The duality between equality and distinctiveness is, in many respects, akin to essentialism of first and second order. Essentialism of first order refers to the assumptions and mechanisms that constitute cultural relativism – the notion of culture as an autonomous totality, defined by some substantial and fixed qualities. Hence, first order essentialism draws attention to basic differences between cultures. By comparison, essentialism of second order refers to the notion of an undifferentiated, abstract human being – a universal subject. Contrary to first order essentialism, therefore, second order essentialism is likely to distract attention away from particular traits, characteristics or identities. However, both involve ahistorical, unified and stable categories that are associated with foundationalism.

2. It must be noted, however, that both Taylor and Larsen highlight the cultural and symbolic structures in their respective accounts of interiorisation, paying less attention to the major institutional structures pertaining to modern societies. In my view, the emphasis on cultural and symbolic structures should be seen as complementary to the institutional approach characteristic of, for example, Foucault's genealogical studies.

3. It is primarily the so-called French post-structuralists and psychoanalysts who have been preoccupied with the reductive opposition between 'us' and the 'others'. The

oppositional relationship is being criticised for ignoring the otherness or the singularity of the 'others' and for rendering the 'others' subordinate. Among those who have deconstructed the logic of opposition along these lines are Jacques Derrida, Gilles Deleuze, Jean-François Lyotard, Michel Foucault, Jacques Lacan, Luce Irigaray, Hélène Cixous and Julia Kristeva. Among those in the field of post-colonialism are Edward Said, Gayatri Spivak, Homi Bhabha and Robert Young.

4. The problem of opposition is related to the inferior position of the 'others'. This matter is addressed by, among others, Edward Said, Homi Bhabha, Gayatri C. Spivak, Robert Young, Franz Fanon, Louis Dumont, Richard Rorty and Jean-François Lyotard. I will return to Lyotard's approach to the problem of opposition in later chapters.

5. When autonomy refers to the subject's freedom from an externality, it denotes not only the independent or indeterminate character of the subject, but also its impurity, incompleteness, insufficiency, deficiency or lack in relation to the omniscient God or, more generally, to the purity of the undifferentiated whole. The concept of autonomy is thus ambiguous in that it denotes human sovereignty or self-sufficiency, on the one hand, and human powerlessness or insufficiency, on the other. When autonomy is taken to mean self-sufficiency, it can also be applied to culture and politics. The term 'cultural autonomy' is frequently used in debates about multiculturalism, while 'political autonomy' is crucial to secular, liberal-democratic politics. The latter corresponds to the ancient Greek concept of autonomy, understood as political independence. Autonomous polities are those that make their own laws (see O'Neill 2000: 40).

6. Derrida and other deconstructionists assume that a thing is defined in relation to what it is not. In this view, the meaning we attach to things arises out of dissociation, either in terms of contrast, which alludes to the logic of opposition, or in terms of differentiation – 'difference of degree'. For instance, black is determined in contrast to white, and it is different from grey. It is the process of differentiation that inaugurates the symbolic order of things. By comparison, radical heterogeneity can be identified neither in oppositional terms nor as a difference of degree. Because it refuses incorporation and escapes our systems of classification, it poses a radical threat to the prevailing order. However, as will be elaborated on in Chapter 4, radical heterogeneity, by virtue of being the excluded outside of our classifications, is the very condition of possibility for social categories, identities, knowledge, intelligibility, etc. The heterogeneity that escapes determination – the constitutive outside – is sometimes articulated in terms of a 'difference of kind' and associated with pathological impurity.

7. Liminality is not always conceptualised within the logic of opposition. Lawrence Grossberg (1996: 91) is among those who associate liminality with radical difference, rather than seeing it as a negation of identity. I will not make any pronouncement concerning the extent to which this is a widespread conceptualisation of liminality. Suffice it to say that there are different ways in which to deploy the term 'liminality'.

8. In Norway, as elsewhere, the designation 'second-generation immigrants' has been severely criticised by researchers and others. In more recent official documents, it has been replaced by categories such as 'persons with two foreign parents' and 'Norwegian-born persons with immigrant parents'.

9. Similar to religious ideas, metaphysical ideas are self-evident, transcendental, unified and unequivocal, devoid of the devil's duplicity, as it were. The term 'devil' dates

back from the ecclesial Latin word *diabolus*, which in turn is drawn from the Greek word *diabolos*. The latter is in the Greek translation of the Hebraic term *Satan* (Eliassen 2002: 25). Significantly, the term 'diabolical' is in some dictionaries listed as an alternative for 'duality' or 'ambiguity'.

10. The word 'end' is characteristically ambiguous by virtue of denoting both 'aim' and 'cessation' (see Lyotard 1991: 29).

11. According to Eliassen (2002: 29), this gives rise to yet another paradox. Inasmuch as death is synonymous with a new beginning, the second in line, it can only be a copy or imitation of the original. It is thus perceived to be immoral and false. Imitation qua simulation is impure because it purports to be something that it is not or cannot be.

12. This point is made by, among others, Adorno and Horkheimer ([1944] 1997: 83). However, they point out an ambiguity in Kant's concepts. On the one hand, they identify the ideal of true universality in terms of utopia, while, on the other, they emphasise that reason constitutes the court of judgement of calculation, which acts upon the world for the ends of self-preservation. The latter denotes functional reason, deprived of hope. As they see it, scientific knowledge, when adhering to systematisation and calculation, is without hope (ibid.: 27, 28). Knowledge becomes tautology and mythology. These critical remarks indicate that Adorno and Horkheimer do not dismiss Enlightenment reasoning – that is, universal or utopian truth – per se. Rather, their principal opponent is 'functionalised reason' and its negative effects within the modern system of production. In terms of functionalised reason, knowledge, they argue, becomes a 'purposeless purposiveness' (a Kantian concept that will be accounted for in Chapter 4), in that it might be attached to all ends (ibid.: 88–89). Within the market economy, knowledge or reason has no end beyond self-preservation, and science is devoid of any intention that would transcend the system (see ibid.: 18). In this regard, the conceptual ambiguity that they identify in Kant seems to be reflected in their own approach. As a number of critics have pointed out, it is somewhat unclear to what extent Adorno and Horkheimer dismiss Enlightenment rationality in general and to what extent they argue in favour of an alternative version – a true version – of Enlightenment rationality.

13. In a different context, Larsen (2002) notes that women and children possess liminal positions in modern societies. On the one hand, they symbolise the uncivilised, the wild – in general, those parts of the physical world that have not yet been domesticated. On the other hand, due to their lack of civilisation, women and children symbolise universal purity. On that account, they are often depicted as uncorrupted, authentic and original – bearers of true human values – and they are believed to possess a non-perverted creativity in their 'innocence' (ibid.: 169). Likewise, Eliassen (2002: 20) notes that a little child is pure in the same manner as it is naive, but it does not know it. If the child came to be aware of its own purity, it would no longer be pure. Childhood is often conceived as the 'lost paradise', the 'pure genesis', manifested in modern psychology by the idea of an inner lost child waiting to be released. Ever since Romanticism, childhood has served as a basis for this kind of nostalgic longing for lost innocence. The notion of innocence is most noticeable in the rhetoric of war: the message is always that the enemy is attacking 'our' communities, accompanied by pictures of mothers trying to shield their children from the enemy. As Yuval-Davis

(1997) points out, women qua mothers are constitutive elements in the notion of imagined ethnic and national communities. Identity politics, associated with ethnic and national strategies of revitalisation, is often motivated and regulated by ideas of (lost) innocence.

14. It was the city's masquerade of false appearances – individuals hidden behind masks of anonymity – that was the object of Rousseau's politics of transparency. This politics aimed at the cultivation of good citizens, understood as a recovery or liberation of the true self (see Donald 1996: 181, 187). However, the process of civic refinement cannot be directly traced back to Rousseau. In fact, Rousseau was an opponent of cultural institutions, as he believed that culture had ruined the original, good human nature. Accordingly, he looked upon schools as phenomena of decline. Unlike the liberal bourgeois, the ideal citizen was considered to be one of a gregarious herd – *les citoyens* – with esteem for the moral law. Because Rousseau looked upon society or community as the most important unity with respect to moral life, society represented the highest moral value. The bourgeois, on the other hand, was believed to be utterly indifferent with respect to the common good and, in Rousseau's view, was mainly preoccupied with his own welfare (Heyerdahl 1993: 218–219).

15. The feminine is most notably associated with the lack, tending to be identified with the immanent, uncivilised and uncultivated (natural, raw, animalistic, wild, etc.) aspects of human life. The masculine, on the other hand, is associated with the cultivated, spiritual and transcendental aspects, standing in league with the sacred, the universal, the whole or the omnipresent to which it aspires. By transcending the basic physical facts of human existence, 'man' is believed to become godlike (Clack 2002; Gressgård 2006). In this regard, the opposition between transcendence and immanence corresponds to the opposition between masculinity and femininity. See, for example, Braidotti (1991) for a discussion of the female lack in contemporary Western philosophy.

16. Rousseau ([1762] 1989) defends a partially cultivated nature that is not yet corrupted by modernity. By contrast, modern society is seen as a fall from nature's original perfection. It is Rousseau's exalted notion of nature that gives rise to his concept of 'the good savage', which denotes a dignified primitivism. This primitivism forms the basis for his critique of modern civilisation by way of critical self-definition via negation.

17. A similar example from the Norwegian integration policy is provided by May Thorseth (1995). In her analysis of the policy regarding refugees, she demonstrates how the official policy deprives the individual refugee of her or his self determination. The problem, she asserts, seems to arise from the democratic principles of equality and autonomy. As long as these principles have the force of law, they escape scrutiny (ibid.: 12).

Chapter 2: Non-modern Holism and Modern Totalitarianism

1. *Modern ideology*: 'The set of common representations that are *characteristic* of modern civilization' (Dumont 1986: 280, glossary).

2. *Holism*: 'We call holist (holistic) an ideology that valorizes the social whole and neglects or subordinates the human individual.... By extension, a sociology is holistic if it starts from the global society and not from the individual supposed to be given independently' (Dumont 1986: 279, glossary).

3. *Value*: 'Under this term, often in the plural, the anthropological literature refers to some extent to what we prefer to call hierarchy. Value is segregated in modern, individualistic ideology; in contrast it is an integral part of representations in holistic ideologies' (Dumont 1986: 280, glossary).

4. A similar point is made by Lyotard, who points to the way in which modern societies separate science from narrative knowledge (e.g. Lyotard 1984). The distinction between science and narrative knowledge does not exist in so-called primitive cultures. In these cultures, all knowledge is narrative knowledge. These narratives are at the same time descriptive or normative, telling us how to act, how to behave. Because no separation is made between different language games (the true, the good and the beautiful), legitimising, external resources (meta-narratives) are unnecessary.

5. *Hierarchy*: 'To be distinguished from power, or command: order resulting from the consideration of value. The elementary hierarchical relation (or hierarchical opposition) is that between a whole (or a set) and an element of that whole (or set) – or else that between two parts with reference to the whole. It can be analyzed into two contradictory aspects belonging to different levels: it is a distinction within an identity, an *encompassing of the contrary*. Hierarchy is thus bi-dimensional' (Dumont 1986: 279, glossary).

6. For instance, Tönnies insisted that both *Gemeinschaft* and *Gesellschaft* are present as principles in modern society. Dumont (1986: 245) responds by stating that the two principles are found on different levels of social life.

7. *Value-ideas*: 'As it is impossible to separate ideas and values in nonmodern forms of thought, one is led to speak of value-ideas or idea-values' (Dumont 1986: 280, glossary).

8. Dumont's exemplary example concerns the division between right and left. The fact that the two poles are unequally valued, the right hand being superior to the left hand, appears to us as an arbitrary, superadded feature, which we are at pains to explain. In order to explain it, he argues, the two hands must be considered as two different parts of a whole: the body. Accordingly, the body is constitutive of the right, the left and their distinctions. Dumont (1986: 248) goes on to suggest that right and left, in their different relation to the body (a right-relation and a left-relation), are different *in themselves*. In other words, the two hands are not two identical entities situated in different places. Rather, the two hands have different places in the hierarchy and thus have different values. The hands and their functions are at once different and ranked. If certain functions are allotted to the left hand, then, in relation to their performance, the right hand will come second, notwithstanding the fact that the right hand is on the whole superior to the left. This example is exemplary in that it clearly demonstrates how the right-and-left pair is both an idea and a value (an idea-value or value-idea).

9. As I pointed out above, this separation dates, at least partly, back to Christianity, notably Calvinism.

10. According to Dumont (1986), the problem relates to the modern division between idea and value, including the value of the individual. As has been pointed out above, the human being qua autonomous individual possesses a free will. Instead of emanating from the society, Dumont remarks, some of the values will be determined by the individual for his or her own use (ibid.: 260). In other words, the (modern) individual as a (social) value demands that society should delegate to her or him a part of its value-setting capacity. The absence of prescription that makes choices possible

is then actually commanded by a superior prescription. From a modern point of view, this is a paradox, which Dumont takes to be the effect of a non-recognised, inherent hierarchical structure.

11. Multiculturalism in general and cultural relativism in particular are predicated upon the modern division of autonomous spheres. On the one hand, the idea of autonomous spheres gives rise to liberal arguments about political independence and culture-free (*Kulturlos*) public debate (see Brown 2006). On the other hand, the division of spheres gives rise to cultural relativism and separate moral universes. As Dumont (1986: 264) sees it, what happens in the anthropological view (and in the case of multiculturalism, we might add) is that every ideology is relativised *in relation to the others*. It is not a matter of absolute relativism, he argues, because the unity of humankind sets limits to the variation. Paradoxically, therefore, it is a unity – a holism – that constitutes the backdrop for cultural relativism and, more generally, the division of autonomous spheres. Dumont goes on to argue that each particular configuration of ideas and values is contained with all others in a universal figure of which it is a partial expression (ibid.). Furthermore, he submits that cultures are in fact interacting. Accordingly, we are committed to reducing the distance between our two cases, to reintegrating the modern case within the general one (ibid.: 247). This is quite clearly a rejection of the thesis of incommensurability (cf. Davidson 1984). I will respond to this critique in Chapters 4 and 5.

12. To illustrate his point, Dumont (1986) refers to Marshall Sahlins's analysis of trade in the Huon Gulf: 'Briefly: (1) between two commercial partners, each of the exchanges in a series is unbalanced, alternatively in one and the other direction, in approximation to a balance reached in the end, i.e., for the series as a whole; equality is thus reached through a succession of somewhat unequal exchanges; (2) each particular exchange is thus not closed but remains open and calls for the next one; the stress is on the continuing relationship more than on instantaneous equivalence between goods. All aspects of our problem are here contained in a nutshell: the difference between hierarchy and equality is not at all what we are wont to suppose' (ibid.: 266n).

Chapter 3: Heterogeneity and the Singular Subject

1. In his introductory remarks, Pluhar explains the background of Kant's critique of aesthetic judgement. He notes that Kant, in this Third Critique, employs the term 'aesthetics' in the narrow sense, dealing with the standards of perfection that sense perception must meet in order for us to perceive beauty; 'it is the science (or art) of the beautiful and of taste, i.e., of the power to cognize beauty' (Kant ([1790] 1987: xlix). Pluhar moves on to argue that Kant uses the term 'aesthetics' in accordance with rationalistic, formal aesthetic theory (similar to Baumgarten's and Mendelssohn's interpretations). As for the definition of 'taste', Kant is informed by 'the philosophy of taste' (Hutcheson and Burke). Contrary to the rationalists, but in line with the philosophers of taste, Kant holds that aesthetic judgements are not objective but rather subjective. In accordance with the rationalists, Kant maintains that judgements of taste must be universally valid.

2. A priori judgements denote propositions based on principles that are universal and necessary, which means that they are not merely empirical, psychological and, as

such, trivial. They are universal by way of applying to any experience that we can have of the world and by saying something necessary about the world. A priori knowledge can thus be attained in advance of experience. It is knowable independently of experience and, as such, is presupposed by any experience. Yet the judgements of taste are not analytic but synthetic. Writes Kant ([1790] 1987: §36:288): 'We can readily see that judgments of taste are synthetic; for they go beyond the concept of the object, and even beyond the intuition of the object, and add as a predicate to this intuition something that is not even cognition: namely, [a] feeling of pleasure (or displeasure).' In a judgement of taste, therefore, a non-cognitive 'predicate', a feeling, is connected with the mere intuition of an object, and to this extent the judgement is singular and empirical (Pluhar in ibid.: lix; cf. ibid.: §37). However, in Kant's view, an aesthetic judgement is not merely a judgement of sensation, but a formal judgement of reflection that requires the liking (that accompanies the object's presentation) from everyone as necessary (ibid.: §36). Aesthetic judgement must be based on something as its a priori principle. In other words, the problem of the critique of judgement pertains to the a priori principles that the pure power of judgement uses when it makes aesthetic judgements. According to Kant, we may think of this problem as follows: 'How is a judgment possible in which the subject, merely on the basis of his *own* feeling of pleasure in an object, independently of the object's concept, judges this pleasure as one attaching to the presentation of that same object *in all other subjects*, and does so a priori, i.e., without being allowed to wait for other people's assent?' (ibid.: §36:288). The problem of the critique of judgement, Kant asserts, is part of the general problem of transcendental philosophy: how are synthetic judgements possible a priori?

3. In the English translation of the Third Critique from 1987, Pluhar prefers the term 'power' to 'faculty' when our ability to make (individual) judgements (*Urteile*) is concerned. The term 'power', he states, is more appropriate in that it disassociates 'Kant's theory (of cognition, desire, etc.) from the traditional *faculty psychology*'. However, he makes clear that '"power" is never used to mean anything like *strength* or *forcefulness* (of concepts, desire, and so on)' (Kant ([1790] 1987: 167n3).

4. It should be noted that reflective judgement comes in two versions. One is teleological judgement, while the other is aesthetic judgement of taste. Kant is preoccupied with the latter.

5. In Book I in the first part of the Third Critique, Kant ([1790] 1987) discusses the 'analytic of the beautiful', which is an examination of the conditions that must be fulfilled in order for judgement of taste to be universally valid. The judgement of taste is rendered in light of the four logical 'moments': quality, quantity, relation and modality. Quality and relation concern the conditions for asserting that something is beautiful, while quantity and modality are a matter of discovering what is required for calling a judgement an authentic judgement of taste, that is, a judgement of the beautiful. In Book II, Kant (ibid.) develops a transcendental deduction. Here, he submits a transcendental justification of the claim to subjective universality, that is, a justification of the a priori claim of the judgement.

6. In Chapter 1, we saw that autonomy refers to freedom from a metaphysical externality – an indeterminism – that includes self-consciousness. For Kant, self-consciousness is the very condition for judgement. In his view, the passing of synthetic judgements

must be accompanied by an 'I think' in the subject. A synthesis into a unity (of the manifold of intuition) requires a subject that is a unity itself (Storheim 1993: 255).

7. In Greek, *aporia* means 'anxiety' or 'perplexity'. In rhetoric, it refers to a figure of speech in which a speaker purports to be in doubt about what to say, think or do (*Oxford Reference Online*, http://www.oxfordreference.com/).

8. *Noumenon* is listed in *Webster's Encyclopedic Unabridged Dictionary* with the following note: '*Kantianism*, that which can be the object only of a purely intellectual, non-sensuous intuition.' As suggested by the outline above, the Third Critique is based on the assumption that there is something in the world that we cannot possibly know. *Noumenon* denotes this 'something'. Accordingly, *noumenon* cannot be articulated or predicated: it comprises the problem per se and, as such, is closely related to the concept of *aporia*.

9. Lash does not seem to take into consideration that nature may function as a mirror – a reflective horizon – which hints that humans are the final goal of creation (cf. Kant [1790] 1987), despite the fact that this view of nature seems to be implied in Gadamer's hermeneutics. The reason why Lash ignores this aspect of Gadamer's thought is probably because it does not conform to his own line of argument. I shall return to the question of horizon in later chapters, although from a slightly different angle.

10. Lyotard (1992b: 22) remarks that reflective syntheses happen without any 'I think': 'There simply is no aesthetic transcendental *I*. At the most a pre-*I*, a pre-cogito, some sort of floating synthesis between the faculties, whose *I* isn't in charge, but "nature"'. According to Lyotard, the subject is born in this synthesising of the heterogeneous faculties, in this unison. However, it will never be born as such, he notes, because once born, the subject is only the *Ich denke*. 'And the aesthetical pleasure will always come along to disconcert it, to make it be at a loss through its own concert, and its reflexive relation to itself' (ibid.). In other words, the subject will lose itself in its endeavour to determine itself.

11. In Kant's view, the human being (in its natural state) cannot be the final purpose of creation. For this reason, the theosophical proof, which suggests that humans are the purpose of nature and that everything exists for the sake of humans, fails and cannot be justified (Wiggen 1998: 51). (Above in note 9, I suggested that Gadamer draws the opposite conclusion by assuming that the human being is the final purpose of nature. I will return to Gadamer's philosophy in Chapter 5.)

12. A more elaborate argument could include an elucidation of how Kant's attempt at solving a series of antinomies (ostensible contradictions) from his previous Critiques involves an emphasis on the universal validity of the reflective judgement through his concept of the supersensible. By reconciling the two concepts of the supersensible from his former Critiques with a third concept, the Third Critique serves as a bridge between the First and Second Critiques. Kant assumes that there is an indeterminate concept of the supersensible that underlies nature's purposiveness for our cognitive power. Pluhar (in Kant ([1790] 1987: lxiii) suggests that, by switching to this indeterminate concept, Kant suddenly equates the indeterminate concept of nature's purposiveness for our cognitive power with the indeterminate concept of the supersensible basis of that same (subjective) purposiveness. The new concept of the supersensible – that is, the supersensible as underlying nature's subjective purposiveness – thus 'mediates' the 'transition' between the two (the substrate of objects and of ourselves as subjects, on the one

hand, and the supersensible that is practically contained by the concept of freedom, on the other) (see ibid.: lxiv). In this respect, Kant inserts the supersensible as a mediator between the domains of nature and the domain of freedom (e.g. ibid.: §9). For a more comprehensive discussion of this 'third path' in Kant's philosophy, see Pluhar's introduction to *Critique of Judgment* (ibid.: lxi–lxiv, lxxxvi–cix).

13. In Kant's philosophy, autonomy refers both to independence from external causes and to human capacity in terms of a universal rationality. His focus of attention is the human will, in so far as autonomy is considered to be crucial to human freedom and morality. According to Onora O'Neill (2000: 42), Kant regards freedom of the will – negative freedom – as a capacity to work independently of determination by alien causes. Kant conceives of autonomy – positive freedom – as a specific, coherent and reasoned way of using negative freedom. What separates negative freedom from positive freedom is the 'lawlessness' of negative freedom. By contrast, positive freedom entails adopting a 'self-imposed law'. According to O'Neill, Kant is interested in the capacity to adopt principles that could be adopted by all – principles that *can* be universally adopted (which means that they are law-like) – and the rejection of principles that *cannot* be universally adopted (ibid.: 43). However, the principles are not universal in the sense that they are widely accepted or likely to be universally adopted. Rather, they are universal in the sense that a plurality *can* adopt them (ibid.: 43–44). It is precisely this capacity that, according to Kant, makes human beings into moral beings. Significantly, the universal principles constitute moral laws (the categorical imperative). The human being is autonomous in so far as humans can adopt the 'categorical imperative' and are able to act differently than if they had not done so. In this respect, moral law is humanity's *own* law; it is not imposed on humans by an externality (Storheim 1993: 260). This is tantamount to asserting that humans are independent of nature. Accordingly, Kant's concept of autonomy does not denote a human lack; instead, it seems to coincide with the conception of the universal subject's independence from the empirical world.

Chapter 4: Consequences of Heterogeneity

1. In his 'Afterword to the Second German Edition' of *Capital Vol. 1*, Marx ([1873] 1967) takes issue with Hegel's dialectic method, criticising it, in its allegedly mystifying form, for glorifying the existing state of things. According to Marx, dialectic 'must be turned right side up again, if you would discover the rational kernel within the mystical shell.... In its rational form it is a scandal and abomination to bourgeoisdom and its doctrinaire professors, because it includes in its comprehension and affirmative recognition of the existing state of things, at the same time also, the recognition of the negation of that state, of its inevitable breaking up ... because it lets nothing impose upon it, and is in its essence critical and revolutionary' (ibid.: 20). If one, as does Lyotard, criticises dialectical reasoning for reproducing the existing state of things per se, due to its oppositional logic, one could turn Marx's critique against himself, so to speak, claiming that dialectics is a scandal.

2. In his essay 'Rewriting Modernity', Lyotard (1991) elaborates on the procedure of rewriting by reference to Freud's distinction between 'repetition', 'remembering' and 'working through'. Lyotard emphasises that the prefix 're-' in 'reworking' (modernity)

does not signify a return to the beginning but rather a 'working through' (*Durcharbeitung*) – 'a working attached to a thought of what is constitutively hidden from us in the event and the meaning of the event, hidden not merely by past prejudice, but also by those dimensions of the future marked by the pro-ject' (ibid.: 26).

3. In his book *The Postmodern Condition*, Lyotard (1984) uses the terms 'paralogy' and 'paralogism' to designate a practice of destabilisation from within the established frameworks (of art, of science, etc.). However, even if paralogy creates something new, it must be distinguished from the term 'innovation'. Innovation, Lyotard (ibid.: 61) notes, is under the command of the system or at least is used by it to improve its efficiency (cf. Lyotard 1991: 106). As opposed to artistic innovation, which means going in new directions *within* the rules of the language game 'art', paralogism denotes the transgression of established rules, going in an impossible or unpredictable direction.

4. The term 'event' refers to what Heidegger called *ein Ereignis*, denoting an occurrence – a radical difference or a singularity – that refuses incorporation or subsumption under a general concept, rule, law, etc. With respect to the event, we must judge without criteria. The event is thus associated with indeterminate judgement. See Gressgård (2008) for a further elaboration of this concept.

5. In the preceding chapter we saw that the subject, in its experience of the sublime, is subordinated to a power (nature) stronger than itself, which causes a feeling of displeasure. At the same time, the sublime is associated with the feeling of pleasure – a negative pleasure – in so far as the experience of the sublime exhibits and reaffirms the superiority of the mind. This is to say that the experience of the limits in our cognitive powers – the imagination's insufficiency – is accompanied by the feeling that it is the entire world, as it appears to us through our senses (*die Welt der Erscheinung*), that is insufficient in relation to the pure ideas of reason. In their independency of empirical influence, the pure ideas of reason are universal. According to Kasper Nefer Olsen (1989: 110), reason is interested in the sublime because any awakening of ideas of reason contributes to the edification of humankind. The sublime in nature points to that which is exalted in us (as rational creatures). It signifies the supersensible, universal dimension of the subject.

6. Writes Lyotard (1990: 17): 'In defiance of etymology, one needs to understand "exceed" here in terms of the following three Latin verbs taken together: *ex-cedere*, to pass beyond, to go out; *ex-cidere* (from *cadere*), to fall outside of, to be dispossessed from; *ex-cidere* (from *caedere*), to detach by cutting, to excise.'

7. Whereas Kant thought of the sublime as exceeding any time/space perception, the avant-gardes have seen, on the contrary, that by minimising form we 'under-exceed' the threshold of the aesthetical perception, as it were. The avant-gardes thus manage to bring forth a 'pure' impact that does not refer to anything other than the inexpressible, that which no art can depict – the unique *I-now-here* (Nefer Olsen 1989: 114). As pointed out above, this presupposes that the 'now' is not subsumed under a History, order or totality, that is, that the event's *quid* (the fact that it happens) is not annulled by an interpretive *quod* (what actually happens) (see Lyotard 1991: 90). The future, which can no longer be unilaterally depicted as utopia, must be artistically realised in the pure form of the 'now', as a pure event (Nefer Olsen 1989: 116).

8. The event – the sublime now – cannot, in itself, 'take place' because it does not conform to a logic of spatiality. According to Elizabeth Grosz (2001: 141–142), space is

the field of 'differences of degree', that is, linear representations. Hence, we could argue that spatial representation (of that which took place) is a process in which the 'difference of kind' is forgotten. In the sublime, one feels that soon nothing more will take place. 'That "place" is mere "here", the most minimal occurrence' (Lyotard 1991: 84). The legacy of Heidegger's concept of temporal difference, which resists spatialisation, is noticeable in this context.

9. 'The Thing' is borrowed from Lacan's 'La chose freudienne' in *Ecrits*, first published in 1966. For Lacan, 'the Thing' is associated with an individual singularity; it is beyond-of-the-signified. Lyotard, for his part, maintains that 'the Thing' has a philosophical or aesthetic meaning. In his book *The Inhuman*, Lyotard (1991: 142–143) speaks of 'the Thing' in terms of immaterial matter (in relation to form), something that is not addressed, that which does not address itself to the mind: '"The thing" is not waiting to be destined, it is not waiting for anything; it does not call on the mind.... Always forgotten, it is unforgettable.'

10. It should be noted that Lyotard regards Nietzsche's doctrine of the will to power as a repetition of the very metaphysics (of will) harboured by all the philosophical systems of modern Western thought. Despite Nietzsche's proposition that there is nothing that is a primary or originary principle (a *Grund*), and that every discourse is only a perspective, he 'succumbs to the temptation to designate what grounds the perspectivizations, and he calls it the will to power' (Lyotard 1991: 29)

11. According to Lyotard (1988), the conflict is not between humans or entities. Rather, the conflict results from phrases; it is within language, prior to political, ethical or any other conflicts (ibid.: §188). For this reason, Lyotard, in line with other so-called post-foundationalists, takes 'the political' (in language) to be prior to politics and ethics. Whereas 'the political' belongs to ontology, politics and ethics belong to the ontic, empirical level. Hence, 'the political' is not a genre of discourse. The political problem is the question of linkage par excellence (ibid.: §190). Genres of discourse are strategies – of no one (ibid.: §185). As indicated above, Lyotard conceives of language as a battlefield. To speak is to fight, in the sense of playing, and speech acts fall within the domain of a general agonistics. However, this does not mean that one plays in order to win (Lyotard 1984: 10).

12. This is a shift from the rules of formation and linkage that determine the regimen of a phrase to the modes of linking that stem from genres of discourse (see Lyotard 1988: §185).

13. The term 'critique' derives from the Greek noun *krisis*. In ancient Athens, Wendy Brown (2005: 5) points out, the term *krisis* was a jurisprudential term identified with the art of making distinctions, essential to judging. For the purpose of our discussion in this chapter, we could say that the making of distinctions (separation) – and the grouping of sentences – is the basis for judgement (see Brügger 1989: 67n24). In Chapter 5, we shall see how the ancient Greek meaning of *krisis* comes into play in my conceptualisation of critical distance.

14. Lyotard takes the Kantian 'so dass' to mean 'as if' rather than 'so that' (Stjernfelt 1989: 141).

15. In his book *Remnants of Auschwitz: The Witness and the Archive*, Agamben (1999) enters into a dialogue with Levi on the paradox of testimony.

16. For example, 'the differend' seems to resemble the term 'illegitimate paternalism'. Contrary to illegitimate paternalism, legitimate paternalism entails that the involved parties are rational and that they would have given their assent if they had been totally informed (Thorseth 1995: 19). Conversely, legitimate paternalism corresponds to 'litigation'.

17. The practice of offering a gift is judged as illegal based on a Norwegian principle of gender equality. If, however, the practice of gift offering had been evaluated on the basis of regular and institutionalised gender-related practices in Norwegian society, such as the nuptial morning gift to the bride, a different conclusion might have been reached.

18. According to Lyotard (1988: §8), the dilemma contains the mechanism of the 'double bind' (referring to the Palo Alto school of which the most prominent member was Gregory Bateson). Lyotard considers the mechanism to be a linchpin of Hegelian dialectical logic, in which one applies to two contradictory propositions, p and *not-p*, two logical operators, exclusion (*either ... or*) and implication (*if ..., then*). So, at once [(*either p or not-p*) and (*if p, then not-p*)].

19. As I pointed out above, this principle applies also to other areas in society. When Lyotard reaches an idea of justice that does not involve consensus, the first step is an acknowledgement of the heterogeneity in language, including the genres of discourse, which calls for openness to silences.

Chapter 5: Conditions for Dialogue

1. In a similar vein, Alasdair MacIntyre (1988: 380) points out: '[F]rom the fact that two communities with ... rival belief-systems are able to agree in identifying one and the same subject matter as that identified, characterized, and evaluated in their two rival systems and are able to recognize that the applicability of certain of the concepts in the one scheme of belief precludes certain concepts in the other scheme from having application, it does not follow that the substantive criteria which govern the application of those concepts – the standards, that is, by which truth or falsity and rational justification or the lack of it are judged – cannot differ radically.'

2. As Arendt (1973) illuminates in her book *The Origins of Totalitarianism*, totalitarian regimes can indeed suppress the subject's will to such a degree that subjectivity appears to be lost. Accordingly, we may ask if the limit of the subject's will amounts to physical death. Or is a 'living dead' in the concentration camp deprived of all her or his freedom, too? I will not pursue this question here. Suffice it to say that the object of dominance, irrespective of whether or not the domination is total, is to strip the freedom of the subject.

3. According to Vetlesen and Nortvedt (1994: 73), 'moral' concerns people's welfare – that is, what violates their rights and welfare in a situation – and, conversely, what promotes its realisation.

4. Empathy refers, in this context, to humanity's basic emotional faculty – the capacity that forms the basis for an entire range of particular emotional associations to others, such as sympathy, compassion and concern. It denotes a non-calculating engagement in the situation of others (Vetlesen and Nortvedt 1994: 60).

5. This discourse rests on two formal premises: 'ideal speech situation' and 'unconstrained dialogue'.

6. Habermas has, in his later writings, modified his view on this matter. However, he still does not seem to think that emotions have a role to play in the justification of actions; actions and norms are to be justified through rational argumentation. Accordingly, his discourse ethics presupposes a marked distinction between perception and judgement, and the capacity for empathy is confined to the level of perception.

7. The aesthetic of the sublime was promulgated by Nicolas Boileau-Despréaux via his 1674 translation of the book *On the Sublime*, whose author was thought to be Cassius Longinus (a Hellenistic rhetorician), but the author's real name is unknown. In this book, the sublime is depicted as thought-provoking – 'from the sublime springs a lot of reflection' (cited in Lyotard 1991: 94).

8. Some seem to think that an ethics of difference, deconstruction or dissensus is necessary in order to address the heterogeneity that escapes categorisation or determination – the otherness of the 'others'. In addition to those I have mentioned in the preceding chapter, there are a number of scholars, coming from different theoretical positions, who see the need for an ethics that checks the totalising effects of postconventional politics, ethics and reasoning (e.g. Ahmed 1998; Bell 2007; Critchley 1992, 2007; Irigaray 1993; Spivak 2003; Trey 1998; Ziarek 2001). Some scholars draw on Levinas's ethics of alterity in their conceptualisation of ethical responsibility and accountability. The ethics of alterity is considered to interrupt the homogenising character, authoritarian tendencies and formal abstraction of conceptual frameworks. At the same time, it is depicted as a resistance to – or a neutralisation of – power, that is, a check on politics. Although beyond both classical universalism and cultural relativism, this turn to ethics sometimes involves a constitutive extra-political element. Accordingly, it risks taking attention away from the constitutive power of ethics itself and, in doing so, is likely to perpetuate the problem that it aims to resolve.

9. Butler (2000) seems to adhere to a notion of radical difference without presupposing ontological difference. She takes issue with, among others, Ernesto Laclau's (1996) notion of the universal due to its ontological dimension. She seems to be of the opinion that the universal, instead of being 'located' in the ontology of language, constitutes a dimension of a particular socio-political, normative *claim* – a claim for universality. And qua claim, the universal has to be articulated through a certain set of cultural conventions in a recognisable venue (Butler 2000: 35). In response to Laclau's notion of the universal as an empty place, she maintains that it is empty only because it has already disavowed or suppressed the content from which it emerges (ibid.: 34). The emptiness is an effect of politics, not grounded in ontology. However, as my line of argument has suggested, ontological difference does not have to be conceived as extra-political. The following statement by Marchart (2007: 171) encapsulates the mutual subversion of the ontological and the ontic: 'Every ontology, which necessarily will be *less* than a pure ontology, has to be grounded in an "ontic", which necessarily will be *more* that a mere ontic.'

References

Adorno, Theodor ([1951] 2005), *Minima Moralia*, http://www.marxists.org/reference/archive/adorno/1951/mm/ch02.htm.
Adorno, Theodor and Horkheimer, Max ([1944] 1997), *Dialectic of Enlightenment*, (trans.) John Cumming (London: Verso).
Agamben, Giorgio (1993), *The Coming Community*, (trans.) Michael Hardt (Minneapolis: University of Minnesota Press).
_____ (1998), *Homo Sacer: Sovereign Power and Bare Life*, (trans.) Daniel Heller-Roazen (Stanford, CA: Stanford University Press).
_____ (1999), *Remnants of Auschwitz: The Witness and the Archive*, (trans.) Daniel Heller-Roazen (New York: Zone Books).
_____ (2005), *State of Exception*, (trans.) Kevin Attell (Chicago, IL: University of Chicago Press).
Ahmed, Sara (1998), *Differences That Matter: Feminist Theory and Postmodernism* (Cambridge: Cambridge University Press).
Ålund, Aleksandra (1991), 'Immigrant Culture as an Obstacle to "Partnership"', in *Paradoxes of Multiculturalism*, (ed.) Aleksandra Ålund and Carl-Ulrik Schierup (Aldershot: Avebury), 69–87.
Anderson, Benedict (1983), *Imagined Communities* (London: Verso).
Arendt, Hannah (1973), *The Origins of Totalitarianism* (New York: Harvest Book).
Badiou, Alain (2005), *Metapolitics*, (trans.) Jason Baker (London: Verso).
Barry, Brian (2001), *Culture and Equality* (Cambridge: Polity Press).
Barth, Fredrik (ed.) (1969), *Ethnic Groups and Boundaries: The Social Organisation of Culture Difference* (Oslo: Universitetsforlaget).
Barthes, Roland ([1957] 1993), *Mythologies*, (trans.) Annette Lavers (London: Harvester Wheatsheaf).
Bell, Vikki (2007), *Culture and Performance: The Challenge of Ethics, Politics and Feminist Theory* (Oxford: Berg).
Benhabib, Seyla (1986), *Critique, Norm, and Utopia: A Study of the Foundations of Critical Theory* (New York: Columbia University Press).
Bhabha, Homi (1994), *The Location of Culture* (London: Routledge).

_____ (2004), 'A Global Measure: Writing, Rights, and Responsibility', paper presented at the Humanitas Series Lecture, American Cultures and Global Context Center, University of California, Santa Barbara, http://www.uctv.tv/search-details.aspx?showID=8903.

Blum, Lawrence (1980), *Friendship, Altruism, and Morality* (London: Routledge and Kegan Paul).

_____ (1998), 'Recognition, Value, and Equality: A Critique of Charles Taylor's and Nancy Fraser's Accounts of Multiculturalism', in *Theorising Multiculturalism*, (ed.) Cynthia Willett (Malden, MA: Blackwell), 73–99.

Bologh, Roslyn W. (1990), *Love or Greatness: Max Weber and Masculine Thinking* (London: Unwin Hyman).

Borchgrevink, Tordis (2002), 'Noen religionsmøter på norsk – og et forsøk på å ikke holde hånden for det ene øyet' [Some religious encounters in Norway – and an attempt at not covering one eye with one's hand], in *Internasjonal migrasjon og etniske relasjoner 1997–2001: Resultater fra 20 forskningsprosjekter* [International migration and ethnic relations 1997–2001: Results from 20 research projects] (Oslo: Norwegian Research Council).

Braidotti, Rosi (1991), *Patterns of Dissonance* (Cambridge: Polity Press).

Brown, Wendy (1995), *States of Injury: Power and Freedom in Late Modernity* (Princeton, NJ: Princeton University Press).

_____ (2005), *Edgework: Critical Essays on Knowledge and Politics* (Princeton, NJ: Princeton University Press).

_____ (2006), *Regulating Aversion: Tolerance in the Age of Identity and Empire* (Princeton, NJ: Princeton University Press).

Brügger, Niels (1989), 'Om sprogspillet der forsvandt' [On the language game that disappeared], in *Filosofiske forskydninger* [Philosophical displacements], (ed.) Niels Brügger and Finn Frandsen (Århus: Akademisk Forlag), 37–67.

Butler, Judith (1992), 'Contingent Foundations: Feminism and the Question of "Postmodernism"', in *Feminists Theorise the Political*, (ed.) Judith Butler and Joan W. Scott (New York and London: Routledge), 3–21.

_____ (1997), *Excitable Speech: A Politics of the Performative* (New York and London: Routledge).

_____ (1999), *Gender Trouble: Feminism and the Subversion of Identity*, 10th Anniversary Edition (New York: Routledge).

_____ (2000), 'Restaging the Universal: Hegemony and the Limits of Formalism', in *Contingency, Hegemony, Universality: Contemporary Dialogues on the Left*, (ed.) Judith Butler, Ernesto Laclau and Slavoj Žižek (London and New York: Verso), 11–43.

_____ (2004a), *Undoing Gender* (New York and London: Routledge).

_____ (2004b), *Precarious Life: The Powers of Mourning and Violence* (London and New York: Verso).

_____ (2005), *Giving an Account of Oneself* (New York: Fordham University Press).

_____ (2009), *Frames of War: When Is Life Grievable?* (London: Verso).

Butler, Judith and Spivak, Gaytari C. (2007), *Who Sings the Nation-State?* (London and Calcutta: Seagull Books).

Carroll, David (1990), 'Foreword: The Memory of Devastation and the Responsibilities of Thought: "And let's not talk about that"', in *Heidegger and 'the jews'*, Jean-François Lyotard, (trans.) Andreas Michel and Mark Roberts (Minneapolis: University of Minnesota Press), vii–xxix.

Clack, Beverly (2002), *Sex and Death* (Cambridge: Polity Press).

Critchley, Simon (1992), *The Ethics of Deconstruction* (Oxford: Blackwell).

_____ (2007), *Infinitely Demanding: Ethics of Commitment, Politics of Resistance* (London: Verso).

Davidson, Donald (1984), *Inquiries into Truth and Interpretation* (Oxford: Clarendon Press).

Dean, Mitchell (1999), *Governmentality: Power and Rule in Modern Society* (London: Sage).

Deleuze, Gilles ([1967] 1991), *Masochism: Coldness and Cruelty*, (trans.) Jean McNeil (New York: Zone Books).

_____ ([1969] 1990), *The Logic of Sense*, (trans.) Mark Lester and Charles Stivale (London: Athlone Press).

Derrida, Jacques (1992), 'Force of Law: The "Mystical Foundation of Authority"', in *Deconstruction and the Possibility of Justice*, (ed.) Drucilla Cornell, Michel Rosenfeld and David Gray Carlson (New York and London: Routledge), 3–67.

_____ (1993), *Aporias*, (trans.) Thomas Dutoit (Stanford, CA: Stanford University Press).

_____ (1997), *Of Grammatology*, (trans.) Gayatri C. Spivak (Baltimore, MD: Johns Hopkins University Press).

_____ (2000), *Of Hospitality*, (trans.) Rachel Bowlby (Stanford, CA: Stanford University Press).

Donald, James (1996), 'The Citizen and the Man About Town', in *Questions of Cultural Identity*, (ed.) Stuart Hall and Paul du Gay (London: Sage), 170–190.

Douglas, Mary (1984), *Purity and Danger: An Analysis of Concepts of Pollution and Taboo* (London: Ark Paperbacks).

Dumont, Louis (1970), *Homo Hierarchicus: The Caste System and Its Implications*, (trans.) Mark Sainsbury (Chicago, IL: University of Chicago Press).

_____ (1986), *Essays on Individualism: Modern Ideology in Anthropological Perspective* (Chicago, IL: University of Chicago Press).

Egeland, Cathrine and Gressgård, Randi (2007), 'The Will to Empower: Managing the Complexity of the Others', *Nordic Journal of Women's Studies (NORA)* 15, no. 4: 207–219.

Eliassen, Knut Ove (2000), 'Det urenes estetikk' [The aesthetics of the impure], *Samtiden* 110, no. 1: 10–23.

_____ (2002), 'Urenhetens metafysikk' [The metaphysics of impurity], in *Fanden går i kloster: Elleve tekster om det andre* [The devil joins the convent: Eleven texts on the other], (ed.) Randi Gressgård and Siri Meyer (Oslo: Spartacus), 13–34.

Eriksen, Tore (1990), 'Postmodernisme og antihumanisme' [Postmodernism and anti-humanism], *Arr: Idéhistorisk Tidsskrift* 2, no. 1: 42–46.

_____ (1995), 'Habermas og Lyotard – eller forsøk på å introdusere Lyotard til en debatt' [Habermas and Lyotard – or an attempt to introduce Lyotard to a debate], in *Fornuftens Former: Habermas og Lyotard* [The forms of reason: Habermas and Lyotard], (ed.) Tore Eriksen and Knut Ove Eliassen (Oslo: Spartacus), 247–280.

Erikson, Erik H. (1964), *Insight and Responsibility: Lectures on the Ethical Implications of Psychoanalytic Insight* (New York: W.W. Norton).

Falzon, Christopher (1998), *Foucault and Social Dialogue: Beyond Fragmentation* (London and New York: Routledge).

Favell, Adrian (2001), *Philosophies of Integration: Immigration and the Idea of Citizenship in France and Britain* (Basingstoke and New York: Palgrave).

Foucault, Michel (1979), *Discipline and Punish: The Birth of the Prison*, (trans.) Alan Sheridan (London: Penguin).

_____ (1980), *Power/Knowledge: Selected Interviews and Other Writings by Michel Foucault* (New York: Pantheon Books).

_____ (2000), 'Different Spaces', in *Aesthetics, Method, and Epistemology: Essential Works of Foucault 1954–1984, Vol. 2*, (ed.) James D. Faubion (London: Penguin Books), 175–186.

Gadamer, Hans-Georg (1975), *Truth and Method*, (trans.) Garrett Barden and John Cumming (London: Sheed & Ward).

Gehlen, Arnold ([1940] 1988), *Man: His Nature and Place in the World*, (trans.) Clare A. McMillan and Karl A. Pillemer (New York: Columbia University Press).

Gennep, Arnold van ([1909] 1960), *The Rites of Passage*, (trans.) Monika B. Visedom and Gabrielle L. Caffe (London: Routledge and Kegan Paul).

Gombrich, E. H. (1969), *Art and Illusion: A Study in the Psychology of Pictorial Representation* (Princeton, NJ: Princeton University Press).

Gray, John (1995), *Enlightenment's Wake: Politics and Culture at the Close of the Modern Age* (London: Routledge).

Gressgård, Randi (1997), *Det sosiale bymiljøet som visuelt felt: Et grunnlagsteoretisk fokus på forholdet mellom språk, estetikk, moral og sosiabilitet* [The urban space as a visual field: A theoretical focus on the relationship between language, aesthetics, morality and sociability], Mphil thesis, Department of Sociology, University of Bergen.

_____ (2005), 'Hva mener regjeringen med flerkulturelt mangfold?' [What does the government mean by multi-cultural plurality?], *Nytt Norsk Tidsskrift* 22, no. 1: 72–79.

_____ (2006), 'The Veiled Muslim, the Anorexic and the Transsexual: What do They Have in Common?', *European Journal of Women's Studies* 13, no. 4: 325–341.

_____ (2008), 'Mind the Gap: Intersectionality, Complexity and "the Event"', *Theory and Science* 10, no. 1: 1–15.

Gressgård, Randi and Jacobsen, Christine (2003), 'Questions of Gender in a Multicultural Society', *Nordic Journal of Women's Studies (NORA)* 11, no. 2: 69–77.

Grossberg, Lawrence (1996), 'Identity and Cultural Studies: Is That All There Is?', in *Questions of Cultural Identity*, (ed.) Stuart Hall and Paul du Gay (London: Sage), 87–107.

Grosz, Elizabeth (2001), *Architecture from the Outside: Essays on Virtual and Real Space* (Cambridge, MA: MIT Press).

Günther, Klaus (1988), *Der Sinn für Angemessenheit: Anwendungsdiskurse in Moral und Recht* (Frankfurt: Suhrkamp).

Habermas, Jürgen (1984), *The Theory of Communicative Action, Vol. 1: Reason and the Rationalization of Society*, (trans.) Thomas McCarthy (Boston, MA: Beacon Press).
_____ (1987), *The Philosophical Discourse of Modernity*, (trans.) Frederick Lawrence (Cambridge, MA: MIT Press).
_____ (1988), 'Law and Morality', in *The Tanner Lectures on Human Values, Vol. 8*, (trans.) Kenneth Baynes, (ed.) Sterling McMurrin (Salt Lake City, UT: Salt Lake University Press), 217–279.
_____ (1989), 'Justice and Solidarity: On the Discussion Concerning Stage 6', in *The Moral Domain*, (ed.) Thomas E. Wren (Cambridge, MA: MIT Press), 224–254.
_____ (1990), *Moral Consciousness and Communicative Action*, (trans.) Christian Lenhardt and Shierry Weber Nicholsen (Cambridge, MA: MIT Press).
_____ (1993), *Justification and Application: Remarks on Discourse Ethics*, (trans.) Ciaran Cronin (Cambridge, MA: MIT Press).
Hammer, Espen (1995), 'Innledning' [Introduction], in *Kritikk av dømmekraften* [Critique of judgment], Immanuel Kant (Oslo: Pax), 13–32.
Hetherington, Kevin (1998), *Expressions of Identity: Space, Performance, Politics* (London: Sage).
Hewitt, Roger (2005), *White Backlash and the Politics of Multiculturalism* (Cambridge: Cambridge University Press).
Heyerdahl, Grete B. (1993), 'Jean-Jacques Rousseau', in *Vestens tenkere, Vol. 2* [The philosophers of the West, vol. 2], (ed.) Trond B. Eriksen (Oslo: Aschehoug), 204–221.
Irigaray, Luce (1993), *An Ethics of Sexual Difference*, (trans.) Carolyn Burke and Gillian C. Gill (Ithaca, NY: Cornell University Press).
Jacobsen, Christine M. (2010), *Islamic Traditions and Muslim Youth in Norway* (Leiden: Brill).
Kant, Immanuel ([1781] 1996), *Critique of Pure Reason*, (trans.) Werner S. Pluhar (Indianapolis, IN: Hackett Publishing).
_____ ([1790] 1987), *Critique of Judgment*, (trans.) Werner S. Pluhar (Indianapolis, IN: Hackett Publishing).
Kapferer, Bruce (1988), *Legends of People: Myths of State* (Washington, DC: Smithsonian Institution Press).
Kögler, Hans Herbert (1999), *The Power of Dialogue: Critical Hermeneutics after Gadamer and Foucault*, (trans.) Paul Hendrickson (Cambridge, MA: MIT Press).
Kymlicka, Will (1989), *Liberalism, Community and Culture* (Oxford: Clarendon Press).
_____ (1995), *Multicultural Citizenship: A Liberal Theory of Minority Rights* (Oxford: Clarendon Press).
Laclau, Ernesto (1996), *Emancipation(s)* (London and New York: Verso).
Laclau, Ernesto and Mouffe, Chantal (1985), *Hegemony and Socialist Strategy* (London: Verso).
Larsen, Tord (1979), 'Er alle stygge andunger egentlig svaner? Tanker om antropologiens moralske sakkyndighet' [Are all ugly ducklings actually swans? Thoughts about the moral competence of anthropology], *Antropolognytt*: 3–16.
_____ (1999), 'Den globale samtalen: Modernisering, representasjon og subjektkonstruksjon' [The global conversation: Modernisation, representation and subject

formation], in *Ambivalens og fundamentalisme: Seks essays om kulturens globalisering* [Ambivalence and fundamentalism: Six essays on the globalisation of culture], (ed.) Thomas H. Eriksen and Oscar Hemer (Oslo: Spartacus), 91–112.

———— (2002), 'Urenhetens metafysikk' [The metaphysics of impurity], in *Fanden går i kloster: Elleve tekster om det andre* [The devil joins the convent: Eleven texts on the other], (ed.) Randi Gressgård and Siri Meyer (Oslo: Spartacus), 13–34.

Lash, Scott (1999), *Another Modernity: A Different Rationality* (Oxford: Blackwell).

Latour, Bruno (1988), *The Pasteurisation of France*, (trans.) Alan Sheridan and John Law (Cambridge, MA: Harvard University Press).

Lefort, Claude (1986), *The Political Forms of Modern Society: Bureaucracy, Democracy, Totalitarianism*, (ed.) John B. Thompson (Cambridge: Polity).

Levi, Primo (1989), *The Drowned and the Saved*, (trans.) Raymond Rosenthal (New York: Vintage Books).

Lévi-Strauss, Claude (1966), *The Savage Mind*, (trans.) John Weightman and Doreen Weightman (Chicago, IL: University of Chicago Press).

Lindstad, Merete and Fjeldstad, Øivind (1999), *Pressen og de fremmede* [The press and the strangers] (Kristiansand: Høyskoleforlaget).

Linke, Uli (1999), *Blood and Nation: The European Aesthetics of Race* (Philadelphia: University of Pennsylvania Press).

Lorde, Audre (1983), 'The Master's Tools Will Never Dismantle the Master's House', in *This Bridge Called My Back: Writings By Radical Women of Color*, (ed.) Cherríe Moraga and Gloria Anzaldúa (New York: Kitchen Table), 98–101.

Lyotard, Jean-François (1984), *The Postmodern Condition: A Report on Knowledge*, (trans.) Geoff Bennington and Brian Massumi (Manchester: Manchester University Press).

———— (1988), *The Differend: Phrases in Dispute*, (trans.) Georges Van Den Abbeele (Minneapolis: University of Minnesota Press).

———— (1990), *Heidegger and 'the jews'*, (trans.) Andreas Michel and Mark Roberts (Minneapolis: University of Minnesota Press).

———— (1991), *The Inhuman*, (trans.) Geoffrey Bennington and Rachel Bowlby (Cambridge: Polity Press).

———— (1992a), *The Postmodern Explained to Children*, (trans.) Don Barry, Bernadette Maher, Julian Pefanis, Virginia Spate and Morgan Thomas (London: Turnaround).

———— (1992b), "Sensus Communis', in *Judging Lyotard*, (ed.) Andrew Benjamin (London and New York: Routledge), 1–25.

———— (1994), *Lessons on the Analytic of the Sublime*, (trans.) Elizabeth Rottenberg (Stanford, CA: Stanford University Press).

Lyotard, Jean-François and Thébaud, Jean-Loup (1985), *Just Gaming*, (trans.) Wlad Godzich (Minneapolis: University of Minnesota Press).

MacIntyre, Alasdair (1988), *Whose Justice? Which Rationality?* (Notre Dame, IN: University of Notre Dame Press).

Madood, Tariq (2007), *Multiculturalism: A Civic Idea* (Cambridge: Polity).

Marchart, Oliver (2007), *Post-Foundational Political Thought: Political Difference in Nancy, Lefort, Badiou and Laclau* (Edinburgh: Edinburgh University Press).

Marx, Karl ([1873] 1967), *Capital Vol. 1: The Process of Production of Capital*, (trans.) Samuel Moore and Edward Aveling (New York: International).
More, Thomas ([1516] 2003), *Utopia*, (trans.) Paul Turner (London and New York: Penguin).
Morken, Ivar (1996), 'Likeverdighetens utematiserte normative forutsetninger' [The underlying normative assumptions of equality], paper presented at the 10th Nordic Research on Migration Seminar, 'Likeverdighet og utestengning – forskningsmessige utfordringer' [Equality and exclusion – research challenges], Bergen.
Mosse, George (1985), *Nationalism and Sexuality: Middle-Class Morality and Sexual Norms in Modern Europe* (Madison: University of Wisconsin Press).
Nancy, Jean-Luc (1991), *The Inoperative Community*, (trans.) Peter Connor, Lisa Garbus, Michael Holland and Simona Sawhney (Minneapolis: University of Minnesota Press).
_____ (2000), *Being Singular Plural*, (trans.) Robert Richardson and Anne O'Byrne (Stanford, CA: Stanford University Press).
Nefer Olsen, Kasper (1989), 'Anæsetik: Det sublime forkaret for elskende' [Anaesthetics: The sublime explained to lovers], in *Filosofiske Forskydninger* [Philosophical displacements], (ed.) Niels Brügger and Finn Frandsen (Århus: Akademisk Forlag), 99–122.
Nietzsche, Friedrich ([1901] 1967), *The Will to Power*, (trans.) Walter Kaufmann and R. J. Hollingdale (New York: Random House).
Odner, Knut (2000), *Tradition and Transmission: Bantu, Indo-European and Circumpolar Great Traditions* (Bergen: Norse Publications).
Okin, Susan M. (1999), 'Is Multiculturalism Bad for Women?', in *Is Multiculturalism Bad for Women?* (ed.) Joshua Cohen, Matthew Howard and Martha C. Nussbaum (Princeton, NJ: Princeton University Press), 7–26.
O'Neill, Onora (2000), *Bounds of Justice* (Cambridge: Cambridge University Press).
Pihl, Joron (2001), 'Government Discourse on Inclusive Education and Its Effects on the Construction of "the Other"', paper presented at the conference 'Genres and Discourses in Education, Work and Cultural Life', Oslo University College.
_____ (2005), *Etnisk mangfold i skolen* [Ethnic plurality in education] (Oslo: Universitetsforlaget).
Polanyi, Michael (1958), *Personal Knowledge* (Chicago, IL: University of Chicago Press).
Priest, Graham (1995), *Beyond the Limits of Thought* (Cambridge: Cambridge University Press).
Puar, Jasbir K. (2007), *Terrorist Assemblages: Homonationalism in Queer Times* (Durham, NC: Duke University Press).
Readings, Bill (1991), *Introducing Lyotard: Art and Politics* (London: Routledge).
Rose, Gillian (1992), *The Broken Middle* (Oxford: Blackwell).
Rousseau, Jean-Jacques ([1762] 1989), *The Social Contract*, (trans.) George D. H. Cole, *Great Books of the Western World*, Vol. 38 (London: Encyclopaedia Britannica), 387–439.
Schmidt, Lars-Henrik and Kristensen, Jens Erik (1986), *Lys, luft og renlighed: Den moderne social-hygiejnes fødsel* [Light, air, and cleanliness: The birth of modern social hygiene] (Århus: Akademisk Forlag).
Scott, Joan W. (1992), 'Experience', in *Feminists Theorise the Political*, (ed.) Judith Butler and Joan W. Scott (New York and London: Routledge), 22–40.

_____ (1996), *Only Paradoxes to Offer: French Feminists and the Rights of Man* (Cambridge, MA: Harvard University Press).
Scruton, Roger (1979), *The Aesthetics of Architecture* (Princeton, NJ: Princeton University Press).
Seidler, Victor J. (1998), 'Identity, Memory and Difference: Lyotard and 'the jews'', in *The Politics of Jean-François Lyotard*, (ed.) Chris Rojek and Bryan S. Turner (London and New York: Routledge), 102-127.
Sejten, Anne Elisabeth (1989), 'Glemselens politikk' [The politics of forgetting], in *Filosofiske Forskydninger* [Philosophical displacements], (ed.) Niels Brügger and Finn Frandsen (Århus: Akademisk Forlag), 69-98.
Sennett, Richard (1976), *The Fall of Public Man* (New York: Vintage).
Skeggs, Beverley (1997), *Formations of Class and Gender: Becoming Respectable* (London: Sage).
_____ (2004), *Class, Self, Culture* (London and New York: Routledge).
SMED (Centre for Combating Ethnic Discrimination) (2001), *Når noen er likere enn andre.... En undersøkelse om bruk av religiøst hodeplagg på arbeidsplassen* [When some are more equal than others.... An investigation of the use of religious headgear at the workplace], annual report.
Spivak, Gayatri C. (1985), 'Three Women's Texts and a Critique of Imperialism', *Critical Inquiry* 12, no. 1: 243-261.
_____ (1987), *In Other Words: Essays in Cultural Politics* (New York: Methuen).
_____ (1988), 'Can the Subaltern Speak?', in *Marxism and the Interpretation of Culture*, (ed.) Cary Nelson and Lawrence Grossberg (Urbane: University of Illinois Press), 271-316.
_____ (1993), *Outside in the Teaching Machine* (New York: Routledge).
_____ (1997), 'Translator's Preface', in *Of Grammatology*, Jacque Derrida (Baltimore, MD: Johns Hopkins University Press), ix-lxxxvii.
_____ (1999), *A Critique of Postcolonial Reason: Towards a History of the Vanishing Present* (Cambridge, MA: Harvard University Press).
_____ (2003), *Death of a Discipline* (New York: Columbia University Press).
Stjernfelt, Frederik (1989), 'Fordi: Lyotards etik mellem dissensus og ubetinget imperativ' [Because: Lyotard's ethics between dissensus and unconditional imperative], in *Filosofiske Forskydninger* [Philosophical displacements], (ed.) Niels Brügger and Finn Frandsen (Århus: Akademisk Forlag), 123-147.
Storheim, Eivind (1993), 'Immanuel Kant', in *Vestens tenkere, Vol. 2* [The philosophers of the West, vol. 2], (ed.) Trond B. Eriksen (Oslo: Aschehoug), 242-264.
Taylor, Charles (1989), *Sources of the Self: The Making of the Modern Identity* (Cambridge, MA: Harvard University Press).
_____ (1994), 'The Politics of Recognition', in *Multiculturalism*, (ed.) Amy Gutmann (Princeton, NJ: Princeton University Press), 25-74.
Thorseth, May (1995), *Sosial integrasjon: Et paternalistisk prosjekt?* [Social integration: A paternalist project?], IFIM Report No. 3 (Trondheim: SINTEF).
Tierney, Nathan L. (1994), *Imagination and Ethical Ideals* (Albany: State University of New York Press).

Trey, George (1998), *Solidarity and Difference: The Politics of Enlightenment in the Aftermath of Modernity* (Albany: State University of New York Press).
Turner, Victor (1969), *The Ritual Process: Structure and Anti-Structure* (London: Routledge).
Vetlesen, Arne Johan (1988), 'Habermas' kritikk av Gadamers tese om hermeneutikkens universalitet' [Habermas's critique of Gadamer's thesis on the universality of hermeneutics], *Norsk Filosofisk Tidsskrift* 23: 27–38.
_____ (1994), *Perception, Empathy, and Judgement: An Inquiry into the Preconditions of Moral Performance* (University Park: Pennsylvania State University Press).
Vetlesen, Arne Johan and Nortvedt, Per (1994), *Følelser og moral* [Emotions and morality] (Oslo: Ad Notam Gyldendal).
Walzer, Michael (1983), *Spheres of Justice: A Defense of Pluralism and Equality* (New York: Basic Books).
White, Hayden (1972), 'The Forms of Wildness: Archaeology of an Idea', in *The Wild Man Within: An Image in Western Thought from the Renaissance to Romanticism*, (ed.) Edward Dudley and Maximillian E. Novak (Pittsburgh: University of Pittsburgh Press), 3–38.
White Paper No. 17 (1996–1997), *Om innvandring og det flerkulturelle Norge* [On immigration and the multicultural Norway] (Oslo: Kommunal- og arbeidsdepartementet).
White Paper No. 49 (2003–2004), *Mangfold gjennom inkludering og deltakelse: Ansvar og frihet* [Diversity through inclusion and participation: Responsibility and freedom] (Oslo: Kommunal- og regionaldepartementet).
Wiggen, Carlos (1998), *Barbari og sivilisasjon* [Barbarism and civilisation] (Kristiansand: Høyskoleforlaget).
Wikan, Unni (1995), *Mot en ny norsk underklasse* [Towards a new Norwegian underclass] (Oslo: Gyldendal).
Wilkerson, T. E. (1973), 'Seeing-As', *Mind* 82, no. 328: 481–496.
Williams, James (1998), *Lyotard: Towards a Postmodern Philosophy* (Cambridge: Polity Press).
Wittgenstein, Ludwig ([1953] 1968), *Philosophical Investigations*, 3rd ed., (trans.) Elizabeth Anscombe (Oxford: Basil Blackwell).
Wood, David (2001), *The Deconstruction of Time*, 2nd ed. (Evanston, IL: Northwestern University Press).
Young, Iris Marion (1990), *Justice and the Politics of Difference* (Princeton, NJ: Princeton University Press).
_____ (1995), 'Polity and Group Difference: A Critique of the Ideal of Universal Citizenship', in *Theorising Citizenship*, (ed.) Ronald Beiner (Albany: State University of New York Press), 175–208.
Yuval-Davis, Nira (1997), *Gender and Nation* (London: Sage).
Ziarek, Ewa P. (2001), *An Ethics of Dissensus* (Stanford, CA: Stanford University Press).
Zerilli, Linda M. G. (2005), *Feminism and the Abyss of Freedom* (Chicago, IL, and London: University of Chicago Press).

Index

Adorno, Theodor, 39; and Horkheimer, 21, 25, 41, 47, 86–87, 127, 136, 142
aesthetic object, 61, 63–64, 69–70; and the singular subject, 61, 63
Agamben, Giorgio, 24, 31, 48, 89, 104, 150n15. *See also* exception
Ahmed, Sara, 152n8
Ålund, Aleksandra, 11, 140n6
Anderson, Benedict, 85
aporia, 58, 59, 82–85, 93, 97, 99, 147nn7–8; and event, 82; between 'is' and 'ought', 95; between the singular and the general, 74, 82, 95–96; between the unidentifiable and the identifiable, 100; between understanding and reason, 91. *See also* conflict; 'differend'; gap; heterogeneity; incommensurability
Aquinas, Thomas, 50
Arendt, Hannah, 30–33, 47–48, 89–90, 93, 151n2. *See also* totalitarianism
arrivant, 85–86, 104. *See also* Derrida; hospitality
assimilation, 7, 11, 14, 19, 23–24, 34, 38, 81, 87, 99, 106–109, 133; and culturalisation, 13, 19, 105–106, 110; and modernisation, 16; and normalisation, 11; and subordination, 12–13, 19, 105–106, 110; of the 'others', 14, 106; recognition by, 13; strategy of, 14

autonomous subject, 22, 28–33, 36–37, 40, 49–52, 55, 66, 70, 102, 133; and the universal subject, 28–33, 54, 102. *See also* autonomy
autonomy, 3, 9, 17, 29, 31–32, 36, 38, 47–48, 58, 60, 67, 141n5, 146n6, 148n13; and cultural relativism, 120; and cultural particularity, 28; and equality, 36–37, 48, 143n17; and freedom, 6; and individuality, 32–33; and intrinsic value, 48; and integrity, 18; and self-development, 39; and uniqueness, 17; cultural, 9, 15–16, 19, 120, 131, 141n5; lack of, 38, 65; of the subject, 28, 72. *See also* autonomous subject; duality; universal subject

Badiou, Alain, 136
Barry, Brian, 4–5, 8, 15, 120
Barth, Fredrik, 138n1
Barthes, Roland, 33, 36, 85
beauty, 59–63, 70–72, 145n1; and ugliness, 71–72; experience of, 60–62, 70; judgement of, 59, 62. *See also* harmony; Kant; pleasure; reflective judgement; taste
Bell, Vikki, 152n8
Benhabib, Seyla, 120
Bhabha, Homi, 8, 19, 134, 141n3, 141n4
Blum, Lawrence, 116–118, 139n2

Bologh, Roslyn, 117
Braidotti, Rosi, 143n15
Brochgrevink, Tordis, 7
Brown, Wendy, xi, 6–8, 11, 19, 38, 109, 111, 125, 136, 139n4, 140n7, 145n11, 150n13. *See also* tolerance
Brügger, Niels, 150n13
Buber, Martin, 64
Butler, Judith, xi, 8, 89, 94, 111; on gender perception and aesthetic aspect of norms, 124–125; on norms, performative contradiction and cultural translation, 133–135; on subjectivity, 64; on the universal, 152n9

Caliban, 13–14. *See also* Shakespeare
Carroll, David, 81–82, 104
Christianity, 16, 20, 29, 144
citizens, xi, 29–30, 32–33, 37, 53, 128, 143n14; community of, 71; in a democratic society, 1, 12, 29; equality of all, 29; rights of the, 6. *See also* citizenship
citizenship, 29, 31, 71; institution of, 29. *See also* citizens
Cixous, Helen, 141n3
Clack, Beverly, 143n15
communitas, 23–24, 36, 48, 56, 84, 105; and liminality, 23–25, 27, 101; concept of, 27. *See also* liminality
community, xiii, xv, 9–10, 24, 27, 28, 36, 52, 56, 63–65, 67, 71, 74, 85, 87, 104–105; and dialogue, viii; and identity, x; and judgement, 74; as a work (of itself), 104; as communitas, 105; as 'ground' and middle, 65; based on difference, xiii, xv, 52, 56, 61, 63–64, 67–68, 71, 74, 87, 104–105; based on identity, 56; based on metaphysical ideas, 105; dominant notions of, 104; limit for, 67; of citizens, 71; of communication, 119; of equals, 85; prior to any interest, 85; 73; sense of, 64; without a delimited identity, 104; without community ('nous tous désormais'), 104

conflict, vii, 88, 90–92, 94–95, 97–99, 108, 110, 128, 150n11; a zone of, and paradoxes, 12; as *aporias*, 58; as 'differend' (*différend*), 88, 90–92, 97; as heterogeneity, 97; as irresolvable, 88–89, 91–92, 95, 97–98, 110; as litigation, 91; as solvable, 91; between genres of discourse, 90–92; between feminism and multiculturalism, 3; between heterogeneous phrases, 91; between pure and empirical reason, 28; between the 'people' and the 'elite', x, xi; homogenisation of, 97; over the mode of linking, 90; 'regulation' of, 92, 94; resolution of, 97; two kinds of, 87–88. *See also aporia*; 'differend'; gap; heterogeneity; incommensurability; Lyotard
Critchley, Simon, 152n8
critical distance, 106–107, 113–115, 117, 120–123, 125–126, 130, 135, 15n13; to moral norms, 120; to our evaluative standards, 107, 123; to our own criteria of judgement, 106, 119, 123; to one's own truth claims, 113
critical intervention, xii, 12
cultural distinctiveness. *See* distinctiveness
cultural relativism. *See* relativism
culturalisation, xv, 10, 13–14, 19, 105–106; and assimilation, 13, 19, 105–106; and individualisation, 109; and subordination, 13–14, 19, 36, 48, 105–106, 111; concept of, 109, of immigrants, 10; of inequality, 14; of the 'others', 11, 40, 111. *See also* subordination

Davidson, Donald, 103, 108, 145n11
Dean, Mitchell, 31
Deleuze, Gilles, 23, 28, 126, 141n3; on simulacrum, 83–84
democracy, xii, xi, 12, 39, 94
Derrida, Jacques, 104, 126, 141n3; on deconstruction, xiv, 141n6;

Derrida, Jacques (*cont.*)
  on identity, 86; on law and justice, 102; on the *arrivant*, 85–86, 104. See also *arrivant*; hospitality
determinative judgement, 62, 66, 77, 79, 118, 129, 131; in contrast to play, 66; transcendence of, 66. *See also* judgement; Kant
dialectics, 75, 127, 131, 148n1; scandal of, 75, 128
dialogue, xii–xv, 6–7, 12, 94, 97, 106–107, 110–111, 114–115, 122, 126–131, 150n15, 152n5; and community, viii; and planned pluralism, 126; as monologue, 42, 105; be open to, 129; between equal parties, 15; between the majority and the minority, xii; Gadamer's approach to, 106–107, 110, 114; history as, 129; Kögler's concept of, xiv, 107; organisation of, 107; suppression of, 133; theoretical 'ground' for, vii; with 'others', 130. *See also* multicultural dialogue
'differend' (Lyotard), xiii, 88–93, 95–100, 106, 108, 134; and injustice, 95; as *aporia*, 97; as distinguished from a litigation, 88; as heterogeneity between rules of judgement, 90; as heterogeneity of phrases, 90; as 'illegitimate paternalism', 151n16; as irresolvable conflict, 88–90, 92; attentive to, 100; bear witness to, 97; between genres of discourse, 92–93; between 'us' and the 'other', 106; speak for, 135; testify to, 96; two concepts of, 98–99. See also *aporia*; conflict; gap; heterogeneity; incommensurability; Lyotard
dilemma, xiv, 4, 12–13, 19, 59, 88, 99, 133, 151n18; as a 'double bind', 96; as irresolvable conflict, 88; between equal dignity and distinctiveness, viii, xiv–xv, 12, 14, 16, 20, 22, 49, 52, 87, 105, 118, 126; and paradoxes, 49; of interaction, 2, 88; of representation, 133. *See also* multicultural dilemma
discourse ethics, 107, 119–121, 130, 152n6. *See also* ethics; Habermas
discursive framework, vii, ix, xii, xiv, 12, 135, 137, 140n8. *See also* multiculturalism
disorder, 22–23; and order, 22–23; as impurity, 47; as liminality, 24; as pathology, 23, 72. *See also* impurity; liminality; pathology; ugliness
displacement, xiii, 101–102, 126; as rewriting, 75–76; between modernism and postmodernism, 78, 87, 101–102, 129–130, 135–136; logic of, 101; of identities, 100; philosophy of, 126, 129; relation of, 76; strategy of, xiii, 100, 105, 132
distance. *See* critical distance
distinctiveness, 1–9, 11, 14–15, 18–19, 26, 32, 36–38, 54, 87–88, 134; and culture, 3; and feminism, xv; and equal dignity/equality, vii–viii, 1, 12, 14–16, 20, 22, 49, 52, 87, 102, 105, 126, 137, 140n1; notions of, viii; of the 'others', 7, 14, 139n4; pertaining to communities, xvi; pertaining to cultural relativism, 5; preservation of, 18; recognition of, 1–2, 6–7, 11, 13–14, 16–17, 19, 37–38, 50, 118, 131, 135. *See also* particularity; recognition
domination, 112–113, 126–129, 131–133, 151n2; and collectivity, 47; and power, 111–112; and resistance, 112, 132; relations of, 112; states of, 128; structures of, xv, 19, 115, 132. *See also* Foucault; Kögler; power
Donald, James, 29–30, 32, 143n14
double bind, 96, 151n18
Douglas, Mary, 22–23, 47. *See also* impurity; pathology; purity
duality, 16, 25, 43, 53, 66, 142n9; between equality and distinctiveness, 140n1; between the 'thing' in itself (the Idea) and its image, 83; of

Index

assimilation and culturalisation/subordination, 19; of the child, 30; of ethnocentrism and cultural relativism, 102; of personal autonomy and uniqueness, 17; of the subject, 16–17, 19–20, 22, 28, 32–33, 38, 70. *See also* autonomous subject; universal subject

Dumont, Louis, 16–17, 94, 108, 141n4, 143nn1-2, 144n3, 144nn5-8, 144–145n10, 145nn11-12; on modern and non-modern ideologies, 41–55, 68, 75; on comparison of values, 103; on nationalism and individuality 84–86. *See also* equality; hierarchy; holism; ideology; purity; totalitarianism; value-ideas

egalitarianism, ix, 12, 54. *See also* ideology

Egeland, Cathrine, xvi, 111

Eliassan, Knut Ove, 20, 22, 24, 26, 40, 71–72, 142n9, 142n11, 142n13

empathy, 115–118, 151n4; capacity for, 115; faculty of, 116. *See also* moral performance

enlightenment, 26, 79, 81, 87, 128; and mythology, 21, 41

Enlightenment, the, 17, 20–21, 80, 142n12; and Romanticism, 17; project of, 119; the Age of, 17; critique of, 41; the ideal of, 21, 130; the legacy of, ix. *See also* grand narratives; modernity

equal dignity, 37; and distinctiveness, vii, viii, xiv, xv, 1, 12–13, 16, 22, 102; and gender equality, 3; ideal of, 135; recognition of, 1, 13, 16. *See also* equality

equality, vii–x, xv, 1–5, 11, 16, 29, 31–39, 50–51, 54, 94–95, 118, 135–137, 139n2, 140n1, 140n7, 145n12; among citizens, 12, 29, 37; among groups, ix; among humans, 17; and autonomy, 35, 37, 48, 143n17; and cultural difference/plurality, ix, x, xv, 1; and distinctiveness/difference, vii, viii, 1–2, 14–16, 20, 22, 49–50, 52, 87, 105, 118, 126, 140n1; and gender, 3, 94, 151n17; and freedom, 1, 14, 29, 94; and hierarchy, 50, 145n12; and inclusive humanity, 32; and justice, 34, 107, 118; and respect, 16; and rights, ix, 1, 4, 8; as normalisation and assimilation, 11; boomerang effect of, 39; claims to, 135; democratic form of, 1; ideal of, 7, 16–17, 34, 37–40, 51, 95; embodiment of, 94; of a socio-political nature, 11; paradox of, 39–40; recognition of, 16, 38, 50; respect for, 1; the Christian notion of, 16; the law of, 32; universalist notions of, viii. *See also* equal dignity; recognition

Eriksen, Tore, 78–79

Erikson, Erik H., 45–46

essentialism, 140n1. *See also* strategic essentialism

ethics, 16, 87, 113, 115, 118 – 121, 126, 129–130, 150n11, 152n8. *See also* discourse ethics; moral performance

ethnocentrism, 4, 9, 15, 88, 95, 102, 139n3; and cultural relativism, 2–5, 9, 102; the problem of, 7, 15, 102

event, viii, 78, 80–82, 85–87, 93, 96, 101–102, 107, 149n2, 149n4, 149nn7-8; and *aporia*, 82; bear witness to, 96; testify to, 93, 102. *See also* Lyotard; sublime, the

exception, 89–90, 93; relation of, 89–90; state of, 24, 89. *See also* Agamben

faculty, 57, 59, 80, 146n3, 151n4; and empirical will (to power), 66; of empathy, 116; of imagination, 123; of judgement, 59, 63, 115–116, 118; of presentation, 77, 135; of reason, 57; of understanding, 57. *See also* Kant; power

Falzon, Christopher, 126–133, 137

Fanon, Franz, 141n4

Favell, Adrian, ix, 138n1

feminism, 18; and multiculturalism, 3

Fjeldstad, Øivind, 10
forgotten, the, 81, 86, 105, 128, 136. *See also* Lyotard
Foucault, Michel, 16, 21, 29, 108, 126–128, 140n2, 141n3; on heterotopia and utopia, 27; on objectification and subjectification, 19; on power and domination, 112, 128; on power and freedom, 129. *See also* domination; heterotopia; power
foundationalism, viii, 140n1. *See also* foundations
foundations, viii, 26, 42, 51, 103, 109, 111, 128, 133, 136; contingency of, viii, 111; dissolution of, 85; in modern ideology, 53; need for, viii, 136; quest for, 136. *See also* foundationalism; ground
Fraser, Nancy, 139n2
freedom, xi, xiv, 5–8, 26, 29, 55, 57–59, 64, 69–70, 80, 112, 120, 127, 129, 148nn12–13, 151n2; and equality, 1, 14, 29, 94; and justice, 120; and morality, 148n13; and nature, 69; and power, 112; and rights, 2; and subjectivity, 64; as autonomy, 6, 65, 141n5, 146n6; as idea, 69; as non-normative, 129, 132; domain of, 148n12; from external forces, 25; laws of, 58; loss of, 92; negation of, 112; of choice, 3, 49; of religion, 7–8; of speech, 1; sphere of, 58; vacuum of, 112

Gadamer, Hans-Georg, 65–68, 106–110, 114, 121, 125, 147n9, 147n11; on collective memory and hermeneutical circle, 65–68, 107, 122; on dialogue, 106–110, 114, 127; on solidarity, 121–123
gap, 20–21, 27–33, 58, 60–61, 76, 79, 98, 111, 136; between intuition and intellect, 58; between identity and non-identity, 133; between 'is' and ought', 59, 130; between nature and culture, 60; between the demand and the reaction, 97; between the different spheres, 58; between the good and the non-place, 27; between the ontological and the ontic, 136; between the particular identity and the abstract human being, 33; between the pure and the impure, 21, 28; between the real and the ideal, 119; between the singular/heterogeneous and the general/universal, 93; between the universal and the autonomous subject, 20, 28–29, 33, 54; between understanding and reason, 58–59; between what is told and what cannot be told, 93; between words and things, 98. *See also aporia*; conflict; 'differend'; heterogeneity; incommensurability
Gehlen, Arnold, 65
gender, x, 3, 37, 124; and equality, 3, 94, 151n17; as distinctiveness and deficiency, 30, 32–33
Gennep, Arnold van, 23. *See also* liminality
God, 29, 37, 52, 58, 67–70, 84; and the myth of creation, 44, 84; and the soul, 17; and the supersensible, 70; as guiding principle, 68; as idea of origin, 26; as origin of being, 69; as purity, 22, 84, 141n5
Gombrich, E. H., 125
'good life', 107, 113–116, 118–120, 123, 132; and justice, 116, 118–119, 123; criteria for, 114; level of the, 107
grand narratives, 20, 24, 26, 34, 42, 55, 110, 127, 133. *See also* Enlightenment, the; Lyotard; modernity
Gray, John, 4
Gressgård, Randi, 3, 6, 11, 123, 143n15, 149n4
Grossberg, Lawrence, 141n7
Grosz, Elizabeth, 149n8
ground, vii, 26, 38, 42, 53–54, 63, 67, 69, 74, 78, 120, 136; and utopian ideals, 26; as contingent, 127, 136; as groundless, 61, 63–65, 100–101, 103;

Index

moment of, 136. *See also* foundations; Lash

Günther, Klaus, 119

Habermas, Jürgen, 107, 119–123, 125, 127, 152n6; and solidarity, 121–123; on discourse ethics and post-conventional norms, 107, 119–121; on performative contradiction, 134

Hammer, Espen, 62

harmony, 59–62; between understanding (nature) and reason (freedom, morality), 59; lack of, 59–61, 68; of subject and object, 62. *See also* beauty; faculty; Kant; pleasure; reflective judgement

Hegel, 67, 148n1

hermeneutical circle, 65–66. *See also* Gadamer; hermeneutics

hermeneutics, 66, 106–107, 111, 122, 147n9. *See also* Gadamer; hermeneutical circle; Kögler

heterogeneity, ix, xv, 23, 55–56, 58, 71–72, 73–75, 79, 82, 84, 88, 90–91, 94, 97–99, 101, 111–112, 126–129, 136, 141n6, 152n8; and *aporias*, 59; and social and political conflicts, 90; and the singular subject, 55; as productive, 111; as difference in kind, 58; as pathology, 23; as 'the differend', 90; as thought-provoking, 130; as unpresentable, 88; between the powers of intuition and reason, 60; consequences of, 74, 92; exclusion of, 128; homogenisation of, 99; in language, 91–92, 97, 99, 103, 151n19; in terms of incommensurability, 55; of phrases, 90; of spheres and faculties, 55–56; ontologisation of, 82, 87, 90, 97, 102; suppression of, 75, 79, 84, 126; of the sublime, 92. See also *aporia*; conflict; 'differend'; gap; incommensurability; Kant; Lyotard

heterotopia, 27. *See also* Foucault; utopia

Hetherington, Kevin, 24
Hewitt, Roger, x
Heyerdahl, Grete B., 143n14
hierarchy, 37, 44, 46–47, 50–51, 83, 85, 144n3, 144n5, 144n8; and equality, 50, 145n12; and holism, 44; as an organising principle, 52; of levels of experience, 44; within the modern configuration, 51. *See also* Dumont; holism; inequality; subordination; totalitarianism

hijab, 8

Hobbes, Thomas, 31

holism, 40–41, 43, 47, 49–55, 103, 143n2, 145n11; and hierarchy, 43; and modern totalitarianism, 40; and totality, 41. *See also* Dumont; hierarchy

Horkheimer, Max, 21, 25, 41, 47, 86, 127, 136, 142n12

hospitality, viii, 86. *See also arrivant*; Derrida

human rights, 4–5, 15; and conventional norms, 4. *See also* rights

humanity. *See* inclusive humanity

ideal, 15–16, 26, 29–39, 54, 94, 122–123; about equal status and equal opportunities, 3; and freedom, 129; as utopian, 21, 26–28, 31, 142n12; of dialogue, 15; of Enlightenment, 21, 130; of equality, 7; 16–17, 31, 34, 37–40, 51, 95, 135; of the political subject's 'enlightenment', 87; of transparency, 32; of purity, 26

ideas, vii, 4, 26, 44, 52, 133, 141n9; about the 'others', 15; and expectations, 113; and images, 85, 104; and thoughts and feelings, 17; and political argument, ix; and terms, 15; and values, vii–viii, 41–43, 52–53, 144n7, 144n10, 145n11; as concepts of reason (Kant), 57–58, 149n5; as legitimising, 53; as metaphysical, 26, 67, 105, 141n9; as regulating, 20, 26, 55; as secular, 21,

ideas (*cont.*)
26; as supersensible (Kant), 72; as utopian, 27–28, 55; in conflict, vii; of divinity, 26; of (lost) innocence, 143n13; normative dimension of, 53; of purity, 20, 26, 103; of omniscience, 28; of origin, 26. *See also* value-ideas
identity, viii, xv, 1, 8, 16, 19, 21–23, 29–34, 41, 43–46, 51–52, 54–56, 82–88, 90, 99–103, 113, 125–126, 129, 131–134, 136, 140n1, 140n6, 141n6, 144n5; among fellow citizens, 32; and community, x, xv, 56, 67, 104–105; and difference, viii, 40, 52, 55, 72, 74–75, 88, 103; and event, 82; and generative/organising principles, 103, 136; and meaning, 21; and non-identity, 60, 97, 99, 132–133; and resistance, 113, 132; and rights, 31; and self-identity, 67; and the *arrivant*, 86; and purity, 100; and subjectivity, 103; and the 'others', 43, 54, 99–100, 105, 115, 133; and totality, xiii; and universality, 103; as civic, 32, 34; as 'common being', 86; as cultural, 1; as inclusive humanity, 31; as national, x, 8, 33, 84; as purity, 40; between people, 51; deconstruction of, 88, 134; formation of, 101, 131–132; level of, 99; logic of, viii, 74, 118; metaphysical ideas of, 67; negation of, ix, 130, 141n7; of Man, 30, 85; of the majority population, 36; of the original, 83; product of, 54; universalisation of, 105. *See also* identity politics
identity politics, 86, 131, 138n1, 143n13. *See also* identity
ideology, vii, 20, 22, 31–33, 36–37, 42–43, 45–47, 49–51, 53–55, 70, 84–85, 94, 102–103, 140n8, 143nn1–2, 144n3, 145n11. *See also* ideology critique; liberal ideology; republican ideology
ideology critique, 113. *See also* ideology
idioms, 88, 93, 96–99, 111; demand for, 99–100, 130; search for, 99, 101, 111, 135. *See also* Lyotard

imagination, 57, 59–60, 62, 77, 80, 93, 101, 115, 117, 122–125, 130, 135, 149n5; and perception and 'seeing-as', 125; and understanding, 62. *See also* faculty; moral performance; 'seeing-as'
immanence, 127; transcendence of, 33–34, 67; and femininity, 143n15
impurity, 20–23, 26–28, 38, 41–42, 47, 72–73, 141nn5–6; and purity, 20–24, 27–28, 42, 47, 51–52, 72, 82, 84, 127, 131; and tolerance, 6; logic of, 28; of the autonomous subject, 28. *See also* disorder; liminality; pathology; ugliness
inclusive humanity, 15–16, 28, 31–34, 37–38, 102, 133–134; and equality, 32; consummation of, 16. *See also* Larsen
incommensurability, ix, 55, 103, 106, 108, 111; and radical difference, 136; and relativism, 113, 129; argument for, 108; as condition for critical reflection, 111; between descriptive and prescriptive, 93; the thesis of, 103, 108, 145n11. See also *aporia*; conflict; 'différend'; gap; heterogeneity; relativism; subordination
inequality, ix, x, 37–39, 50, 140n6, 140n8; and the ideal of equality, 37–39; culturalisation of, 14; problems of, 11. *See also* hierarchy
injustice, 88, 92, 95–96, 108, 118
integration, ix, 5–6, 9–14, 24, 34, 36–38, 49, 86, 94, 140n6; and cultural diversity, ix; and immigration, xii, 6; and recognition, ix, 34; as planned pluralism, 11, 126; as policy, ix, 5, 10–12, 14, 36–38, 49, 94, 143n17; debate on, ix, 6; of the 'others', 12
interiorisation, 16–17, 29, 43, 140n2. *See also* Dumont; Larsen
intervention. *See* critical intervention
Irigaray, Luce, 141n3, 152n8

Jacobsen, Christine M., xvi, 3, 6, 26
Jews, 7, 92

Index

'jews, the', 81. *See also* Lyotard
judgement, viii, xiv, 5, 8, 56–63, 68, 69, 72, 74, 78–79, 83, 88, 90, 96, 101–102, 106, 113, 115–116, 118–119, 121, 125, 130, 134, 138n1, 142n12, 145nn1–2, 146nn2–6, 149n4, 150n13; and cognition, 62; and knowledge, 101; and perception and action, 115–116, 152n6; and understanding, 110, 130; as mediating power, 59; condition of possibility for, 101; context of, 56, 59; criteria of, 91, 106, 108, 115, 119, 123; heterogeneous conditions of, 78–79; justification of, 58; lack of universal rule of, 88, 90, 92, 96; misuse of, 124; Moment of, 63; of beauty, 59, 62, 146n5; of taste, 56–57, 59, 61–63, 145n1, 146n2, 146nn4–5; of the sublime, 59; standard of, 15, 26, 39, 42, 88, 94–95, 111, 114, 125; postponement of, 130; two types of, 56; will to, 123. *See also* determinative judgement; reflective judgement
jurisdiction, 36, 82, 88–89, 93, 95. *See also* judgement; Lyotard
justice, viii, x, 4, 35, 37–38, 94–95, 101–102, 107, 113–114, 116, 118–121, 123–124, 126, 128–130, 140n8, 151n19; and equality, 37–38, 94, 107, 118; and freedom, 120; and the 'good life', 116, 119, 123; and morality, 120; and truth, 94; as non-determinative, 101–102, 113; for the 'others', 95

Kant, Emmanuel, xiii, 28, 55–63, 65, 67–74, 78–80, 82–83, 91–92, 96, 98, 100, 105, 120, 142n12, 145n1, 146nn2–6, 147n9, 147nn11–12, 148nn12–13, 149n7. *See also* beauty; determinative judgement; faculty; God; harmony; heterogeneity; *noumenon*; reflective judgement; sublime, the; ugliness
Kapferer, Bruce, 33
Kögler, Hans Herbert, xiii–xiv, 106–115, 117, 120, 123, 125–127, 129–130, 132. *See also* dialogue; domination; hermeneutics; power; truth; totalitarianism
Kristensen, Jens Erik, 22, 27, 65
Kristeva, Julia, 141n3
Kymlicka, Will, 3–5

Lacan, Jacques, 141n3
Laclau, Ernesto, 127, 133, 136, 152n9
Larsen, Tord, 2, 9, 13–19, 140n2, 142n13. *See also* duality; inclusive humanity; interiorisation; liminality; opposition; Shakespeare; subject
Lash, Scott, xiii, 56–59, 61, 63–68, 72, 74, 85–86, 100–101, 103–104, 127, 147n9. *See also* aesthetic object; community; difference; gap; ground; judgement; reflexivity; singular subject; transcendence
Latour, Bruno, 27
law, xii, 1, 4, 61, 65, 89, 91, 94, 96, 101, 104, 107, 113, 118–120, 141n5, 143n14, 143n17, 148n13; and articles, 7; and cultural relativism, 119; and exception, 89; and totalitarianism, 94; and tolerance, 6–8; and equality, 32, 34; and freedom, 58–59; and morality, 120; and nature, 61–62, 92, 85; and rights, 89; and Roman society, 29; as some universal, 56, 61, 91, 149n4; the plural representability of, 118, 131
Lefort, Claude, 84
Levi, Primo, 93, 150n15
Lévi-Strauss, Claude, xiii
liberal ideology, 28, 31 32. *See also* ideology
liminality, 23–24, 27, 101, 141n7; and communitas, 23–24, 27, 101. *See also* Gennep; Larsen; Turner
Lindstad, Merete, 10
litigation, 88, 91, 97–98, 151n16. *See also* Lyotard
Locke, John, 31
Lorde, Audre, xiv

Lyotard, Jean-François, xiii, 26, 30, 53, 73–84, 86–94, 96–105, 108, 110–113, 118, 126–127, 129–130, 132–133, 136, 141n3, 141n10, 144n4, 147n10, 148nn1–2, 149n3, 149nn6–7, 150nn8–12, 150n14, 151nn18–19, 152n7. *See also* conflict; 'differend'; event; forgotten, the; grand narratives; heterogeneity; idioms; 'jews, the'; litigation; *Nachträglichkeit*; postmodernism; silence; sublime, the; wrong, a

MacIntyre, Alasdair, 33, 37, 110–111, 117–118, 151n1
Madood, Tariq, 12
Marchart, Oliver, 136, 152n9
Marx, Karl, 148n1
media, ix, xi, 10, 95
metaphysics, 26, 150n10; of purity, 13, 19, 21–22, 25, 34, 66, 74. *See also* purity
modernism, 74, 76–78; and postmodernism, 76–78, 129. *See also* Lyotard; postmodernism
modernity, xiii, 24, 26, 56, 74–75, 80, 105, 143n16, 148n2; grand narratives of, 24. *See also* Enlightenment, the; grand narratives
moral performance, 115, 121. *See also* empathy; ethics; imagination; perception; Vetlesen
More, Thomas, 27. *See also* utopia
Morken, Ivar, 38
Mosse, George, 34
Mouffe, Chantal, 127, 136
multicultural dialogue, vii–iv, xii, 11–12, 42, 106–107, 115, 126, 130–131. *See also* dialogue
multicultural dilemma, vii, xv, 1, 22, 34, 38, 42, 88, 102, 105–106. *See also* dilemma
multicultural paradox, xv, 11, 36, 42. *See also* paradox
multiculturalism, xii, 3, 13, 17–18, 54, 145n11; and feminism, 3; and integration, 49; as a political doctrine, 4; 12; debate on, vii–viii, xii, xiv, 1–3, 12, 15, 18, 20, 50, 118, 138n1, 141n5; discourses on, viii; framework of, vii–ix, 135; paradox of, 140n8; parameters of, 49; politics of, x, xii; 'soft' version of, xi

Nachträglichkeit, 80–81. *See also* Lyotard
Nancy, Jean-Luc, 64, 67, 104
narratives. *See* grand narratives
nation state, viii–ix, 5, 11, 30–31, 53
nationalism, 67, 84
Nefer Olsen, Kasper, 80, 87, 149n5, 149n7
Nietzsche, Friedrich, 16, 65, 150n10
norms, 2–5, 32–35, 75, 85, 94–95, 107, 118–120, 123, 128, 131, 135, 139n5; aesthetic aspect of, 124; and human rights, 4; and principles, 107, 118; and values, 3–4, 7–8, 11, 15, 37; application of, 119; destabilisation of, 132; for communicative ethics, 120; justification of, 119, 152n6; of dominance, 136; of freedom, 120; of gender equality, 3; of justice, 120; of the bourgeoisie, 85; of the majority, 5; particularity of, 119; transgression of, 129; universality of, 34, 119. *See also* values
Nortvedt, Per, 115–118, 151nn3–4
nostalgia, 77; for an original state of nature, 25; for lost origins, x; for the unattainable, 76
noumenon, 59, 147n8. *See also* Kant

object. *See* aesthetic object
Odner, Knut, 48
Okin, Susan Moller, 3–5, 15
O'Neill, Onora, 141n5, 148n13
opposition, ix, 18, 24, 41, 52, 54, 56, 75; between culture/freedom and nature, 69; between masculinity and femininity, 143n15; between 'people' and 'elite', xi; between purity and impurity, 21, 47; between transcendence and immanence, 143n15; between 'us'

Index

and the 'others', xv, 13, 23, 36, 52–53, 105, 140n3; logic of, xv, 9, 20, 23, 34, 40–41, 47, 55–56, 75, 102, 105, 141n3, 141nn6–7; the problem of, 18–19, 38, 42, 54, 75, 87, 102, 105, 141n4; to the whole, 45

paradox, xv, 3, 5, 11–12, 22, 24, 39, 42, 49–50, 54, 85, 99; and *aporia*, 100; and death, 27; and dilemmas, 42, 49, 99; and hierarchy, 144n5; and holism, 49–50; and liminality, 24; and planned pluralism, 5; and the sublime, 81; and totalitarianism, 85; of (in)equality, 39–40; of modern ideology, 22; of modern subjectivity, 33; of multiculturalism, 140n8; of the future (*post*) anterior (*modo*), 78; of testimony, 93. *See also* multicultural paradox

particularity, 12; and contingency, 110; as cultural, 28, 36; as opposed to universality, 4; of norms, 119; of standards, 140n8. *See also* distinctiveness

pathology, 23. *See also* disorder; impurity; ugliness

perception, 73, and action and thought of others, 112; as aesthetical (Kant), 145n1, 149n7; and emotions, 123; and imagination and 'seeing as', 123–125, 135; and judgement and action, 115–116, 152n6; as ethical/moral, 29, 115–116. *See also* moral performance

performative contradiction, 134–135. *See also* Butler; Habermas

Pihl, Joron, 35, 37

planned pluralism, xv, 5, 10–11, 86, 126, 136. *See also* Ålund

pleasure, 59–60, 62, 70, 72, 101, 146n2, 147n10; and pain, 101; and solace, 101; feeling of, 59, 62, 71, 96, 100, 146n2, 149n5, sense of, 60; as negative, 60, 71, 149n5. *See also* beauty; harmony; Kant; reflective judgement

pluralism. *See* planned pluralism

Polanyi, Michael, 20

post-colonialism, 141n3

postmodernism, 76–79. *See also* Lyotard; modernism

power, 111–113, 128–129; and community, 104; and domination, 111–112, 128, 133; and critique, 113; and freedom, 112; and hierarchy, 144n5; and individuality, 113; and modern man, 32; and (post-)colonialism, 19; and resistance, 152n8; as constitutive, 152n8; as faculty, 55, 57, 59–62, 65, 68–71, 73–74, 76–77, 79–81, 91–92, 115, 117, 123, 125, 127, 130, 145n1, 146nn2–3, 147n12, 149n5; as influence, 6, 129; as inviting, 86; as productive, 76; as subversive, 76; nonlegal mode of, 8; of a people, 84; of imams, 10; of indoctrination and control, 5; of historical traditions, 138n1; of language, 134; will to, 65–66, 68, 70, 112, 129, 150n10. *See also* domination; faculty

Priest, Graham, 82

Prospero, 13–14, 18. *See also* Caliban; Shakespeare

proximity, 113–115, 121, 123; and distance, 113, 115, 121

Puar, Jasbir K., xi

purity, 20–23, 25–27, 42; aesthetic of, 72; and children, 142n13; and danger, 22; and identity, 101; and impurity, 20–24, 27–28, 42, 47, 51–52, 72, 82, 84, 127, 131; and the caste system, 47; and the whole, 44, 141n5, as cultural, 23; as metaphysical, 20–24, 26–28, 42, 51; ideals of, 26; logic of, 28; metaphysics of, 13, 19, 21–22, 25, 34, 66, 74; totalitarian ideas of, 103. *See also* metaphysics

racism, x

Readings, Bill, 78, 94, 102, 114, 119

recognition, xv, 1, 3, 8, 12–15, 18–19, 34, 50, 61, 99, 118, 133; and assimilation,

recognition (*cont.*)
    14, 34; and hierarchy, 50; and 'others', 13–14, 133; and rights, 138n1; of cultural distinctiveness/difference, vii–ix, 1–2, 5–7, 11, 13–17, 19, 36–38, 50, 118, 135; of equality/equal dignity, vii–viii, 1, 13–17, 38, 50, 118; of individuals, 1; of groups, 2; politics of, vii–viii, 2, 14–15, 17, 20, 28, 34, 38; of the existing state of things (Marx), 148n1. *See also* assimilation; distinctiveness; equal dignity; equality
reflective judgement, 56, 61–62, 64, 66, 68, 70–71, 79, 118, 146n4, 147n12. *See also* beauty; harmony; judgement; Kant; pleasure; sublime, the; taste
reflexivity, 64; and freedom and existential meaning, 64; deficit of, 66. *See also* Lash
Reformation, 16–17
relativism, 118, 145n11, 152n8; and incommensurability, 113, 129; and determinative judgement, 118, 131; as cultural, 2–5, 9, 95, 102, 108, 118–120, 131, 133, 140n1, 145n11, 152n8; in terms of 'anything goes', 118; with respect to evaluative standards, 108. *See also* incommensurability
republican ideology, 28–31, 32. *See also* ideology
resistance, xv, 112–113, 129, 132–135, 137; alliances of, 133; against domination, 132; against totalitarianism, 126, 132; and dialogue, 132; and strategic essentialism, 134; as a strategy of displacement, 132; organisation of, 132, 135
rights, vii, ix, x, 1–8, 10, 15, 18, 29, 31, 89–90, 94, 118, 131, 138n1, 151n3; and equality, viii, 4, 8; and freedom, 2; and human dignity, 3, 10; and opportunities, 50; justification of, 118; the vocabulary of, 18. *See also* human rights
Romanticism, 16, 142n13; as opposed to Enlightenment, 17
Rorty, Richard, 108, 141n4

Rose, Gillian, 64–65
Rousseau, Jean-Jacques, 29–32, 36, 143n14, 143n16

Said, Edward, 141n4
Schmidt, Lars-Henrik, 22, 27, 65
Scott, Joan, 22, 111
Scruton, Roger, 125
'seeing-as', 123–125, 135. *See also* Tierney; Wittgenstein
Seidler, Victor J., 105
Sejten, Anne Elisabeth, 92
Sennett, Richard, 29, 32
September 11, xii, 89
Shakespeare, 13, 18. *See also* Caliban; Prospero
silence, 91, 93–95, 99–100, 105, 151n19; and *aporia*, 93; being put to, 94–95; following from a wrong, 93–94. *See also* wrong, a
simulacrum, 83–85
singular subject, 55–56, 63–64, 68, 103; and aesthetic object, 61, 63–64, 68; and community, 56, 61, 63–64. *See also* autonomous subject; subject
Skeggs, Beverley, 33–34
solidarity, 28, 121–122; and community, 122; and hospitality and justice, viii; and rational discourse, 122; and truth, 121, 123; and understanding and interpretation, 122. *See also* Gadamer; Habermas; Vetlesen
Spivak, Gayatri C., xiii–xiv, 14, 18, 134, 141nn3–4, 152n8; and equality and recognition, 135; and strategic essentialism, 132; and the problem of opposition, 19, 54, 75; and the subaltern woman, 133. *See also* strategic essentialism
Stjernfelt, Fredrik, 150n14
Storheim, Eivind, 147n6, 148n13
strategic essentialism, 132–134. *See also* essentialism; Spivak
subject. *See* autonomous subject; duality; singular subject; universal subject

Index 173

sublime, the, 59–61, 67–68, 70–74, 132, 149nn7–8, 152n7; analytic of, 79–80; and ugliness 71–73; as thought-provoking, 130; in Kant's philosophy, 67–72, 74, 79, 92; in Lyotard's philosophy, 79–82, 87, 92, 96–98, 101, 127, 130, 149n5, 150n8; judgement of, 59; representation of, 60. *See also* gap; heterogeneity; judgement; Kant; Lyotard; reflective judgement

subordination, 11, 24, 39–40, 44, 51, 54, 72, 140n8; and assimilation, 12–13, 19, 105–106, 110; and culturalisation, 13–14, 19, 36, 48, 105–106, 111; chain of, 17; in relation to the whole, 52. *See also* culturalisation; domination; power

supersensible, 68, 70–72, 74, 79, 147n12, 148n12, 149n5. *See also* Kant

taste, 57, 63, 145n1, 146n2; consensus of, 76; judgement of, 56–57, 59, 61–63, 145n1, 146n2, 146nn4–5. *See also* beauty; harmony; judgement; Kant; reflective judgement

Taylor, Charles, 1, 17, 107, 118, 139n2, 140n2

Thorseth, May, 11, 143n17, 151n16

Tierney, Nathan L., 123–125. *See also* 'seeing-as'

tolerance, 2, 6–8, 86, 136–137. *See also* Brown

totalitarianism, xv, 40–41, 47, 54–55, 84, 93–94, 106–107, 131, 151n2; and *aporia*, 84; and holism, 47, 54; and the 'differend', 89, 93; and silence (following from a wrong), 93–94; and pre-judgement, 107; and unity of people, 84; in practice, 94; of truth, 106–107, 114, 123, 131; resistance against, 126, 132

transcendence, 34, 66–67; and masculinity, 143n15; and play, 66–67; and survival, 65–66; in finitude, 68; of determinative judgement, 66; of immanence, 34, 67; of nature, 66; of the limits of understanding, 58; of the pre-established agreement, 122; quest for, 27

Trey, George, 152n8

truth, viii–ix, 59, 78, 93–94, 100, 106, 108–110, 113–114, 118, 123, 130, 142n12, 151n1; ahistorical epistemologies of the, 20; and Enlightenment, 21; and justice, 94; and meaning, 101; and rational consensus, 120; and solidarity, 121; fear of, 41; totalitarianism of, 106–107, 114, 123, 131

Turner, Victor, 24. *See also* liminality

ugliness, 71–72, 98. *See also* disorder; impurity; Kant; pathology

ultimate foundations. *See* foundations; ground

universal subject, 22, 28, 51, 64, 68, 70, 94, 103, 113, 140n1, 148n13; and the autonomous subject, 28–33, 54, 102; the 'death' of, 103. *See also* autonomous subject; duality

universalisation, 17; and strategic essentialism, 134; of norms, 33; of 'our' identity, 105; of 'our' rationality, 107; of the Western subject, 17. *See also* universalism

universalism, 131, 152n8; and historical totalitarianism, 131; and identity, 67; value of, 85. *See also* universalisation

utopia, 27–28, 39, 50, 55, 110, 142n12, 149n7; of death, 27. *See also* ideals; More

value-ideas, 44–45, 94, 144n7. *See also* Dumont; ideas; values

values, vii, xi, 3–5, 9, 14–15, 25, 36–37, 40–45, 47–50, 52–54, 75, 138n2, 140n8, 144n3, 144n5, 144n8, 144n10; absolute forms of, 100–101; and facts, 44, 54; and ideas, vii–viii, 41–43, 52–53, 144n7, 144n10, 145n11; and loyalties, xi; and norms, 3–4, 7–8, 11,

values (*cont.*)
    15, 37; and purity, 52; and recognition, 50; and truth, 109; and ways of life, xi; as human, 1, 47–48, 142n13; comparison, of, 103; levels of, 43; of cultural diversity, 5; of society, 10, 36, 48, 143n14, 144n10; of universalism, 85. *See also* norms; value-ideas
Vetlesen, Arne Johan, 115–120, 122, 151nn3–4. *See also* ethics; moral performance; solidarity

Walzer, Michael, 4
White, Hayden, 14, 35
'white backlash', x–xi. *See also* Hewitt
Wiggen, Carlos, 68–71, 85, 147n11

Wikan, Unni, 35–36, 53
Wilkerson, T. E., 125
Williams, James, 96
Wittgenstein, Ludwig, 114, 117, on 'seeing-as', 123–124
Wood, David, 119, 136
wrong, a, 88–89, 92–94, 96–98; and silence, 93–94; testify to, 88, 93–94, 97–98. *See also* Lyotard; silence

Young, Iris M., 32, 34, 37, 140nn7–8
Young, Robert, 141nn3–4
Yuval-Davis, Nira, 138n1, 142n13

Zerilli, Linda M. G., 135
Ziarek, Ewa P., 152n8